MW00335263

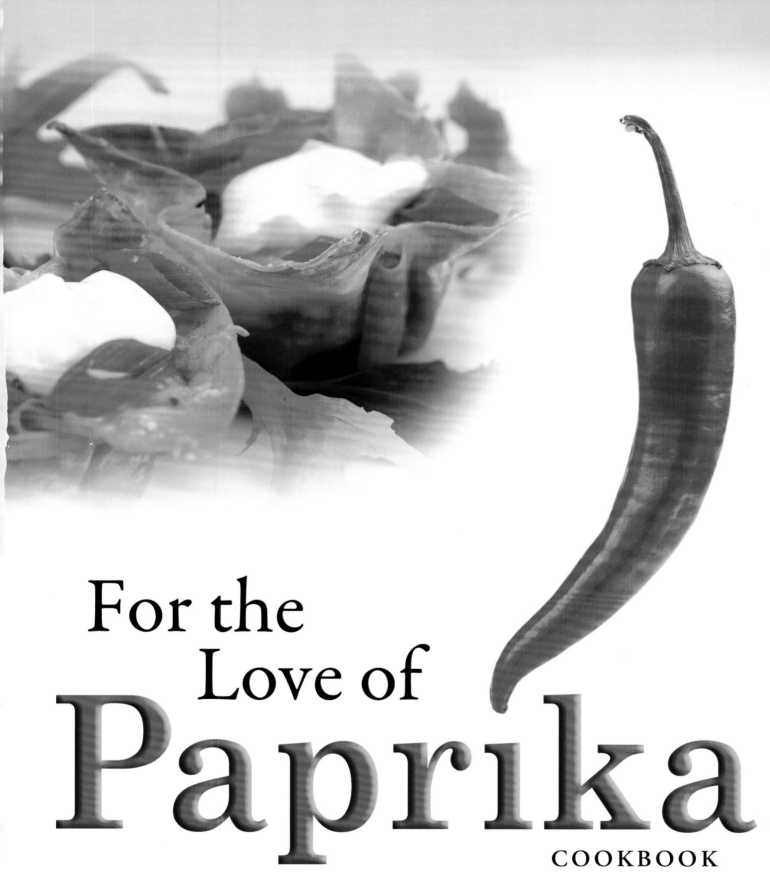

For the
Love of
Paprika
COOKBOOK

John Czingula

ÉdenLili Publishing Company LLC

For the Love of Paprika by John Czingula

© 2013 John Czingula. All rights reserved.

No part of this book may be reproduced in any written, electronic, recording, or photocopying
without written permission of the publisher or author. The exception would be
in the case of brief quotations embodied in the critical articles or reviews and pages
where permission is specifically granted by the publisher or author.

Although every precaution has been taken to verify the accuracy of the information contained herein,
the author and publisher assume no responsibility for any errors or omissions.
No liability is assumed for damages that may result from the use of information contained within.

Books may be purchased by contacting the publisher and author at:

ÉdenLili Publishing Co., LLC

4155 E. Jewell Avenue, Suite 1118

Denver CO 80222

Cover Design: Nick Zelinger, NZ Graphics, Inc.

Interior Design: Rebecca Finkel, F+P Graphic Design

Publisher: ÉdenLili Publishing Co., LLC

Editor: Mira Perrizo

Indexing: John Maling

Book Consultant: Judith Briles, The Book Shepherd

Library of Congress Catalog Number: 2013938180

ISBN: 978-0-9893130-0-1

1. Food and Wine International 2. Quick and Easy 3. Hungary

First Edition Printed in China

I dedicate this book to two wonderful people, my parents Dezsö Czingula and Irén Czingula, who dedicated and sacrificed their lives to bring me and my siblings up through incredible hardship, during and after the Second World War in Europe followed by the dungeons of darkness with the Soviet occupation and communism in Hungary.

I did not realize as a small child and teenager the enormous sacrifice they had endured for us. Not until I came to the United States as a refugee after the revolution of 1956 and could compare life here and what my parents went through to make sure we survived those inhumane days and know the truth. As children we thought that's life, that's how it has to be.

But as my Father and Mother would teach us, back then—that's not how it has to be! God bless them. I shall never forget them.

JOHN CZINGULA

Acknowledgments

The creation of *For the Love of Paprika* was a true team effort. Without them, it wouldn't be in your hands. In Hungary, we say, "Köszönöm." Thank you. Each has earned my deep gratitude and respect for guiding me through this complex journey.

Ten-year-old **Éden Czingula,** my talented granddaughter, created the many illustrations that were inspired by the stories of my youth as only a child could interpret them. What fun it was to have her share her talent in her drawings with me.

Nick Zelinger of NZ Graphics quickly grasped the cover concept, bringing to life the uniqueness that paprika is far more than a few red sprinkles that garnish foods. My surprise was that Nick is also the chief cook in his house, so his enthusiasm for all things paprika came through in the cover. Chorizo Won Ton Flowers on the cover and not goulash … indeed!

Rebecca Finkel of F + P Graphic Design dove into the interior with a true paprika relish. Her use of the vibrant paprika color throughout created the perfect ambiance for any cook to just start reading and discover the true joy of paprika. Rebecca brought a crisp flavor and attitude to each page to highlight this wonderful spice and the recipes within.

Mira Perizzo is the perfect editor for a cookbook. Not only is she a cook; she "got" the recipes, and quickly knew when a teaspoon should have been a tablespoon and how many people can really eat the proportions being suggested. To my surprise, she quickly told me that she would be a buyer and a user of the finished book.

Judith Briles was The Book Shepherd. Introducing each member of my new team to me, she kept all on track, adding insights and a dimension that none of us had thought about. Learning more about my history, she insisted that I share the stories of my youth, bringing and bridging my old world with the new one that I embraced. Impossible isn't in her vocabulary.

Judi Monsour is the last word on all the recipes that are shared. Testing, tasting and retesting each, she has honored the many recipes of my homeland and merged them to embrace the American palate. Judi's vision in creating Judi's Univer Store, our online market that carries all the products mentioned within, is one of the key components contributing to the Univer Foods USA success.

Bill Monsour's knowledge of gourmet dining as a restaurant owner has been invaluable. Whether it's exquisite dining or just a simple dish, his expertise on how to present and how to prepare is simply articulated to the everyday cook. His expertise as a businessman and his knowledge of marketing have been instrumental in the success of Univer Foods USA.

Contents

 **Goulash Cream**

 **Sweet Ann**

 **Red Gold**

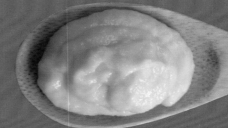 **Garlic Cream**

 **Strong Seven**

 **Horseradish with Vinegar**

Appetizers 28

Soups and Stews 58

Beef 82

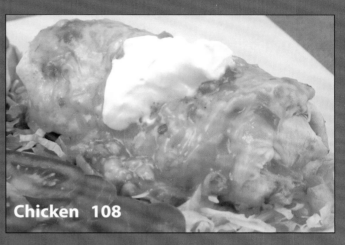

Chicken 108

Pork 140

Seafood 166

Side Dishes 188

Butters, Dressings, Sauces, and More 218

Foreword

For the Love of Paprika is about this wonderful red spice that Hungary is known for. The word "Paprika" is a Hungarian word. In this cookbook, you will learn that Paprika, known to scientists as Capsicum Annuum, is a powerful spice that both enhances taste, improves your health, as well as giving food great coloring created by nature. Among other nutrients it is high in Vitamin C, important in boosting the immune system and fighting infections and it contains a variety of minerals to help the body to stay healthy. In addition to health assisting nutrients, it adds flavor to ordinary foods, turning them into gourmet foods. Ranging from sweet-mild to hot, Hungarian Paprika provides a special secret to cooking that makes food extraordinary.

As the son of a master chef who was voted the outstanding chef in the world at the World Congress of Chefs in Geneva, Switzerland, I naturally developed a discerning palate at a young age. Following in my father's footsteps professionally, this has served me well in owning and managing different restaurants and food service establishments. I was always looking for that distinguishing taste—and that special look—to a dish that would separate my restaurant cuisine from the ordinary. Being unique is paramount to survival in the restaurant industry. Each dish on my menu was crafted to have that special taste that would bring customers back for more—again and again.

In the United States, paprika is not used often as a seasoning agent; it is more an addition to food just for its color. A sprinkle of paprika is often used to enhance the look of deviled eggs as well as other buffet items. The main reason for this is simple. Paprika is not often used in cooking because we do not have access to and therefore have not experienced the right kind.

Hungarian paprika creates such a uniqueness and gave my dishes a special, hard-to-put-your-finger-on-it taste. The good news: you can do this with your own cooking at home as well. You can discover ways to transform your dinner party foods from "good" to "outstanding" with this little known secret: Hungarian paprika. Your guests will comment on your delicious offerings and want to know your secret. Hungarian paprika, unlike the paprika commonly used, enhances flavor within the dish rather than modifying its taste.

John Czingula, as a boy, lived in Hungary during World War II under both the German and Russian occupations. He introduces each chapter with stories during that time of how important food was to him and his family during those trying, dangerous times. They were fortunate to be able to grow their own food, but often they had to do without because of the demands of the German and Russian military during the occupations. Food, in addition to dodging bullets, became a driving force in their survival.

John has created For the Love of Paprika because of how important good food—not just ordinary food, but food correctly seasoned and prepared—has been in his life. Hungarian paprika has been an important part of that experience, and he wants to share with you that experience with these recipes and the inclusion in them of these special Hungarian paprika relish and paste products.

I hope you will enjoy this book as much as I have and learn how to create outstanding dishes that will delight you, your family and your guests.

PAUL H. LAESECKE
Senior Lecturer, Fritz Knoebel School of Hospitality Management, Daniels College of Business
Director of Creativity & Entrepreneurship LLC, Living and Learning Communities, University of Denver

Introduction

Paprika, ranging from mild to very hot, is the much-loved spice of Hungary, and Europe in general. American cooks use paprika primarily as a coloring agent, and indeed, flavor has all but been bred out of domestic paprika. Cooks in this country are pleasantly surprised to find that Hungarian paprika has a robust taste unlike anything they have ever encountered.

Centuries of careful breeding and propagation have resulted in the crowning of Hungary as the paprika capital of the world. Over forty varieties are grown there, and the annual August and September harvest renders the fields bright with eye-catching red color from the crops. With its long sunny days, Hungary produces tons of the appetizing spice each year. Used to flavor and color foods from stews to sausages, paprika is a go-to spice for wise European chefs.

Harvesting is an interesting and colorful undertaking. The paprika is ripened on the plant; when they turn red, they are picked and strung up to dry by the sun. The red paprika are tied to long strings and hung out to dry in the open air. Making powder out of the dry paprika is a century's old tradition in Hungary.

The new tradition is the paprika paste—in this form one can brush the paprika on meats, chicken, or fish. Or one can flavor and naturally color any dish, soup, or even your scrambled eggs. It can be used very creatively in cooking, in your favorite pasta sauce, potatoes, rice, and vegetables. Use it liberally with meat, poultry, and fish. A little can make store-bought or homemade soups a gourmet treat.

Paprika, also known as Capsicum Annuum, is a spice generally made from ground-up dried fruits. Its flavor can range from mild to very hot. Hungarian paprika is rich in vitamin C and other vitamins, antioxidants, minerals, and was once even used as a tinting agent for hair coloring.

Paprika for western countries is graded by color. The amount of pigment is measured by the ASTA—American Spice Trade Association. The range runs from 80 ASRA to 240 ASRA, which is a beautiful dark red. Dr. Albert Szent-Györgyi, a Hungarian biochemist, discovered that paprika has more vitamin C than citrus fruits. Szent–Györgyi was awarded the Nobel Prize in 1937 for his achievement and became a national hero in Hungary.

The original home of paprika was probably Central America. It was an exotic plant brought from the New World by Christopher Columbus. The Hungarian climate and soil were excellent for the now world-famous plant.

bon appétit

Domestically grown paprika is usually genetically altered to have no taste and no nutritional value. It is primarily used as a coloring agent and is identified as such on the food label. It is not necessary to add it to the nutritional portion of the label, since it has little or no nutritional value.

Our factory, Univer Foods, has supplied Europe, Russia, and other areas of the world for over seventy-five years. They craft the paprika into a beautiful aromatic paste and relish, the paprika fruit is crushed, never dried!

The recipes featured in this book use Univer Red Gold Hot or Mild paprika paste—pure paprika cream. Univer Goulash Cream Hot or Mild also is a paprika cream, but it has other spices in it that are needed for a Goulash stew or soup, and anything else that would be improved by fresh paprika. It is also a common table condiment in Hungarian homes and restaurants.

Univer's Strong Steven, a hot paprika relish, and Sweet Ann, a mild paprika relish, are reduced to a lovely sauce with paprika pieces visible.

When the paprika becomes red and ripened on the plant, the ripened paprika is then removed from the plant and made into a paste. Manufacturing it in this way means more vitamin and mineral content of the paprika is preserved and not burned or eliminated by the sun as it dries for making powder out of it. Paprika comes in several varieties.

The growers in Hungary know how to nurture, harvest, and grind the fruits—they have centuries of experience. The knowledge has been passed down through generations. It's like the secret of making a good wine!

Paprika defines the Hungarian nation. It has been part of its history and mystique for centuries. Paprika became the source of hard currency under the Communist era. They bought products needed from the western countries with this hard currency that they otherwise could not get. Paprika Rocks!

In 1957, I came to the United States as a refugee from the Hungarian Revolution that devastated my beloved homeland. I missed my native cooking, and in the ensuing years during visits back to my village, I always returned home to America with a few paprika products and other favorites tucked away in my suitcase. My friends begged me to share, and I began thinking of introducing authentic paprika relishes and pastes to American chefs. That dream became reality in 2004, when I procured the exclusive rights to distribute Univer Hungarian Paprika and other select products to the United States.

Now living the American dream, I have successfully pursued multiple careers in acting, real estate, and alternative energy. My first love has always been cooking, though, and my beloved paprika is always at hand in my kitchen. Please enjoy these recipes and "Jó étvágyat!" (Bon appétit!)

My Father the Horticulturalist

My father was a very hard working and diplomatic man. He was a "gentleman;" I learned the meaning and refinement of the word gentleman when I learned English. He was truly a gentleman. But hearing the stories of his youth, I learned he wasn't always like that.

On his side, all the men going back to the late eighteen hundreds were Rail Road men. Even my older sister worked for the Rail Road before she got married. I did too, for about a year until the 1956 Hungarian Revolution against the occupying Soviet Union.

Joining the rail road was not by choice. I did the same thing that my Father did at the time when he was about my age. Over time, that choice determined the rest of both of our lives. We both left Hungary; he did it after World War I by choice, and I did it after the second World War by necessity. The difference was that he returned. I could not, at least while Hungary was still controlled by the Communists.

As an only child, Father was a rebel in his teens according to stories from him and his father, my Grandfather. Grandfather was a Rail Road Man working as a Station Master. In those days before the war, especially in the early nineteen hundreds it was a very respectable and responsible job working for the Rail Road. All the men had nice looking uniforms and were ranked like the military. They saluted each other and were very serious about their occupation which was for a lifetime.

My Grandfather was in charge of permitting trains to enter into the Rail Road Station or stopping them before entering. It depended, of course, on how busy the rails were and whether a given rail line into the station was free for an approaching train. He did this job by working what was called "the semaphore." He would control the semaphores outside the station by pulling large levers in his tower. These levers, through a series of wires and pulleys, would work the semaphores outside of the station, sometimes quite far away. If the semaphore—at the top of a tall metal pole—was pointing up at forty-five degrees, then the train could proceed into the station. If it was in a horizontal position, the train would have to stop.

On this particular occasion, my father and a buddy of his decided to find out how the semaphore worked, so they climbed up the metal pole to investigate. Little did they know there was a train approaching. When my Grandfather pulled the lever to allow the train to enter the station without stopping, my father was caught and squeezed in the arm of the semaphore, preventing it from raising to the correct 45 degree position. Instead of continuing on into the station, the engineer of the train thought he could not proceed. So he stopped!

Of course this was a complete disaster for my Grandfather, especially when he found out it was his very own son that caused this stoppage. The train was about 45 minutes late by the time the rail road men got my father down from the top of the pole (they had to dismantle some parts of the semaphore before they could do it), and the train could go into the station. This almost ended the rail road career of my Grandfather. He was put before the equivalent of a military tribunal—a Rail Road Court Martial—and almost lost his job. This was a job in those days that elevated a man to a respectable position in life and a higher level in society. He almost lost that prestigious job, and his name and rank was tarnished, all because of his son.

Needless to say, my father, for the first time in his life, was severely punished by his father. This was a profound and significant turn of events for him in his young life!

Because of this shame, he left home. He was without resources, however. He had no money; he had no trade, craft or profession. He didn't know what to do, but it was at the beginning of World War One. So he lied about his age and enlisted in the Hungarian Army! They soon discovered that he was under age, but he was by that time in army uniform and undergoing basic training. Instead of discharging him, the Army put him on an Army Hospital Train as an assistant to the medical team. His main job on the train was to carry severed limbs up front to the steam engine to be burned in the fire box. He told us many years later that that difficult job made him a man and changed his life forever.

When the war was over, he did not return home; instead he travelled from Eastern to Western Europe, working from country to country doing odd jobs to survive. One day he got a job in a large facility where they grew all kinds of plants, trees and flowers, a job he found he really enjoyed. It meant he had found his calling!

He stopped drifting, went to school to study and got a degree in Horticulture. He was twenty six years old when he finally returned to Hungary, a grown man with a special trade. After all those years, he reunited with his Father, my Grandfather, who was still a Rail Road man . . . a lucky break for my father.

The Hungarian Rail Road had five or six large horticultural establishments with different locations in the country. Each one of these had two or three hundred people working for them. These establishments would grow trees, flowers and design parks around the Rail Road Stations all over the country. They would actually plant fruit trees along the Rail Road tracks throughout the country, and they allowed the fruit trees to be picked for free by the local people who lived nearby.

Surprisingly, my father was able to continue our family's tradition of working for the Hungarian Rail Road. Why? He became a Manager and ranking Rail Road official wearing a Uniform! He was hired to run one of those large Horticultural Rail Road establishments. He oversaw two to three hundred workers, and managed many green houses, laboratories and park designers.

Then the Second World War came. Germany occupied Hungary and we subsequently were bombed by the Russians, English and Americans. Since my Father was the head of one of these Horticultural establishments, the government considered it an important enough job so that he was not drafted into the army to fight the Russians, at least not until 1944. This was the time when the Germans were losing the war on both the Eastern and Western fronts.

My father was drafted and sent to the Russian Front. The Germans would routinely send Hungarians as well as other ethnic soldiers to the front to fight the Russians. Luckily my father was not killed; but he was captured by the Russians along with another officer. When the war was over, he managed to escape from the Russians and returned to us in the spring of 1946.

We were at Grandma's house, trying to clean up the ravages of war, when father appeared. I remember it took me, as a child, a few minutes to recognize him. At first I was actually afraid of him; he was skin and bones with a long beard on his face. The reunion was an unforgettable event.

My Grandmother had five acres of land and lived just on the outskirts of town. About six hundred feet from us was a project that had hot ground water from which the city's public swimming pools were supplied. The excess hot water that the City could not use flowed in a ditch right by the front of Grandma's house . . . and it was still hot!

My father had a plan! Grandma had nearly five acres of land right there and capable of growing food. The future of our economy was unpredictable; it was unknown when the economy would return to a state where people could work, make a living and not starve to death. Growing our own food was an imperative. Father's plan for that was to design a year-round garden, a garden with three greenhouses that would be heated by the hot water going to waste in the very front of our property. One greenhouse would be placed perpendicular to the ditch where the waste hot water was flowing. A second greenhouse was to sit parallel to the road and the ditch, and the third greenhouse would be placed perpendicular to the road in the back of the house. His plan would let the hot water flow through all three greenhouses and then back out to the ditch.

The greenhouses would be built into the ground so that the roofs would nearly touch the earth. Father, my five year old brother and I (eight years old) started to dig the holes for the greenhouses. We dug until their bottoms were below the ditch carrying the hot water so that it would flow into the greenhouses. We then built a channel out of concrete and brick we got from bombed out structures close by. We covered these channels with quarter inch thick steel panels which we got from the destroyed German tank in front of our house and from another tank about sixty yards from us. These were panels hanging from their sides to shield them from bullets, and fortunately, they were quite easy to remove.

Among the explosives in the German tank, we found a whole case of champagne, but my father destroyed it in case the contents were poisoned. Each of these panels were identical and about a square meter in size. Father designed the width of the channels for that same size, so the panels would perfectly cover the channels. This was so that when the hot water flowed through the channels, it would not emit steam into the green house, but would heat the steel panels and in turn create heat in the greenhouses, vital for plant growth in the fall and winter.

When the green houses were done, we let the hot water in from the ditch and it flowed perfectly. My parents and Grandma were elated. Of course my brother and I became heroes as well, especially in our mother's eyes.

Not long after that, the government wanted my Father to come back to the Rail Road and run the Rail Road greenhouses and manage the workers under the new communist government, now controlled by the Russians. He was delighted about that until he learned that in order to get his rank back, he would have to join the communist party. He refused. It was a bitter fight with the communist agitators to get him into the party. Their argument was that he could not be the leader—the manager of two hundred or so people—if he didn't become a communist. He still refused!

He got the job but never got his Rail Road rank back, nor did he get his full salary back. He got only an ordinary worker's salary, yet was required to run the whole project. The man who was designated the manager of the project was a communist party member but did not have the knowledge or the education to take on and properly run the project. My father did it, but was paid only as a common laborer.

He managed to turn this whole thing into a positive, however. Since he was a Rail Road man, our whole family was entitled to free Rail Travel. This was a blessing. When Christmas approached in the dead of winter, we were the only supplier of green lettuce in the whole country. The whole family would pack our suitcases with lettuce and travel to Budapest. In time, the resellers would line up at the train station waiting for us and our lettuce. We were the only suppliers for quite a long time, thanks to father and the free hot water.

In the meantime, father planted carnations, violets, roses and other flowers which my Grandmother and Mother sold in the local farmers markets and in front of cemeteries. People bought them to put on the graves of their loved ones buried there. It was truly lucky for us during that time that this had always been a great tradition in Hungary.

Essential Components for Your Kitchen

Stocking a well-working kitchen depends a lot on what and how you cook. If you are vegan, you probably don't need a meat cleaver. If you have a big family, you need bigger pots for spaghetti and potatoes, etc. If it's just you and your partner, you can probably get by with a 5- or 6-quart Dutch oven. If you entertain a lot, put some money into attractive serve-ware and table settings, glassware, linens, etc.

Before you begin what can be an expensive process, sit down with a cup of coffee or tea and really analyze how you will use your kitchen and who will use the kitchen. Also take into consideration your storage availability. You may like shopping at the big warehouse stores, but you may not have anywhere to put those larger packages.

We have divided this chapter into two sections, food and kitchen utensils.

Section 1: Food

Univer Products: This cookbook is designed to use our wonderful line of fresh, never powdered, paprika and complementary products. We believe our paprika and garlic cream is superior to powdered paprika and garlic cloves. By using our products, you can add a layer of flavor that most American cooks are unfamiliar with—real paprika taste.

Most paprika peppers grown in this county have been genetically modified to eliminate flavor and vitamins, leaving the powdered product a cheerful red color but with no taste or nutritional value. This was done deliberately so food manufacturers could use this domestic paprika as a coloring agent in other foods. By removing nutrients, the manufacturers eliminate the need to list them on the nutrition label, because it does not have any nutrients.

When you read an ingredient label that states the product contains "natural coloring," you can just about guarantee that the color comes from domestic paprika. There is nothing wrong with this, except that most American cooks have never tasted real paprika! They, in fact, use it as a coloring agent, too—on deviled eggs, potato salad, and other dishes that could benefit from a dash of color. Taste is irrelevant, just the color matters.

Throughout For the Love of Paprika, we will let you know when the Univer Products will enhance your cooking and eating experience. Watch for: Sweet Ann, Strong Steven, Red Gold, Goulash Cream, Garlic Cream (a key staple), Horseradish with Vinegar, Horseradish with Mayonnaise, Mustard, and Mayonnaise.

One of our favorite quotes is by food authority Craig Claiborne. He noted, "The innocuous powder which most merchants pass on to their customers as paprika has slightly more character than crayon or chalk. Any paprika worthy of its name has an exquisite taste and varies in strength from decidedly hot to pleasantly mild, but with a pronounced flavor."

Dried paprika can be substituted in some recipes in this cookbook, but not all. We do not recommend sautéing with dried paprika because it burns easily. For dishes containing liquid, such as soups and stews, add the dried paprika to the liquids. Use a good quality imported dried paprika for the best results. Remember, this cookbook is designed to use our line of fresh, never powdered, paprika and complementary products. Using a dried paprika may alter the texture and taste.

Our Gourmet Garlic Cream is simple genius. Garlic is not a generic plant whose cloves will taste or cook up with the same results every time. Garlic heads are not consistent due to heat, watering conditions, soil conditions, etc. Garlic is grown in many parts of the world and is influenced by surrounding conditions. Univer Garlic is grown in a specific region and prepared under the same stringent rules each time. Our garlic cream has a higher flash point, so it does not burn as readily as chopped or minced garlic. This means you can add it to a hot frying pan without worrying about it burning as quickly and turning bitter. It also means that creamy garlic will blend more readily into any dish, eliminating the problem of overworking meats for burgers and meatloaf. It makes better dips, gravies, and sauces since it is thoroughly incorporated into the other ingredients.

If you are out of this terrific product, use minced garlic. Two to three cloves of minced garlic is the equivalent of 1 teaspoon of Gourmet Garlic Cream. Remember, garlic cloves burn easily and become bitter, so watch your frying pan closely.

Univer Horseradish with Vinegar is a true find for people who like the flavor of horseradish, but not the "sinusy" bite that accompanies most horseradishes. Our horseradish is hot and has great flavor, but Univer has lessened the nasal impact.

Our other products are mainstays in European kitchens, as well. We invite you to try a selection of our paprikas and other creations, prepare a few recipes in this book, and enjoy the ensuing applause from your family and friends.

And now, let's move on.

Spices and herbs! Grow your own fresh herbs as much as possible, or buy them, then wrap them in a damp paper towel and store in a zipped storage bag for maximum storage life. Never harvest more than one-third of an herb plant at any one time. Dried herbs and spices have a pretty short shelf life. Buy the smallest tins or jars of the herbs you use least and write on the container the date you opened it.

White pepper, red pepper, and black pepper have different heat levels and affect the palate in different places. Keep all three in your kitchen for dishes that have complex heat, such as Cajun and Creole. Try a course ground pepper if you really like pepper and like the look of it on your dish.

There are so many salts on the market today it can be confusing. Kosher salt and regular table salt are the basics for every kitchen. Just remember when using kosher salt that it is not as strong as table salt. Experiment with sea salts and the colored salts. Here's a tip—in your kitchen, you control the salt shaker. Taste before you salt, remember that other ingredients may also contribute salt, and remember that you can always add more.

Oils: Canola oil has little flavor and can cook at higher temps without burning. This makes it ideal for deep-frying, frying, baking, and as an all-purpose oil. A good olive oil or two is a must. Keep in mind that olive oils have a lower flash point and will burn more quickly. Adding a little butter or other oil will allow you to turn up the heat a little.

There are many other oils and many specialty oils. A lot of them come in smaller bottles so you can experiment without blowing your budget. If you are trying a specialty oil for the first time or need it for a once-a-year recipe, buy the smallest size you can find. Store oils in a cool, dark place.

Pantry: There are a few basics. This food selection really depends on your shopping habits. If you buy for a week or more at one time, you'll need more canned goods on hand. If you are a daily shopper or hit the stores two or three times a week, you'll need fewer. Keep an inventory of canned tomatoes, broth, and a soup or two. Tea, coffee, sugar, flour, breadcrumbs and/or panko, powdered sugar, brown sugar, a selection of vinegars, rice, and pasta will help round out the basics. Before shopping, take a cell phone photo of your pantry and the inside of your refrigerator. It can help you remember if you already have the ingredients on hand.

Here are a few secrets you don't have to share:

   Jarred Alfredo sauce—a quick, cheesy topping for veggies, burritos, eggs, etc.

   Instant mashed potatoes—stir into too-thin gravy when you know you just can't add any more flour or cornstarch.

   Instant coffee—add a dash to gravies and sauces for a richer flavor.

   Instant dried gravy—will also save a gravy that just won't thicken.

Fresh Produce: Could include potatoes, onions, lemons, limes, and some fruit. Add basic salad ingredients like lettuce, cucumbers, and tomatoes.

Section 2: Kitchen Utensils

- **A large, stable cutting board.** We prefer wood, but some cooks like the antibacterial factors of the newer plastics. You might want to get another board reserved just for poultry.

- **Decent cookware.** The more you cook, the more you need pots and pans that won't easily warp, pit, or scratch. Cookware is an item you don't replace often, no matter how much the pot wobbles when it's full of boiling water. Let the primary cook make the buying decision. Before you decide, hold the new pots and pans to feel how the handles work with your hands, how heavy the pot is going to be when filled with food or liquids, how the lids fit, and how the steam is released from the lid (to the side or directly in your face). We have a large frying pan that we love, but when it's full of gumbo we have to call for help to lift it! The reason is not the weight of the full pan, it's the length of the handle. It's so long that we can't get decent weight distribution. A big frying pan with two handles is a real winner in our book!

- **Dry goods and cleaning supplies.** Storage bags, foil, cling wrap, trash bags, napkins, paper towels, dish soap, dishwasher soap, an all-purpose cleaner, a mop of some sort, a broom of some sort, some storage containers, and linens.

- **Colander for draining and straining.** We use them all—stainless, plastic and mesh.

- **Choose good knives and keep them sharpened.** Dull knives are dangerous to you, and they make a mess of your food. You can't cut a pretty tomato wedge or slice bread properly unless you use the right knife, well-sharpened. Select the right size knife with a handle that is comfortable in your hand. You may prefer a heavier weight but your cooking partner may prefer a light-weight handle with a different curve. Buy both—it's safer, and it will make you a better cook.

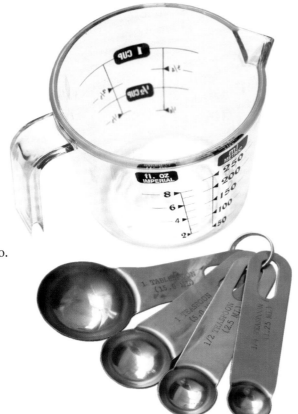

- **Scissors that are dishwasher safe are a must.** A definite must!

- **A decent set of measuring cups and spoons.** We use glass; our spoons are metal.

- **Cheesecloth for straining** just about anything (think thawed spinach that needs to be dried).

- **Butcher's twine.** Kitchen twine or string works also.

- **A decent can opener** that won't hurt your wrists.

- **A trusty meat thermometer.**

- **A good deep fry/candy thermometer.**

- **An oven thermometer** if you suspect your oven isn't "true" to temperature.

- **Microplane grater.**

- **A new toothbrush** will make quick work of cleaning a microplane or grater.

- **Clothespins** to keep bags closed, such as chips and cookies. You can usually buy three dozen for a buck at a dollar discount store.

- **Produce keeper for the fridge.** We like Rubbermaid,™ but we've never tried any other brand. We love this product because it keeps lettuce and other greens fresh for a couple of weeks. *Here's a tip:* Don't cut the lettuce with a knife before storing in the keeper. You can pull it apart with your hands, but cutting with a knife will brown the lettuce and reduce the storage life.

Tips, Tricks and Notes

Below are a variety of tips, tricks, and notes that have enhanced our cooking experiences. We will also sprinkle them throughout to remind you when to use in a specific recipe.

- **Mix dry ingredients with dry ingredients and wet with wet.** For example, add dry spices to breadcrumbs and liquid ingredients to eggs when dredging. What you are striving for is a mixture of ingredients that will blend together with no clumps of any one ingredient standing out. No one likes a dish that doesn't have the garlic evenly distributed.

- **Easily remove excess moisture** from thawed spinach by putting it in cheesecloth and twisting until the liquid is gone.

- **Save those vegetable trimmings** to boost the flavors of stocks and broths. Just clean and freeze them until ready for use. No need to thaw—throw them in the pot frozen.

- **To remove garlic, onion, and fishy smells** from your fingers, slide your fingers over the side of the blade of a stainless steel knife under cold running water. (And yes, be careful.) Better yet, use a stainless steel spoon!

- **When the pasta is cooked and drained,** put it back in the warm pot to dry it a little before adding sauce. If not using immediately, dress the pasta with a little sauce or Goulash Cream to prevent clumping (or use Gourmet Garlic Cream if you are a serious garlic fan!).

- **If you need to boil a large pot of water quickly,** try boiling the water in two smaller pans, then combining the water into a larger pot, returning the water to a boil.

- **Veggies cooked in water or broth** will benefit from being put back in the warm pan to dry a bit before serving.

- **When serving a large group at tables** (think holidays), consider using multiple platters that can hold turkey, ham, and beef. Each of the tables can have a meat platter, so they don't have to be passed. Buy inexpensive yet sturdy platters at a discount store. Put a bowl of potatoes, a bowl of veggies, etc. on each table. This way, the food doesn't get cold before it reaches everyone. Don't forget multiple baskets for the rolls, with a dish of butter for each table. Several boats of gravy or sauce are also a must! Inexpensive salt and pepper shakers can be purchased for each table. Feel free to mix and match place setting serve-ware.

- **Do not rely on gravy or sauces** to reheat your meal at the table. If you need to serve a soup dish first, keep the entrée warm in the kitchen before taking it to the table.

- **Keep the potato skins on** whenever possible—that's where the most nutrients are found.

- **Sniff before you season!** Check tinned spices and herbs frequently and replace when the aroma is diminished. Some spices, such as curry and cumin, have a pretty short shelf life. If your recipe calls for a teaspoon of an herb or spice you've had for several months, you may need to add a little more.

- **Don't store spices above your stove or other heat source.** Keep them in a cool, dark place for maximum shelf life.

- **If the avocado you want to use tonight** is just not quite ripe, cut it open as usual and remove the seed. Take a teaspoon and scrape the flesh in thin strips. It still won't be ripe, but it will blend much better into a dip or sauce.

- **When you go to the supermarket,** take a cell phone photo of your pantry and your refrigerator. It will help you remember if you need an item or if you already have it!

- **If you are cooking at altitude,** check with your local college extension service for adjustments to your recipes. For example, melting chocolate for fudge at 5,000 feet reaches the softball stage at a lower temperature than at sea level.

- **Save that turkey carcass or big ham bone to make stock.** It's easy and so handy to have it in the freezer for later use.

- **If the potatoes have a green tinge when peeling,** just keep peeling until it's gone. The green flesh is not only bitter, but toxic when eaten in quantities.

- **Use a muffin tin** to hold several potatoes for baking at the same time.

- **If you prefer a soft potato skin** on your baked potato, wrap them in foil. Otherwise rub a little fat and Garlic Cream on them and place directly on the oven rack.

- **Leftover mashed or baked potatoes** can go directly into a stew or soup as a thickener—dice the baked potatoes.

- **Don't throw out herbs** (dried or fresh) or citrus peels; toss them in the garbage disposal to freshen it.

- **Brine those birds!** A simple ⅔ kosher salt to ⅓ sugar dissolved in water, with some added herbs for flavor, will make your meat much tastier. We like to rinse off the brine when ready to cook, but many cooks just pat the bird dry. If you don't rinse, remember to add additional salt very sparingly.

- **Meat MUST rest after cooking,** especially off a hot grill. Resist the urge to plunge your knife into hot meats and poultry. Resting will help the juices redistribute for maximum moisture when sliced. Let small cuts rest about 5 minutes, big cuts at least 10, and large roasts or turkeys about 30 minutes. Tent loosely with foil to keep warm.

- **Don't overcrowd the pan when frying** or deep frying foods. You will lose the heat needed to really sear the outside of the food and instead the food will steam.

- **Don't worry too much about cleaning the stems** from soft herbs like parsley and cilantro. They taste just as good as the leaves! Just chop finely and add to your dish. Do trim stems from woody herbs such as rosemary.

- **We prefer bone-in meats and poultry.** The flavors are better and the meat retains more moisture, but if you dislike bones, these recipes can use either cut.

- **To slice meat into thin strips** for fajitas or stir-fry, put it in the freezer for a bit and it will slice easily.

- **Remove meat from the fridge** about 30 minutes before cooking or grilling so it can get some of the chill off.

- **Leftover soups and stews** can be stretched by serving them over rice, noodles, mashed potatoes, or hash-brown potatoes.

- **If you are going to serve a dish at a buffet** that includes rice, remember that rice will keep absorbing any liquid until it becomes mushy. If you can, keep the rice separate from the sauce—serve the sauce over the rice. If you must combine them, make additional sauce to serve over the dish, but keep it separate. Sounds counterintuitive, but this tip really works.

- **Choose a cutting board** that has enough room to easily hold all the food you are chopping.

- **Reduce a liquid** by letting it simmer gently until the desired thickness is achieved. The flavor of a reduction liquid is more intense.

- **No fireplace matches to flambé your dish?** Use a piece of uncooked spaghetti. (Also good for lighting lots of candles.)

- **After browning meat and veggies** for spaghetti sauce and soups, don't throw away that liquid in the pan. Deglaze with wine or broth and add to the sauce for another layer of flavor.

- **Cook bacon in the oven** on a cookie sheet with a rack and it will stay flat and crispy. Start it in a cold oven and the fat will render slowly and reduce shrinkage (350–400° F to desired doneness).

- **One slice of bacon** equals about 1 tablespoon crumbled.

- **If you are using a recipe,** read it thoroughly before you start cooking to make sure you have the ingredients and the time to finish the meal as instructed. If you are rushed and have to cook at too high a heat, your meal will not be the end result you wanted. Be creative if you have to substitute an ingredient. No canned tomatoes? Will a jar of salsa work instead?

- **When adding fresh eggs** to a mixture, break the eggs into a small bowl first so you can remove any shell bits before adding to the mixture. (Especially if your mixture is white, as in pancake or a cake batter.)

- **Old carrot skins and cores** can be bitter and tough—peel the skins and trim out the core to make the carrots tender. Fresh carrots and baby carrots can be served with the skin on, just wash and prepare as directed for your recipe.

- **Warming dinner plates and chilling salad bowls** elevate your meal presentation to a professional level.

- **Keep your good knives** out of the dishwasher, as well as wooden utensils.

- **Chop and slice foods with love,** not speed. Chop only at the pace at which you are comfortable—no need to keep up with TV chefs! That's just an accident waiting to happen.

- **For those large cooking events,** such as big family functions and holiday dinners, figure out how many serving pieces you will need in advance. At large buffets, you may wish to have two serving stations, and you may forget to double the serving pieces you will need.

- **Taste as you cook!** There is no substitute, not even your nose!

- **A damp paper towel** placed over your bowl of liquid in the microwave will help catch the occasional blowups of the liquid.

- **Clean as you go.** Trying to cook with a mess all around you is discouraging.

- **Don't play with your food when cooking!** Leave it alone and let the heat do its job. Breaded food that loses its breading when flipped is a sign you are flipping too early. Food like steaks and chops won't stick to the pan when they are ready to turn. That beautiful crust on hash browns—you can't get it by constantly moving the potatoes around.

- **Check out your local ethnic markets** for less expensive produce and make friends with some unfamiliar veggies. The produce manager will be happy to answer questions and provide cooking tips.

- **Open a drawer to temporarily hold a baking sheet** if you are short on counter space. Be careful if there are children running about.

- **A long wooden spoon laid** over a boiling pot will help prevent the liquid from boiling over. However, if you fear the pot will boil over, you probably have the heat too high.

- **We've never understood the mushroom/water relationship.** If mushrooms will get soggy if we wash them, why don't they get soggy in our sauce? If they are really dirty, we say give them a quick rinse and be done with it!

- **If your mushrooms just need a spot cleaning,** use a paper towel dampened with lemon juice to keep them from browning.

- **Paprika in its raw form** (all Univer paprika products) contains vitamin C. One teaspoon of Red Gold has 2 percent of vitamin C, based on a 2,000-calorie diet. By actual weight, paprika contains more vitamin C than lemon juice.

- **If you need softened butter,** grate it instead of using the microwave. The consistency is better and it will soften quickly.

- **Forgot to take the cream cheese out to soften?** Just cut into small pieces and it will soften fast.

- **A little milk** added to the cooking water will keep cauliflower pretty and white.

- **When making homemade French fries,** let the cut potatoes stand in cold water for about 20–30 minutes. Pat dry. The fries will be nice and crispy.

- **Add a few teaspoons of white vinegar** to simmering water when poaching eggs; it will help the whites stay together better.

- **Rinse sauerkraut in the colander** to remove some of that briny taste; drain before using. Instead of warming in water or broth, try beer!

- **Sauerkraut benefits** from a light sprinkling of caraway seeds and absolutely sings with chopped fried bacon!

- **When using a slow cooker,** put the vegetables in the bottom of the crock first, then cover with meat.

- **Sautéing vegetables?** Add a tablespoon of Red Gold or Goulash Cream Paprika, Hot or Mild. Both add fabulous flavor and appealing rich color.

- **Bell peppers** (any color) are an excellent way to present dips to your family and guests. Slice off the top and remove the ribs and stems, then fill with dip. (If the pepper is a little unsteady, support it with lettuce on the plate.) Also great for egg and tuna salads!

- **Blend** in a little Red Gold or Goulash Cream to the butter or oil before sautéing veggies.

- **Garlic Cream is the first thing we reach for in the kitchen.** This lovely white cream is our staple garlic and we use it in all our savory dishes. Use Garlic Cream in place of garlic cloves. Add it to oil along with Univer paprika before sautéing. Use it in dips, dressings, etc. One teaspoon equals about 2–3 cloves of chopped garlic.

- **Fresh garlic bread is a snap.** Mix Garlic Cream with butter, spread on bread and top with Parmesan cheese.

- **Brush clean, dry potatoes** with Garlic Cream, and then bake as usual. Mix with mashed potatoes for instant Garlic Potatoes.

- **Add a dollop** of Red Gold or Goulash Cream to stews, gravies, and sauces. We use it in both red and white pasta sauces.

- **We love Sweet Ann** in our scrambled eggs. It also gives hash browns beautiful color.

- **Cook pasta and drain well.** Mix some Red Gold or Goulash Cream into the pasta and stir to coat. Great flavor, creamy texture. Top with sauce as usual.

- **A roast beef sandwich** just cries out for our Mayonnaise with Horseradish spread thickly on the bread!

- **Horseradish with Vinegar** is perfect for those who love the taste of horseradish, but don't like the "sinusy" bite it has.

- **Spread celery sticks and crackers** with equal parts peanut butter and Horseradish with Vinegar. Crazy? We call these Colorado Nachos!

- **Horseradish with Vinegar** is superb with beef. Spread it on when the steak is hot off the grill and resting.

- **Add a hint of Horseradish with Vinegar** to coleslaw and potato salad, especially if they are store-bought. It will boost the flavors and your guests will wonder where the great taste is coming from.

- **Horseradish with Vinegar mixed** with ketchup and a splash of Worcestershire sauce makes the perfect seafood sauce.

- **Add some Sweet Ann to a couple cups of cooked rice,** and it really perks up the flavor. Or, just add it to the cooking water.

- **Use Univer Paprika products in dips and sauces.** Great mixed into sour cream, cream cheese, mayonnaise, and yogurt.

- **Add Univer Paprika to ground meat** for burgers, meatloaf, and meatballs. Add some Garlic Cream right into the meat and mix well.

- **Fried chicken or pork chops?** Add Strong Steven to the egg batter. It brightens the flavor with a nice spiciness that doesn't overpower the taste.

- **Add a squirt of Red Gold or Goulash Cream to hot dog water**—turn cheap hot dogs into wonder dogs!

- **When slicing rolls and buns** for sandwiches, don't cut them completely apart. This way, everyone will have a top and a bottom when assembling their sandwich.

- **To easily extract juice from lemons and limes,** microwave them for about 10–15 seconds, and then roll them around on a cutting board with the palm of your hand.

- **Keep citrus shells** after you have juiced them—freeze the shells to use later to stuff baked birds.

- **And here is one of our all-time favorite tips:** Never bring the host/hostess fresh flowers unless they are in a vase! She must stop everything she is doing to find a vase, fill the vase, cut the stems to fit the vase, and then find a place to put the vase. Never bring anything that will require her to stop what she is doing and tend to your gift!

appetizers

Belgian Endive with Garlicky Avocado Spread, see page 31

Hungarian Appetizers

Appetizers were not very common in Hungary. At least not when I was growing up before, during, and after the Second World War. They still aren't. Our main course began with soup—always with soup—and some simple second course like Paprikás Krumpli (Paprika Potato). Cooked with lard, one would sauté some onions, put a goodly amount of delicious red paprika on them, add the potatoes, cover them with water, add salt, and cook until the potatoes were nice and soft. As simple as that. And delicious.

The word appetizer was something that we, as children, didn't understand. We thought it was something that only rich people served.

Oh yes, occasionally Mother would bake Pogácsa, which is a biscuit. One version would be baked with butter and another with fragments of "tepertö," created when bacon is fried in large pieces to make lard. What remains from that frying process is the tepertö, small pieces of which she would crush and mix in the biscuit dough and bake. Anytime some important guest would come to the house, there always would be freshly baked Pogácsa in anticipation of their arrival, ready to serve them before lunch or dinner.

Another of what you might call an appetizer would be "Lángos," or Bread Puffs—my very favorite to this day. They are deep-fried in oil using my favorite—sunflower oil. These bread puffs are irresistible. They are especially good when you take a clove of garlic and rub it all over the Lángos until it is down to your fingernails. Top it with sour cream and shredded cheese. Awesome! The closest thing I've found in the U.S. is the Indian flatbread, Naan.

I also have to mention "Körözött," a cheese spread made with butter, some goat cheese, chopped onions, garlic, and of course, Hungarian powder or paste paprika, making this a sensational spread.

Oh! The real and traditional appetizer for the Hungarians for centuries is the all-important Pálinka. Legend has it that it originated in the ninth century, when people settled in the present site of Hungary.

When I think back to my childhood and to this day, there always has been Pálinka in our house and, I think, most other Hungarian households. That was and is the real appetizer. It is actually served both before and after the meal. The "before," prepares the stomach for the meal, the "after" helps digest it. Logical, isn't it?

What Is It?

Pálinka is a strong alcoholic beverage—it has an alcohol content of 35–85 percent! It is loved by, and enjoys the reverence of, all Hungarians for its punch, flavor, and fragrance. It is truly a Hungarian invention. So much so that now the European Union has granted and patented the name Pálinka only to Hungary. It is not Pálinka if it is not made in Hungary! Just like it is not true Champagne if it is not made in the Champagne region of France.

Pálinka is made of fruits that grow in Hungary—plums, apricot, cherries, and others. Making Pálinka is an art. There are many artisans there but many more people who enjoy the fruits of their labor. A shot before or after the meal—or both—will help with the digestion of food and keep you in good health. There are those who just gulp it down in one shot and there are the connoisseurs who sip and savor the drink. If anything can be called an appetizer in Hungary, it is the Hungarian Pálinka.

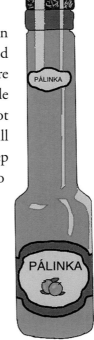

Yield about 5 cups
Preparation time 10 minutes
Cooking time 25 minutes
Ready in 35 minutes

Avocado Cilantro Salsa

This can also be used as a chilled side dish for meat and poultry.

ingredients

1 (16 oz) package frozen corn kernels, thawed

1 medium red bell pepper, chopped

1 medium onion, chopped

1 cup black olives, roughly chopped

1 cup green cabbage, shredded

2 Tbs cilantro, chopped

2 tsp Univer Gourmet Garlic Cream

⅓ cup olive oil

¼ cup lemon juice

¼ cup cider vinegar

1 tsp dried oregano

½ tsp salt

½ tsp pepper

3 medium avocados, peeled and diced

Tortilla chips

In a large bowl, mix corn, red bell pepper, onion, black olives, cabbage, and cilantro. Set aside. In a small bowl, whisk Garlic Cream, olive oil, lemon juice, cider vinegar, oregano, salt, and pepper. Pour into the corn mixture and toss to evenly coat. Cover and chill in the refrigerator for 2 hours. Add avocados just before serving. Stir to combine. Serve with tortilla chips.

Yield about 4 cups
Preparation time 10 minutes
Cooking time 25 minutes
Ready in 35 minutes

An all-time classic with a bit of a twist using green chilies.

Artichoke and Spinach Dip with Green Chilies

ingredients

1 (14 oz) can artichoke hearts, drained and chopped

½ cup grated Parmesan cheese

1 (10 oz) package frozen chopped spinach, thawed and squeezed dry

1 (4 oz) can mild green chilies, chopped

⅓ cup heavy cream

½ cup sour cream

1 Tbs Univer Gourmet Garlic Cream

1 cup shredded mozzarella cheese

Tortilla chips and bread chunks

Preheat oven to 350° F. Lightly grease or spray a 9x13-inch baking dish. In a medium bowl, mix artichoke hearts with Parmesan cheese. Add spinach, green chilies, heavy cream, sour cream, Garlic Cream and mozzarella cheese. Stir to combine. Spoon into prepared baking dish and bake for 25 minutes or until cheese is melted. Serve with tortilla chips and bread chunks.

After you have dried the spinach, check that it is really chopped. If you find a lot of stringy pieces, grab your knife and give it a bit more of a chop.

"My doctor told me to stop having intimate dinners for four ... unless there are three other people."
—Orson Welles

Serves 8

Preparation time 15 minutes

Ready in 15 minutes

A pretty, very refreshing appetizer that is light on the palate! The endive is crisp against the creaminess of the avocado.

Belgian Endive with Garlicky Avocado Spread

ingredients

2 heads Belgian endive, separated into leaves

2 Tbs Univer Mayonnaise

1½ tsp Univer Garlic Cream

1 Tbs grated Parmesan cheese

2 Tbs milk, more or less

1 medium avocado, mashed

3 Tbs shredded Parmesan cheese

Salt and pepper to taste

Wash the endive thoroughly in cold water and pat dry. Combine the Mayonnaise, Garlic Cream, grated Parmesan, and milk. Mash the avocado and add to mixture, stirring well. Add shredded Parmesan, salt, and pepper. Adjust milk to achieve desired consistency. Spread on ends of endive leaves.

Don't be intimidated by the price of the endive— 2 heads weigh very little.

Yield about 7 cups

Preparation time 15 minutes

Cooking time 35 minutes

Ready in 50 minutes

Beef, onions, and cheese— what more could a football fan want?!

Beefy Onion Dip

ingredients

1 lb lean ground beef

1 medium onion, chopped

¾ cup green bell pepper, chopped

½ cup celery, chopped

1 Tbs Univer Red Gold Mild

1 (6 oz) can tomato paste

1 cup water

2 tsp Univer Gourmet Garlic Cream

2 tsp Univer Red Gold Hot

1 tsp Worcestershire sauce

¼ tsp pepper

1 cup shredded Mexican cheese blend

Corn and tortilla chips

In a large frying pan over medium high heat, brown and crumble ground beef for about 10 minutes. Add onion, bell pepper, celery, and Red Gold Mild. Cook until onion is translucent, about 5 minutes. Drain excess fat. Stir in tomato paste and water. Add Garlic Cream, Red Gold Hot, Worcestershire sauce, and pepper. Bring to a boil. Cover, reduce heat, and simmer 20 minutes, stirring occasionally. Remove from heat and pour into a serving dish. Top with cheese and serve with corn chips and tortilla chips.

Don't store spices above your stove or other heat source. Keep them in a cool, dark place for maximum shelf life.

"I've been on a constant diet for the last two decades. I've lost a total of 789 pounds. By all accounts, I should be hanging from a charm bracelet."

—Erma Bombeck

Yield about 5 cups
Preparation time 15 minutes
Cooking time 15 minutes
Ready in 2 hours, 15 minutes

Substitute any type of beans for the black beans—creating dips and salsas are a great way to use up leftovers and clean out the pantry!!

Serves 4
Preparation time 10 minutes
Cooking time 5 minutes
Ready in 2 hour, 15 minutes

Black Bean and Avocado Salsa

Border Town Antichucos

A favorite at street festivals, this version really turns up the heat.

ingredients

1 (15 oz) can black beans, rinsed and drained

1 (16 oz) package frozen corn kernels, thawed

½ cup green onions, thinly sliced

½ cup black olives, roughly chopped

½ cup red bell pepper, chopped

2 Tbs fresh cilantro, chopped

1 (16 oz) jar chunky salsa

1½ tsp fresh lime juice

2 tsp Univer Strong Steven

1 tsp Univer Gourmet Garlic Cream

1 tsp ground cumin

1 medium avocado, peeled and diced

Tortilla chips

ingredients

½ cup Univer Strong Steven

½ cup low-sodium beef broth

1 Tbs Univer Gourmet Garlic Cream

1 large onion, grated medium fine

2 lbs top sirloin steak, cut into 1½-inch chunks

Combine beans, corn, onions, olives, red bell pepper, and cilantro in a medium bowl. In another bowl, combine salsa, lime juice, Strong Steven, Garlic Cream, and cumin. Mix until well blended and pour over vegetable mixture. Chill at least 2 hours. Just before serving, peel and dice the avocado and add to mixture. Serve with tortilla chips.

For the marinade, in a large mixing bowl, whisk together Strong Steven, beef broth and Garlic Cream. Grate the onion over a plate to catch juices. Squeeze the onions over the bowl to release juices, and then add onions to Strong Steven mixture and stir. Add meat to the mixture, cover and refrigerate for 2 hours. Divide meat evenly between metal skewers. Grill over very high heat for 2–3 minutes per side for medium rare. Baste with marinade at each turning.

Please note that the cumin was added to the wet ingredients. Cumin and other relatively strong herbs and spices should be added to a liquid so they are evenly distributed throughout the dish; otherwise you might get a big bite of cumin that wasn't incorporated well.

Serves 12

Preparation time 10 minutes

Cooking time 10 minutes

Ready in 20 minutes

Cheesy Mushrooms

Easy stuffed mushrooms are an instant hit at the cocktail table.

ingredients

24 large fresh mushrooms

2 Tbs olive oil

1 Tbs Univer Goulash Cream Hot

1 tsp Univer Gourmet Garlic Cream

¼ cup green onions, sliced, including green tops

⅔ cup Italian seasoned bread crumbs

½ cup shredded Cheddar cheese

1 Tbs fresh parsley, chopped

Preheat oven to 425° F. Lightly grease or spray a cookie sheet. Clean mushrooms and remove stems. Place mushroom caps on a cookie sheet. Chop enough stems to make about 1 cup. In a medium-size frying pan over medium heat, heat oil, Goulash Cream Hot, and Garlic Cream. Sauté chopped mushroom stems and green onions for 5 minutes. Remove from heat; stir in breadcrumbs, cheese, and parsley. Spoon crumb mixture into caps. Bake for 10–12 minutes or until heated through. Drizzle the caps with any accumulated pan juices and serve hot.

Use Goulash Cream Mild for a less spicy version.

Serves 16

Preparation time 20 minutes

Cooking time 5 minutes

Ready in 25 minutes

Try this as an alternative to garlic bread.

Cheesy Bruschetta

ingredients

1 cup cream cheese, softened

6 Tbs sour cream

2 Tbs Univer Mayonnaise

2 tsp Univer Gourmet Garlic Cream

1 cup shredded Italian cheese blend, divided

¼ cup grated Parmesan cheese

2 Tbs parsley, chopped

1 Tbs green onions, chopped

2 (1 pound) loaves French bread, cut diagonally in 1-inch slices

1 tsp ground black pepper

Preheat the broiler. In a medium bowl, blend cream cheese, sour cream, Mayonnaise, and Garlic Cream with an electric mixer until smooth. Stir in half of the Italian cheese blend. Add the Parmesan cheese, parsley, green onions and stir to blend. Arrange bread slices in a single layer on a large baking sheet. Lightly toast under the broiler. Remove from heat.

Spread French bread slices with the cream cheese mixture. Sprinkle with remaining cheese. Broil approximately 1½ minutes, until cheese is melted. Remove from heat and sprinkle with ground black pepper.

Forgot to take the cream cheese out to soften? Just cut into small pieces, and it will be ready soon.

Serves 8

Preparation time 20 minutes

Ready in 50 minutes

What a great way to use up leftover chicken!

Chicken and Olive Pinwheels

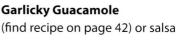

ingredients

1 cup cooked chicken, shredded or finely chopped

1 (4 oz) can mild green chilies, chopped

¼ cup black olives, chopped

¼ cup pimento-stuffed green olives, chopped

¼ cup green onions, chopped

8 oz cream cheese, softened

1 Tbs Univer Goulash Cream Mild

1 tsp Univer Gourmet Garlic Cream

¼ tsp black pepper

1 cup shredded Monterey Jack cheese

8 (10 inch) flour tortillas

Garlicky Guacamole
(find recipe on page 42) or salsa

In a large mixing bowl, combine the chicken, green chilies, black and green olives, and green onions. In a separate bowl, using a mixer, blend the cream cheese, Goulash Cream Mild, Garlic Cream, and pepper. Add cheese and stir to combine. Add cheese mixture to chicken mixture and stir well. Spread the mixture in a thin layer on the tortillas. Roll the tortillas up, cover and chill 30 minutes. Cut the tortilla rolls into ½-inch slices. Serve with Garlicky Guacamole or salsa.

"Never eat more than you can lift."
—**Miss Piggy**

Serves 4
Preparation time 15 minutes
Ready in 1 hours, 15 minutes

Chicken Salad Croissants

This is a lovely dish for a baby or wedding shower, and the guys love it, too!

2 cups chicken, cooked and cubed

¾ cup Univer Mayonnaise

1 Tbs fresh dill, chopped

1 cup seedless red grapes, sliced

1 (11 oz) can Mandarin oranges, drained and halved

½ cup walnuts, chopped

salt and pepper to taste

4 miniature croissants

In a large bowl, mix chicken and Mayonnaise. Gently fold in dill, grapes, mandarin oranges, and walnuts. Season with salt and pepper. Cover and refrigerate at least 1 hour. Serve the mixture on miniature croissants.

If you are short on time, rotisserie chicken from the supermarket works fine.

Serves 6
Preparation time 15 minutes
Ready in 45 minutes

Kid-friendly finger food that grownups like, too.

Chile and Black Bean Pinwheels

4 oz cream cheese, softened

½ cup shredded Mexican cheese blend

¼ cup sour cream

1 (4 oz) can mild green chilies or jalapeños, drained and chopped

½ tsp Univer Gourmet Garlic Cream

¼ tsp onion powder

1 cup refried black beans

3 large flour tortillas

Salsa

Mix cream cheese, Mexican cheese, sour cream, green chilies, Garlic Cream, and onion powder with mixer on medium speed until well blended. Place refried black beans in a bowl and stir for a minute to break up chucks and make them easier to spread. Spread a thin layer of beans on each tortilla; spread cheese mixture over beans. Roll tortillas up tightly and chill for 30 minutes. Cut into ½-inch slices. Serve with salsa.

"Thank you, I really love this paste and will be giving it as gifts."
—Delighted Paprika Fan

Serves 5 cups
Preparation time 15 minutes
Cooking time 30 minutes
Ready in 45 minutes

Restaurant-style Queso right from your kitchen!

Chile Con Queso

1 lb lean ground beef

1 Tbs Univer Goulash Cream Hot

1 tsp Univer Gourmet Garlic Cream

1 cup onions, chopped

2 (4 oz) cans chopped green chilies

1 cup tomatoes, seeded and diced

8 oz process cheese loaf, cubed

⅓ cup half and half cream

1 (1.25 oz) package taco seasoning mix

Tortilla chips

In a frying pan, brown and crumble ground beef; add Goulash Cream Hot and Garlic Cream. Stir into meat. Add onion and cook until transparent, about 5 minutes. Add green chilies and tomatoes. Stir to combine, then drain excess fat. Add cheese and slowly melt into meat mixture. Meanwhile, mix taco seasoning with cream. Slowly blend in cream mixture. Keep warm and serve with tortilla chips for dipping.

An electric fondue pot will keep this dip at just the right temperature.

Serves 12
Preparation time 5 minutes
Ready in 5 minutes

Sweet-Hot Apricot Spread

Many dips and salsas are quite tasty when served over softened cream cheese. Next time you make one, imagine it with cream cheese as a "base."

1 (12 oz) jar apricot preserves

1 Tbs Univer Mustard

1 Tbs Univer Horseradish with Vinegar

1 (8 oz) package cream cheese, softened

freshly ground black pepper to taste

Crackers

In a medium-size bowl, combine apricot preserves, Mustard, and Horseradish with Vinegar. Place the cream cheese on a serving plate and spoon the apricot mixture over the cream cheese. Grind fresh pepper over the top. Serve with crackers.

If the preserves have been refrigerated, warm them a little in the microwave or on the stovetop so they will be easier to blend.

Serves 12

Preparation time 20 minutes

Cooking time 20 minutes

Ready in 40 minutes

One of our most popular appetizers, this makes a beautiful presentation on a pretty tray. The stuffing can also be used for mushrooms.

Chorizo Wonton Flowers

ingredients

1 lb ground chorizo pork sausage, or sausage of your choice

1 cup shredded Mexican cheese blend

1 cup salsa, drained

1 Tbs Univer Goulash Cream Hot

24 (3.5-inch square) wonton wrappers

½ cup sour cream

½ cup green onions, chopped

Preheat oven to 350° F. Lightly grease or spray a miniature muffin pan. In a large frying pan over medium high heat, brown and crumble sausage. Drain excess fat. Stir in cheese, salsa, and Goulash Cream Hot; set aside.

Press wonton wrappers into the prepared muffin pan so that edges are extending. Spoon a heaping tablespoon of the sausage mixture into each wonton wrapper. Bake 10 minutes, or until edges begin to brown. Transfer to a serving dish. Put a dollop of sour cream on each wonton and sprinkle with green onions.

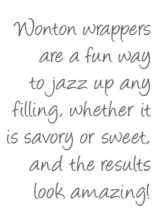

Wonton wrappers are a fun way to jazz up any filling, whether it is savory or sweet, and the results look amazing!

Serves 3
Preparation time 10 minutes
Cooking time 10 minutes
Ready in 50 minutes

Sophisticated and timeless, crab cakes are a lavish appetizer. You can also double this recipe to serve as an entrée.

Crab Cakes

ingredients

¼ cup Univer Mayonnaise

1 Tbs Univer Mustard

1 tsp Univer Gourmet Garlic Cream

1 tsp Univer Red Gold Hot

1 large egg

½ cup green onions, finely chopped, including green tops

¼ cup frozen corn, thawed

¼ cup celery, finely chopped, with some leafy tops

1 lb crabmeat, picked over

½ cup plain breadcrumbs (or more)

2 Tbs butter

2 Tbs olive oil

Panko (Japanese-style bread-crumbs) for dredging

Spicy Red Mayonnaise
(find recipe on page 230)

In a large mixing bowl, whisk together Mayonnaise, Mustard, Garlic Cream, Red Gold Hot, and egg. Fold in the green onions, corn, and celery. Mix to combine. Add crabmeat and gently stir, being careful to keep larger crab pieces intact. Add enough bread-crumbs so crab mixture just holds together when shaped into a cake. Cover and chill for about 30 minutes so mixture is easier to handle and breadcrumbs can absorb most of the moisture.

Shape mixture into 8 small cakes. Heat butter and oil in a frying pan. Dip cakes into the panko on both sides and brush off excess. Cook on medium heat for about 5 minutes on each side, or until browned and cooked through. Do not crowd pan. Drain and serve warm with Spicy Red Mayonnaise.

Don't overcrowd the pan when frying or deep-frying foods. You will lose the heat needed to really sear the outside of the food and instead the food will steam.

Serves 4
Preparation time 5 minutes
Ready in 5 minutes

Colorado Nachos

Make plenty! Your guests will love this unique little snack.

ingredients

16 whole wheat crackers

6 Tbs peanut butter

6 Tbs Univer Horseradish with Vinegar

3 slices bacon, cooked and finely crumbled

Mix together peanut butter and Horseradish with Vinegar. Spread on crackers. Top with bacon crumbles and serve.

For variety, use slices of cucumber and jicama. Great on celery sticks, too!

Serves 6
Preparation time 20 minutes
Cooking time 10 minutes
Ready in 2 hours, 30 minutes

Always a favorite with the kids; try this for the ball game instead of wings! Serve with a Buffalo-style sauce if you want to punch up the heat.

Crispy Chicken Fingers

ingredients

4 boneless skinless chicken breasts, cut into ½-inch strips

1 egg

1 cup buttermilk

1 Tbs Univer Goulash Cream Mild

1½ tsp Univer Gourmet Garlic Cream

1 cup flour

1 cup seasoned breadcrumbs

1 tsp baking powder

1 quart oil, for frying

Spicy Red Mayonnaise (find recipe on page 230) or **Horseradish Mustard Sauce** (find recipe on page 232)

Place chicken strips into a large, re-sealable plastic bag. In a small bowl, whisk together the egg, buttermilk, Goulash Cream Mild, and Garlic Cream. Pour mixture into the bag with chicken. Seal and refrigerate at least 2 hours, turning occasionally. In another large, re-sealable plastic bag, combine the flour, bread-crumbs, and baking powder. Remove chicken from bag and shake to remove excess moisture. Discard buttermilk marinade. Place chicken in flour mixture bag. Seal, and shake to coat.

Heat oil in a large, deep pan to 375° F. Carefully place coated chicken in hot oil a few pieces at a time. Fry until golden brown and juices run clear, about 10 minutes. Drain on paper towels. Serve with Spicy Red Mayonnaise or Horseradish Mustard Sauce.

These look very tasty when served in a basket with a checkered napkin!

Serves about 1 cup

Preparation time 5 minutes

Ready in 35 minutes

Yummy with crispy cold veggies, or spread on trimmed celery sticks.

Curried Mayonnaise Dip

ingredients

1 cup Univer Mayonnaise

1–2 tsp curry powder

1 tsp lemon juice

1 tsp honey

¼ tsp black pepper

½ tsp Univer Red Gold Hot

Fresh veggies and pita crisps

In a bowl, combine all ingredients and stir until well blended. Cover and chill for 30 minutes. Serve with fresh vegetables and pita crisps.

Curry powder can be quite strong, especially when freshly opened. Try one teaspoon to begin with, then add more to taste.

Red Gold Hot
A few suggested uses:

- Add a spicy boost to stews, soups and gravies
- Glaze a sizzling steak or chop
- Mix into ground meats
- Add to marinades
- Sauté onions and vegetables
- Create wonderful dips
- Mix into salsa to enhance the flavor
- Add to ranch dressing to make Southwestern dressing with a kick
- Lightly brush onto hot grilled pineapple
- Gluten-free; no trans fats

Yield about 2½ cups
Preparation time 10 minutes
Ready in 2 hours, 10 minutes

Garlic Vegetable Dip

Fresh dips and spreads are so quick and simple to make. This one is good on baked potatoes, too!

ingredients

1 cup Univer Mayonnaise

1 cup sour cream

1 Tbs Univer Mustard

1 tsp Univer Gourmet Garlic Cream

3 Tbs green onions, finely chopped

3 Tbs green olives, finely chopped

1 Tbs fresh parsley, chopped

salt and pepper to taste

Fresh vegetables and crackers

Whisk together the Mayonnaise, sour cream, Mustard, and Garlic Cream until well blended. Add the green onions, green olives, and parsley. Season with salt and pepper and stir to combine. Cover and chill for at least 2 hours. Serve with fresh vegetables and crackers.

Yiel;d About 3½ cups
Preparation time 15 minutes
Ready in 1 hour, 15 minutes

Gourmet Garlic Cream really shines in any dip recipe because it blends perfectly.

Garlicky Guacamole

ingredients

2–3 large ripe avocados

3 Tbs fresh lime juice

2 tsp Univer Gourmet Garlic Cream

1 jalapeño, seeded and diced

2 small tomatoes, seeded and diced

1 small red onion, finely chopped

¼ cup fresh cilantro leaves, finely chopped

salt and freshly ground pepper, to taste

Tortilla chips

Halve and pit avocados and scoop flesh into a large bowl. Mash avocado with a fork, leaving some chucks for texture. Whisk lime juice with Garlic Cream and add to avocados. Stir in the jalapeño, tomatoes, onion, and cilantro. Blend well. Season with salt and pepper to taste. Cover and chill for at least 1 hour. Stir guacamole again and serve with tortilla chips.

If you don't use jalapeños very often, buy a jar of them in the olive aisle at the supermarket. Keep the jar in the refrigerator and use them as needed.

"The most dangerous food is wedding cake."

—**James Thurber**

Yield about 4 cups
Preparation time 30 minutes
Ready in 2 hours, 30 minutes

So pretty and fresh!

Half Cup Relish

ingredients

½ cup black beans, rinsed and drained

½ cup red bell pepper, finely chopped

½ cup frozen corn kernels, thawed

½ cup tomatoes, seeded and diced

½ cup green cabbage, shredded

½ cup red onion, finely chopped

2 Tbs jalapeño peppers, seeded and finely chopped

2 Tbs cilantro, finely chopped

1 Tbs Univer Strong Steven

2 tsp Univer Gourmet Garlic Cream

½ tsp ground cumin

1 cup sour cream

Tortilla chips

In a medium-size mixing bowl, mix all the vegetables. Add jalapeño, cilantro, Strong Steven, Garlic Cream, and cumin; fold in sour cream. Cover and refrigerate 2 hours. Serve with tortilla chips.

Leftovers? Serve on a bed of lettuce for a great salad.

Yield about 2½ cups
Preparation time 10 minutes
Ready in 10 minutes

Green Chile Cheese Spread

This is not only a great spread, but it makes a good topper for a bowl of hot chili, too!

ingredients

1 (8-oz) package cream cheese, softened

1 Tbs Univer Red Gold Hot

1 tsp Univer Gourmet Garlic Cream

1 (4.5 oz) can chopped green chilies, drained

2 Tbs jalapeño peppers, seeded and chopped

1 cup shredded Mexican cheese blend

3 green onions, chopped

Crackers, tortilla chips and cut vegetables

In a medium mixing bowl, mix cream cheese with Red Gold Hot and Garlic Cream until combined. Add chilies, jalapeños, cheese, and green onions. Blend well. Spoon into a crock or serving dish. Serve with crackers, tortilla chips, and cut vegetables.

Serve at room temperature for best flavor.

Makes 24 pieces

Preparation time 30 minutes

Ready in 2 hour, 30 minutes

An attractive appetizer brightened with fresh basil.

Ham and Sun-Dried Tomato Roll-Ups

ingredients

1 (8 oz) package cream cheese, softened

1 Tbs Univer Goulash Cream Mild

6 (10-inch) flour tortillas

12 slices deli ham

4 oz fresh basil

1 cup sun-dried tomatoes, drained

6 leaves red leaf lettuce

In a small mixing bowl, blend cream cheese and Goulash Cream Mild until combined. Spread each tortilla lightly with cream cheese mixture. Arrange two ham slices across the middle of each tortilla. Add a layer of basil, then a layer of tomatoes. Top with lettuce layer. Do not place ingredients too close to tortilla edges. Starting at one end, tightly roll up each tortilla, securing with toothpicks at regular intervals. Cover and refrigerate for 2 hours. Slice each roll into four evenly sized pieces. Remove toothpicks to serve.

Sun-dried tomatoes have a wonderful, intense flavor. If you haven't used them before, you'll soon be adding them to many of your favorite dishes.

Yield about 5 cups
Preparation time 15 minutes
Cooking time 50 minutes
Ready in 1 hour, 5 minutes

Delicious, hearty, and great for any occasion.

Ham and Swiss Dip Bread Bowl

ingredients

1 lb round loaf of bread

2 Tbs olive oil

8 oz cream cheese, softened

8 oz sour cream

1 Tbs Univer Goulash Cream Mild

½ tsp Worcestershire sauce

1 cup shredded Swiss cheese

1 (10 oz) package frozen broccoli florets, thawed and chopped

1 cup deli ham, diced

½ cup green onions, chopped

Bread chunks, chips, and crackers

Preheat oven to 350° F. Slice off top of bread loaf; reserve top. Hollow out loaf of bread, making a shell, being careful not to cut through sides or bottom. Cut hollowed out bread into chunks, set aside. Brush olive oil on the outside of bread bowl. Place on a baking sheet, and bake for 10 minutes. Beat cream cheese until smooth; add sour cream and beat until creamy. Stir in Goulash Cream Mild and Worcestershire sauce. Add cheese, broccoli, ham, and green onions. Stir again; spoon into the bread bowl. Cover with reserved bread top.

Cover loosely with foil and continue baking for 30 minutes until bread bowl is nicely browned and dip is bubbly. Toast reserved bread chunks 7–10 minutes, until golden. Serve with bread chunks, chips, and crackers.

This recipe is fun for a potluck; wrap it in foil to keep it warm.

Serves 5
Preparation time 20 minutes
Cooking time 30 minutes
Ready in 50 minutes

Hot Reuben Dip

One of our most sought-after recipes—be prepared to share this one!

ingredients

1 cup Univer Mayonnaise

1 cup sour cream

2 Tbs Univer Horseradish with Vinegar

1 Tbs Univer Mustard

1 (16 oz) can sauerkraut, drained, squeezed dry, and chopped

1 small onion, finely chopped

¼ lb deli corned beef, finely chopped

1 cup shredded Swiss cheese

1 Tbs dried caraway seeds

Rye bagel chips or party rye bread

Preheat oven to 350° F. Lightly grease or spray a 1-quart baking dish. In a medium mixing bowl, whisk together the Mayonnaise, sour cream, Horseradish with Vinegar and Mustard. Add the sauerkraut, onion, corned beef, Swiss cheese, and caraway seeds. Spoon into prepared baking dish. Bake for 30–40 minutes, or until bubbly and heated through. Serve with rye bagel chips or party rye bread.

Leftovers? Spread on slices of rye bread, broil lightly, and serve open-faced.

Serves 8
Preparation time 5 minutes
Cooking time 10 minutes
Ready in 15 minutes

Olive Crostini

Crostini offers a nice alternative to traditional garlic bread. Try it on your next pasta night.

ingredients

2 (6 oz) cans black olives, pitted and drained

3 Tbs olive oil

2 Tbs pine nuts, toasted

1 tsp Univer Gourmet Garlic Cream

½ tsp Univer Goulash Cream Mild

black pepper to taste

1 French bread, baguette-style, sliced into 8 pieces

8 slices roasted red peppers

Preheat oven to 350° F. In a food processor, purée olives, olive oil, pine nuts, Garlic Cream, and Goulash Cream Mild until smooth. Season olive purée with pepper to taste. Place bread slices in single layer on baking sheet. Bake for 10 minutes, or until lightly toasted. Spread olive paste on toast. Top with roasted pepper pieces. Serve immediately.

Toast pine nuts in a frying pan over medium heat, stirring frequently, for about 4–5 minutes until lightly browned and fragrant.

Serves 10
Preparation time 15 minutes
Cooking time 25 minutes
Ready in 40 minutes

There's something special about a hot dip that people really enjoy. Maybe it's the extra little effort that's so appreciated.

Hot Swiss and Spinach Dip

ingredients

1 cup Univer Mayonnaise

1 tsp Univer Gourmet Garlic Cream

1 tsp Univer Goulash Cream Mild

1 (10 oz) package frozen chopped spinach, thawed and squeezed dry

1 (4 oz) can chopped green chilies, drained

1 cup shredded Swiss cheese

¾ cup grated Parmesan cheese

¼ tsp ground black pepper

1 tomato, seeded and diced

Crackers and vegetables

Preheat oven to 350° F. In a medium bowl, whisk together Mayonnaise, Garlic Cream, and Goulash Cream Mild. Add spinach, chilies, Swiss cheese, Parmesan cheese and black pepper. Stir to combine. Spoon mixture into 9-inch ungreased pie pan. Bake 25 to 30 minutes, until bubbly and lightly browned. Top with diced tomatoes and serve warm with crackers and vegetables.

Seeding the tomato will help prevent the dish from becoming watery.

Yield about 24 meatballs

Preparation time 10 minutes

Cooking time 30 minutes

Ready in 40 minutes

These succulent little gems will go fast. You may also make them to serve with pasta and your favorite sauce.

Hungarian Meatballs

ingredients

1 Tbs extra virgin olive oil

1 Tbs butter

3 Tbs Univer Red Gold Hot, divided

1 medium onion, chopped

¾ lb ground beef

¾ lb ground pork

1 Tbs Univer Gourmet Garlic Cream

1 cup seasoned breadcrumbs

1 cup grated Parmesan cheese

1 egg

Bill's Zookie Sauce
(find recipe on page 231)

Preheat oven to 350° F. Grease or spray a baking sheet. In a large frying pan, heat oil, butter, and 1 tablespoon of Red Gold Hot; sauté onions until translucent, about 5 minutes. Meanwhile, mix together the meat, Garlic Cream, breadcrumbs, cheese, 2 remaining tablespoons Red Gold Hot, and egg. Add sautéed onions and mix until blended. Roll into bite-sized balls and place on baking sheet. Bake about 30 minutes or until done. Remove to a platter and serve with Bill's Zookie Sauce.

If you are short on time or patience, you may add the chopped onion raw to the meat mixture. It gives a slightly different consistency and a stronger onion taste, but the meatballs are still very good. If you do not sauté the onions, eliminate the oils and use 2 tablespoons of Red Gold Hot.

Serves 6

Preparation time   20 minutes

Ready in   20 minutes

Welcome the stuffed egg back to the appetizer table.

Paprika Stuffed Eggs

ingredients

6 eggs, hard boiled, shelled,
  cut in halves, yolks reserved

2 Tbs pickle relish, dill or sweet

2 Tbs Univer Mayonnaise

1 Tbs Univer Mustard

1 Tbs Univer Goulash Cream Mild

1 Tbs grated Parmesan cheese

celery seed, for garnish

freshly ground black pepper,
  for garnish

In a medium-size mixing bowl, break up cooked egg yolks. Add relish and mix together. Add Mayonnaise, Mustard, Goulash Cream Mild, and Parmesan cheese; stir to combine. Spoon yolk mixture into egg halves. Arrange on an attractive serving dish and garnish with celery seed and fresh black pepper.

Egg filling is largely a matter of taste and consistency. Add the relish to the yolks first, because the relish has a lot of moisture. Taste as you mix, and you will find the perfect ratio of ingredients. The measurements above are approximate; adjust to your own tastes.

Yield about 10 cups
Preparation time 30 minutes
Cooking time 50 minutes
Ready in 1 hour, 20 minutes

Paprika (Goulash Cream Mild or Hot) enhances the flavor of this classic dip. If you use Goulash Cream Hot, you may want to back off the amount of jalapeños.

Picadillo Chip Dip

ingredients

½ lb lean ground beef

½ lb ground pork

2 tsp Univer Goulash Cream Mild

2 tsp Univer Gourmet Garlic Cream

½ tsp black pepper

1 (14 oz) can low-sodium beef broth

4 medium tomatoes, seeded and diced

4 green onions, chopped, including tops

1 (12 oz) can tomato paste

2 jalapeño peppers, seeded and finely chopped

½ tsp dried oregano

¾ cup diced pimentos

¾ cup raisins

¾ cup toasted sliced almonds

Tortilla chips

In a large frying pan over medium-high heat, brown and crumble meats. Drain excess fat. Add Goulash Cream Mild, Garlic Cream, pepper and stir into meat. Add beef broth to meat mixture, cover and bring to a boil. Reduce heat and simmer 20 minutes. Add tomatoes, green onions, and tomato paste. Stir to combine. Add jalapeños, oregano, pimentos, raisins, and almonds. Cover and bring to a boil, reduce heat, and simmer for 30 minutes. Serve warm with tortilla chips.

Golden raisins add a pretty touch, but dark raisins are just fine. This dish freezes well.

Yield about 4 cups
Preparation time 10 minutes
Cooking time 15 minutes
Ready in 25 minutes

Pizza Dip

If you love pizza, this is the best dip ever!

ingredients

8 oz cream cheese, softened

½ cup sour cream

1 tsp Univer Strong Steven

1 tsp Univer Gourmet Garlic Cream

1 tsp dried oregano

1 cup prepared pizza sauce

½ cup pepperoni, chopped

¼ cup green onions, sliced

¼ cup green peppers, chopped

½ cup shredded Italian cheese blend

Tortilla chips

Preheat oven to 350° F. In a medium bowl, mix together cream cheese, sour cream, Strong Steven, Garlic Cream, and oregano. Spread mixture in an 8-inch square pan. Top with pizza sauce. Evenly spread pepperoni, green onions, and green peppers over the pizza sauce. Bake for 10 minutes. Remove from oven and top with cheese and bake another 5 minutes, or until cheese is melted and mixture is heated through. Serve with tortilla chips.

There are so many variations to this dip! What's your favorite pizza? Adjust the meat and veggies accordingly!

Yield about 5½ cups
Preparation time 10 minutes
Cooking time 30 minutes
Ready in 40 minutes

Ranchero Bean Dip

A handy take-along dish that will serve a hungry crowd.

ingredients

1 (16 oz) can refried beans with jalapeño peppers

1 cup picanté sauce (any heat level)

2 cups shredded Mexican cheese blend

1 cup sour cream

1 (3 oz) package cream cheese, softened

1 Tbs Univer Red Gold Hot

1 tsp Univer Gourmet Garlic Cream

½ tsp ground cumin

½ cup green onions, chopped

Chips and crackers

Preheat oven to 350° F. Lightly grease or spray a 13x9-inch baking pan. In a medium bowl, combine refried beans, picanté sauce, cheese, sour cream, cream cheese, Red Gold Hot, Garlic Cream, and cumin. Mix until well blended. Transfer to the prepared baking pan. Bake for 30 minutes, or until cheese is melted and bubbly. Remove from oven and top with green onions. Serve with your favorite chips and crackers.

Serves 8
Preparation time 15 minutes
Cooking time 20 minutes
Ready in 35 minutes

Tasty and fast, this could also be a great dinner for mid-week.

Quesadilla Turnovers

ingredients

1 lb lean ground beef

1 Tbs Univer Red Gold Hot

1 tsp Univer Gourmet Garlic Cream

1 medium onion, chopped

¾ cup chunky salsa, medium heat, drained

1 (4.5 oz) can chopped green chilies, drained

2 cups shredded Mexican cheese blend

16 flour tortillas (8-inch)

olive oil

Sour cream or **Garlicky Guacamole** (find recipe on page 42)

Preheat the oven to 450° F. Lightly grease or spray a large baking sheet. In a large frying pan, brown and crumble the ground beef over medium heat until nearly done. Add the Red Gold Hot and the Garlic Cream; stir into meat. Add the onions and sauté for about 5 minutes. Drain off the excess liquid. Add the salsa and chilies; mix well, then stir in the cheese. Spoon about ¼ cup of the mixture over half of each tortilla; fold each in half and place on a baking sheet. Lightly brush the tops of the tortillas with olive oil and bake for 8 to 10 minutes, or until the tortillas are lightly browned and crisp. Serve with a dollop of sour cream or Garlicky Guacamole.

Leftovers? Toss them with some eggs to make a delicious Mexican scramble!

Yield about 6 cups
Preparation time 10 minutes
Cooking time 25 minutes
Ready in 35 minutes

Sweet Ann Paprika lends a beautiful color and wonderful flavor. You may add more, to taste.

Roasted Red Pepper Dip

ingredients

1 (8 oz) package cream cheese, softened

1 cup Univer Mayonnaise

2 Tbs Univer Mustard

1 tsp Univer Gourmet Garlic Cream

1 tsp Univer Sweet Ann

1 (7 oz) jar roasted red peppers, drained and diced

¼ cup onion, finely diced

2½ cups shredded Monterey Jack cheese

Tortilla chips and crackers

Preheat oven to 350° F. In a medium mixing bowl, blend cream cheese, Mayonnaise, Mustard, Garlic Cream, and Sweet Ann. Add roasted red peppers, onions, and cheese. Mix to combine. Spoon into a baking dish and bake for 25 minutes, until lightly browned and bubbly. Serve with tortilla chips and crackers.

Paprika in its raw form (all Univer paprika products) contains vitamin C. One teaspoon of Sweet Ann has 6 percent of vitamin C, based on a 2,000-calorie diet. By actual weight, paprika contains more vitamin C than lemon juice.

"Learn how to cook— try new recipes, learn from your mistakes, be fearless, and above all, have fun!"
—Julia Child

Yield about 5 cups
Preparation time 15 minutes
Ready in 3 hours, 15 minutes

Salmon and Spinach Dip

Try serving this dip in a hollowed-out bread bowl, using the bread as dippers.

ingredients

1 (7.5 oz) can salmon

1 (10 oz) package frozen chopped spinach, thawed and squeezed dry

1½ cups Univer Mayonnaise

2 tsp Univer Goulash Cream Hot

½ cup fresh parsley, chopped

½ cup green onions, chopped

¾ tsp dill weed

½ tsp dried basil

½ tsp lemon zest

Veggies and crackers

Drain salmon and place in a medium-size mixing bowl. Flake with a fork; add spinach and stir to combine. In a small mixing bowl, whisk together Mayonnaise, Goulash Cream Hot, parsley, green onions, dill weed, basil, and zest. Add to salmon mixture and stir to blend well. Cover and refrigerate for 3 hours to blend flavors. Serve dip with raw vegetables and crackers.

Yield about 4 cups
Preparation time 15 minutes
Cooking time 25 minutes
Ready in 40 minutes

An Italian spin on the Mexican classic 7-Layer Dip.

Seven Layer Italian Dip

ingredients

1 (8 oz) package cream cheese, softened

1 Tbs Univer Gourmet Garlic Cream

1 Tbs Univer Goulash Cream Mild

½ cup grated Parmesan cheese, divided

1 tsp dried oregano

½ cup pepperoni, chopped

½ cup salami, chopped

⅓ cup prepared pesto

1 (4 oz) jar diced pimentos, drained

½ cup black olives, chopped

¼ cup Italian Giardiniera mix, drained and chopped

½ cup shredded Italian cheese blend

Crackers or sliced Italian bread

Preheat oven to 350° F. Mix cream cheese, Garlic Cream, Goulash Cream Mild, ¼ cup Parmesan cheese, and oregano with an electric mixer on medium speed until well blended. Spread mixture on the bottom of a 9-inch pie pan. Mix pepperoni and salami and layer on top of cream cheese mixture.

Layer, in this order, the pesto, pimientos, black olives, Giardiniera mix, Italian cheese, and remaining Parmesan cheese over the meats. Bake for 25 minutes or until thoroughly heated. Serve with crackers or sliced Italian bread.

Giardiniera may be found in the olive and jarred pepper section of most supermarkets.

Yield about 5 cups

Preparation time 15 minutes

Cooking time 35 minutes

Ready in about 50 minutes

An old favorite now in dip form!

Sausage, Peppers, and Onions Dip

ingredients

1 lb bulk hot Italian sausage

1 Tbs Univer Goulash Cream Mild

1 Tbs Univer Gourmet Garlic Cream

1 cup onions, chopped

½ cup green bell peppers, chopped

1 cup sour cream

½ cup Univer Mayonnaise

¼ cup grated Parmesan cheese

1 (2 oz) jar diced pimento peppers

¼ cup green onions, chopped

Crackers and cocktail breads

Preheat oven to 350° F. Lightly grease or spray a medium baking dish. In a frying pan over medium high heat, brown and crumble sausage until nearly done. Add Goulash Cream Mild and Garlic Cream; stir into meat. Add onions and bell peppers; sauté about 5 minutes. Drain fat and set meat mixture aside.

In a mixing bowl, combine sour cream, Mayonnaise, Parmesan cheese, and pimentos. Add sausage mixture and stir to blend. Spoon mixture into prepared baking dish. Bake for about 25 minutes, or until bubbly and slightly browned. Garnish with green onions. Serve warm with crackers and cocktail breads.

"A nickel will get you on the subway, but garlic will get you a seat."
—**Old New York Proverb**

Serves 8
Preparation time 10 minutes
Cooking time 45 minutes
Ready in about 1 hour

Strong Steven Chicken Wings

These are spicy hot, garlicky and a big hit as an appetizer.

ingredients

7 lbs chicken wings

1 (7.4 oz) jar Univer Strong Steven

1 Tbs Univer Gourmet Garlic Cream, or more to taste

1 large onion, grated medium fine

Garlic Ranch Dressing
(find recipe on page 227)

Preheat oven to 350° F. Prepare chicken wings by cutting off wing tips and discarding. Split at the joint to make two portions. In a medium-size mixing bowl, whisk together Strong Steven and Garlic Cream. Grate the onion over the bowl to catch juices.

Place wings in large roasting pan and pour Strong Steven mixture evenly over all. Toss to coat all pieces and spread in a single layer. Cover with foil and bake for 30 minutes. Uncover and bake another 15 minutes, or until chicken is done. For more color, brown wings under the broiler for a few minutes. Serve with Garlic Ranch Dressing.

Yield about 7 cups
Preparation time 15 minutes
Cooking time 30 minutes
Ready in 45 minutes

There are so many variations of Spinach dip; we hope you enjoy this one.

Southwestern Spinach Dip

ingredients

1 Tbs vegetable oil

1 cup chopped onions

1 tsp Univer Goulash Cream Mild

1 tsp Univer Gourmet Garlic Cream

1 cup chunky salsa, drained

1 (10 oz) package chopped spinach, thawed and squeezed dry

2½ cups shredded Mexican cheese blend, divided

1 (8 oz) package cream cheese, softened and cubed

1 cup half and half cream

½ cup sliced black olives

1 (4 oz) can jalapeño peppers, drained and chopped

Tortilla or taco chips

Preheat oven to 400° F. In a frying pan over medium heat, sauté onions in oil, Goulash Cream Mild, and Garlic Cream for 5 minutes. Stir in salsa and spinach, and cook 2 more minutes. Transfer to a baking dish. Stir in 2 cups of the cheese blend, the cream cheese, cream, olives, and jalapeños. Bake for 30 minutes or until hot and bubbly. Cover with foil during last few minutes to prevent over-browning. Remove from oven and top with remaining cheese. Serve hot with chips.

"Red meat is not bad for you. Now blue-green meat, that's bad for you"
—Tommy Smothers

Yield about 6 cups

Preparation time 30 minutes

Cooking time 2 minutes

Ready in about 12 hours, 30 minutes

Great as an appetizer, a martini garnish, or used in salads.

Spicy Marinated Vegetables

ingredients

6 cups fresh vegetables, such as cauliflower, broccoli, asparagus, carrots, onions, and bell peppers, cut into florets and chunks

1 gallon water

2 Tbs salt

1 (8 oz) package Mozzarella cheese, cubed

1 cup olives, black, green, or mixed

1 (4 oz) jar pimento slices, including marinade

Marinade

2½ cups extra virgin olive oil

1½ cups white wine vinegar

2 Tbs Univer Mustard

2 Tbs Univer Red Gold Hot

1 Tbs Univer Gourmet Garlic Cream

1 tsp freshly ground black pepper

1 tsp dried rosemary leaves

1 tsp dried thyme

1 tsp dried oregano

In a large pot or Dutch oven, add water and salt; cover and bring to a hard boil; add vegetables and cook, covered, 2 minutes. Drain and rinse with cold water to stop the cooking process. Place vegetables in a large mixing bowl; add the cheese, olives, and pimento slices. To make the marinade, whisk together the oil and vinegar. Add the remaining ingredients and blend well.

Pour the marinade over the vegetables, tossing to coat. Cover and refrigerate overnight. Toss occasionally to evenly distribute marinade. Drain excess marinade; reserve. Serve cold over a bed of red leaf lettuce. If there are leftovers, return to marinade, cover and refrigerate. If not, discard marinade.

I am so excited about discovering your fine products that I have to write and tell you. I have made so many great recipes that there are never any leftovers after dinner."

—Delighted Paprika Fan

Serves about 16
Preparation time 30 minutes
Ready in 30 minutes

Stuffed Green Olives with Garlic and Cheese

Great as a martini garnish, too!

ingredients

4 Tbs grated Parmesan cheese

1 Tbs Gorgonzola cheese

1 Tbs Univer Garlic Cream

8 oz large, marinated unstuffed green olives

Blend together the Parmesan and the Gorgonzola cheeses. Mix in the Garlic Cream to form a smooth paste. Fill a pastry bag with cheese mixture. Using a small round piping tip, pipe paste into olives. Store leftover olives in refrigerator.

Buy marinated olives in the deli. No pastry bag? Use a plastic food storage bag with a tiny snip cut off of one bottom corner.

Serves 10
Preparation time 30 minutes
Cooking time 15 minutes
Ready in about 1 hour, 15 minutes

There are certain appetizers that nearly everyone loves, and mushrooms oozing with cheesy goodness are always welcome!

Stuffed Mushrooms

ingredients

1 lb lean ground beef

2 Tbs Univer Goulash Cream Hot

2 Tbs Univer Garlic Cream

¼ cup margarine

2 lbs fresh mushrooms, stems removed, chopped and reserved

½ cup onions, chopped

½ cup green bell peppers, chopped

3 tsp dried parsley

1 tsp dried basil leaves

1 cup Italian seasoned bread-crumbs

2 cups shredded sharp Cheddar cheese

Preheat oven to 400° F. Lightly grease or spray a large baking sheet. In a large frying pan over medium high heat, brown and crumble beef. Drain excess drippings. Add Goulash Cream Hot and Garlic Cream and toss to coat meat. Remove from pan and place in large bowl. Set aside.

In the frying pan, melt the margarine and stir in the chopped mushroom stems, onions, green bell peppers, parsley, and basil. Cook to soften, about 5 minutes. Add vegetable mixture to the ground beef mixture. Add breadcrumbs and Cheddar cheese and stir to combine. Place the mushroom caps on the baking sheet. Generously stuff each cap with the mixture. Let rest about 30 minutes, and then bake for 15 to 20 minutes, or until the filling is golden brown.

We've never understood the mushroom/water relationship. If mushrooms will get soggy if we wash them, why don't they get soggy in our sauce? If they are really dirty, we say give them a quick rinse, pat dry, and be done with it!

Serves 8
Preparation time 5 minutes
Cooking time 30 minutes
Ready in 35 minutes

Kielbasa can usually be found in the prepared sausage section of the supermarket.

Sweet Kielbasa Sausage with Onions

ingredients

1 cup packed brown sugar
½ cup ketchup
¼ cup Univer Horseradish with Vinegar
2 lbs kielbasa sausage, cut into 1-inch slices
1 medium onion, sliced

In a saucepan, combine the sugar, ketchup, and Horseradish with Vinegar; blend well. Add the sausage and onions, stirring again to coat. Bring to a boil and reduce heat to a simmer. Cover and cook about 30 minutes, until sauce is syrupy and clings to the sausage and onions. Plate sausage with toothpicks for serving.

"We are living in a world today where lemonade is made from artificial flavors and furniture polish is made from real lemons."

—Alfred E. Newman

Yield about 2½ cups
Preparation time 10 minutes
Cooking time 20 minutes
Ready in 30 minutes

Zesty Artichoke Shrimp Dip

A shrimp appetizer is always appreciated. Try something a little different from the standard shrimp cocktail.

ingredients

½ cup Univer Mayonnaise
3 oz cream cheese, softened
½ cup prepared picanté sauce, any heat
1 Tbs Univer Goulash Cream Hot
1 (14 oz) can artichoke hearts, drained and chopped
2 (4 oz) cans small shrimp, drained, rinsed and chopped
¼ cup grated Parmesan cheese
¼ cup green onions, sliced, including green tops
¼ cup sliced black olives

Chips and veggies

Preheat oven to 350° F. In a medium mixing bowl, stir together Mayonnaise, cream cheese, picanté sauce, and Goulash Cream Hot; add artichoke hearts, shrimp, and Parmesan cheese. Spoon into a 9-inch pie pan. Bake for about 20 minutes or until heated through. Garnish with green onions and black olives. Serve with chips and cut vegetables.

If you prefer fresh shrimp, use about 0.5 pound; cook and chop to make about a cup.

soups and stews

Coq Au Vin, see page 65

The World's Best Pea Soup by Aunt Julia

The best times of my childhood were the summers when I was sent to Szerencs, where I was born, to my grandfather's and his sister Julia's house. Actually, the house belonged to my father and mother, but since Dad was working for the railroad, he had been transferred along with my whole family to the second largest city in Hungary, Debrecen, a hundred and fifty kilometers away.

When the summers came, to my great joy, I was sent to my grandfather's and Aunt Julia's for the summer. I loved my grandfather, who was a tall, white-haired man with a white handlebar mustache. In my eyes, he was the epitome of all that was good. And he was a railroad station master! I was going to be one, too, when I grew up.

I had wonderful friends there, and I could hardly wait for summers to come so I could go to Szerencs. But the real reason I always wanted to go there was Aunt Julia's pea soup with dumplings. It was a sheer delight. She always made it from ingredients from her own garden, with freshly picked green peas, which she picked and gathered in her apron by holding the bottom of the apron up, forming a bag to hold the precious cargo.

I always tried to help her pick peas, but she did not let me, because she said I didn't know which ones to pick. If I picked some that were too young or too old, then what were we going to do?

When the right amount was gathered, which she knew by the weight of her apron, we would go in the house and she would gingerly open each green pod and push the peas with her thumb into a dish filled with water. I always tried to help her to do this, too, but I would put a lot of them in my mouth and eat them. I loved those peas; they were tender, soft, and sweet. She would let me eat some, then she would say, "Why don't you go out and spin wheels with your friends or something."

"But Aunt Julia, I want to help you."
"Yes, but you eat a lot of them, then I have to go and pick some more to have enough to cook. I don't have time for that." Actually she had all the time in the world. She was retired.

So, reluctantly, I would go outside and play with my friends on the street in front of the house, never too far from one of the windows because I wanted to be in hearing distance when Aunt Julia or Grandpa would lean out the window toward the street and shout, "Johnny, come on in, the food is ready." That was the best sound I could hear. The pea soup is waiting for me, the ultimate delight. Cooked by Aunt Julia!

Theirs was the biggest house in a two-street community, called Swallow Camp, at the outskirts of a small town filled with great people and friends. I remember them to this day. Everyone knew each other. I still see some of them occasionally when I go to Hungary, the ones who are still alive.

But when I heard Aunt Julia's shrieking voice, "Johnny, come on in, I tell you, the pea soup is going to get cold!" I was right there in a blink of an eye. "Wash your hands, Johnny," she'd say sternly. "Yes, Aunt Julia," thinking that if I don't hurry up, there won't be enough Green Pea Soup left for me. But soon, I would be eating with Grandpa and Aunt Julia the best pea soup in the world with dumplings and fresh parsley. What a smell, what a taste. More than half a century later, I have not tasted any better.

Serves 6

Preparation time 20 minutes

Cooking time 2 hours, 10 minutes

Ready in 2 hours, 30 minutes

Remember goulash at your house when you were a kid?—it was generally leftovers. This is the real deal.

Authentic Hungarian Goulash
(Gulyásleves)

ingredients

2 Tbs lard or shortening

2 onions, chopped

2 lbs beef chuck,
  cut into 1-inch chunks

2 Tbs Univer Sweet Ann

1 tsp salt, divided

4 cups water

2 bay leaves

4 potatoes, peeled and
  cut into large dice

¼ tsp black pepper

Egg Dumplings
(find recipe on page 204)

Sour cream

Melt the shortening in a large frying pan over medium-high heat; sauté onions until lightly browned, about 10 minutes. Add beef, Sweet Ann, and half a teaspoon of salt. Cover and let beef simmer in its own juices for about 1 hour over very low heat. Add water, bay leaves, diced potatoes, remaining salt, and pepper. Cover and simmer until potatoes are done and meat is tender, about another hour. Remove bay leaves before serving. Serve hot with Egg Dumplings and dollops of sour cream.

"I also like to add the Red Gold and the Goulash Cream paprika mix to many of my soups. Just gives it the extra boost of taste. Can't thank you enough."
—Delighted Paprika Fan

Serves 6

Preparation time 20 minutes

Cooking time 2 hours, 15 minutes

Ready in 1 hour, 35 minutes

Beef and Barley Soup

ingredients

1 lb lean ground beef

1 Tbs Univer Sweet Ann

1 tsp Univer Gourmet Garlic Cream

1 medium onion, chopped

6 cups low-sodium beef broth

1 (15 oz) can diced tomatoes, with liquid

2 stalks celery, chopped, including leafy tops

2 carrots, sliced

¾ cup medium barley

1 bay leaf

1 (10 oz) package chopped frozen spinach, thawed and squeezed dry

salt and pepper to taste

In a large stockpot, brown and crumble beef over medium-high heat, about 10 minutes. Add Sweet Ann, Garlic Cream, and onion; sauté about 5 minutes more. Drain pan juices if needed. To the pot, add broth, tomatoes, celery, carrots, barley, and bay leaf. Cover and bring to a boil. Reduce heat; simmer 50 minutes, stirring occasionally. Add spinach and simmer 10 minutes longer. Add salt and pepper to taste. Remove bay leaf before serving.

Easily remove excess moisture from thawed spinach by putting it in cheesecloth and twisting until the liquid is gone.

"A Dutch oven in long-term storage is bad for the soul."

—Blaine Nay

Serves 6

Preparation time 20 minutes

Cooking time 6 hours

Ready in 6 hours, 20 minutes

Beef and Broccoli Soup

Our favorite way to get the kids to eat their broccoli!

ingredients

1 lb lean ground beef

3 cups broccoli florets

1 small onion, chopped

8 oz fresh mushrooms, chopped

2 celery stalks, sliced

6 cups low-sodium beef broth

1 Tbs Univer Goulash Cream Mild

1 tsp thyme

1 tsp oregano

6 Tbs sour cream (optional)

2 cups shredded sharp Cheddar cheese

In a large frying pan, brown and crumble ground beef; drain. Place vegetables in slow cooker and top with ground beef. Add broth, Goulash Cream Mild, thyme, and oregano. Cook on low 6 to 8 hours. Ladle hot soup into bowls and garnish with sour cream and cheese.

Taste as you cook! There is no substitute, not even your nose!

Serves 6
Preparation time 20 minutes
Cooking time 8 hours
Ready in 8 hours, 20 minutes

Beer Stew with Beef and Vegetables

This stew is so good you'll wish it was snowing outside! Really!

ingredients

2 medium potatoes, sliced

2 carrots, sliced

2 celery stalks, sliced

1 large onion, sliced

2 lbs lean beef stew meat, cut in 1-inch cubes

1 cup beer

1 cup low-sodium beef broth

2 Tbs Univer Red Gold Mild

2 tsp Univer Gourmet Garlic Cream

½ tsp freshly ground black pepper

1 tsp dried thyme

Place vegetables in slow cooker; top with meat. In a mixing bowl, whisk together remaining ingredients and pour over meat. Cover and cook on low for 8 to 10 hours.

If you want a thicker sauce, turn slow cooker to high. Combine 2 tablespoons of cornstarch with ¼ cup of cold water and mix well into the juices. Stir occasionally until thickened, about 15 to 20 minutes.

Serves 8
Preparation time 30 minutes
Cooking time 3 hours, 15 minutes
Ready in 3 hours, 45 minutes

A combination of flavorful meats gives depth to the taste and creates a simple and delicious meal

Brunswick Stew

ingredients

1 lb ground pork

1 lb ground beef

1 large onion, chopped

4 stalks celery, chopped

1 green bell pepper, chopped

1 lb cooked chicken, shredded

1 (28 oz) can crushed tomatoes, with liquid

½ cup ketchup

¼ cup Univer Goulash Cream Mild

¼ cup sugar

freshly ground black pepper to taste

Univer Goulash Cream Hot to taste (optional)

2 (15 oz) cans creamed corn

Hot cooked rice (8 servings)

In a large frying pan, brown and crumble pork and beef until no longer pink, about 10 minutes. Add onions, celery, and bell peppers; sauté for about 7 minutes longer. With a slotted spoon, transfer meat mixture to a large stockpot. Over low heat, add the chicken, tomatoes, ketchup, Goulash Cream Mild, and sugar. Season with pepper and Goulash Cream Hot, if using. Cook, stirring occasionally, about 2 hours. Stir in the corn and continue cooking 1 hour longer. Serve over hot cooked rice with rolls and butter.

Leftover soups and stews can be stretched by serving them over rice, mashed potatoes, or hash-brown potatoes.

Serves 4

Preparation time 15 minutes

Cooking time 45 minutes

Ready in 1 hour

Easy and fresher than the restaurant—your guests will want a Mariachi band to sing your praises!

Chicken Tortilla Soup

ingredients

2 Tbs vegetable oil

1 Tbs Univer Red Gold Hot

2 tsp Univer Gourmet Garlic Cream

1 onion, chopped

4 cups low-sodium chicken broth

1 (15 oz) can diced tomatoes, with liquid

1 (4.5 oz) can diced green chilies

1 tsp black pepper

1 tsp Worcestershire sauce

1 tsp ground cumin

1 lb boneless skinless chicken thighs, cubed

salt and pepper to taste

sour cream, for garnish

tortilla chips, for garnish

Heat oil, Red Gold Hot, and Garlic Cream in a large saucepan over medium-high heat. Sauté onions until translucent, about 5 minutes. Add broth, tomatoes, chilies, pepper, Worcestershire sauce, and cumin. Reduce heat and simmer about 30 minutes. Add chicken and simmer 10 minutes longer, or until chicken is done. Adjust salt and pepper. Ladle into soup bowls and garnish with a dollop of sour cream and tortilla chips.

Substitute a 4.5-ounce can of jalapeños for the mild chilies if you want to elevate the heat level.

Serves 8

Preparation time 20 minutes

Cooking time 3 hours

Ready in 3 hours, 20 minutes

Who says traditional has to be boring!?

Chicken Vegetable Soup with Rice

ingredients

2 lbs boneless skinless chicken breasts, cut into 2-inch chunks

2 lbs boneless skinless chicken thighs, cut into 2-inch chunks

6 carrots, sliced

6 potatoes, peeled and sliced

6 celery stalks, sliced

2 onions, sliced

8 oz mushrooms, sliced

4 cups low-sodium chicken broth

2 cups water

2 Tbs Univer Goulash Cream Mild

1 Tbs Univer Gourmet Garlic Cream

½ tsp Univer Goulash Cream Hot

1 cup uncooked rice

Cornbread or croutons

Combine all ingredients except rice in a large stockpot. Bring to a boil over medium-high heat; cover and reduce heat to medium-low. Simmer for 2 hours. Add rice and simmer, covered, 1 hour longer. Serve with cornbread or top with seasoned croutons.

Old carrot skins and cores can be bitter and tough—peel the skins and trim out the core to make the carrots tender. Fresh carrots and baby carrots can be served with the skin on. Just wash and prepare as directed for your recipe.

Serves 6

Preparation time 20 minutes

Cooking time 1 hour, 20 minutes

Ready in 1 hour, 40 minutes

A classic French favorite improved by the addition of Goulash Cream Paprika.

Coq Au Vin

ingredients

6 slices bacon, chopped

3 lbs chicken, cut up

½ cup flour

1 tsp dried thyme

½ tsp freshly ground black pepper

1 onion, sliced

1 carrot, sliced

8 oz fresh mushrooms, sliced

1 cup low-sodium chicken broth

½ cup red wine

1 Tbs Univer Goulash Cream Mild

1 tsp Univer Gourmet Garlic Cream

2 tsp fresh parsley, finely chopped

1 bay leaf

1 tsp fresh basil, finely chopped

In a large frying pan, cook bacon until crisp and fat is rendered. Remove with a slotted spoon and drain on paper towels. Meanwhile, dredge chicken in flour seasoned with thyme and pepper. Brown chicken on both sides in bacon fat; remove to a plate. Brown onions, carrots, and mushrooms for about 5 minutes; drain remaining fat. Add chicken back to frying pan. Add broth, wine, Goulash Cream Mild, and Garlic Cream; stir to combine. Add parsley and bay leaf. Cover and simmer for 1 hour, stirring occasionally. At the end of cooking time, stir in basil and bacon.

Don't worry too much about cleaning the stems from soft herbs like parsley and cilantro. They taste just as good as the leaves! Just chop finely and add to your dish. Do trim stems from woody herbs such as rosemary.

Serves 6
Preparation time 20 minutes
Cooking time 1 hour
Ready in 1 hour, 20 minutes

Creamy Chicken and Barley Soup

An old-fashioned favorite soup updated for today's tastes!

ingredients

1 lb boneless skinless chicken thighs, cut into 1-inch chunks

6 cups low-sodium chicken broth

1 Tbs Univer Red Gold Mild

1 onion, chopped

2 celery stalks, sliced

2 carrots, sliced

¾ cup medium barley

1 bay leaf

½ tsp pepper

1 (10 oz) package frozen baby peas

½ cup half and half cream

To a large stockpot, add all ingredients except peas and half and half. Cover and bring to a boil; reduce heat and simmer 50 minutes, stirring occasionally. Add peas and gently fold in cream. Stir to combine and simmer, covered, 10 minutes longer, or until heated through. Remove bay leaf before serving.

Find barley in the rice section of your supermarket.

Serves 6
Preparation time 10 minutes
Cooking time 40 minutes
Ready in 50 minutes

Potatoes, bacon, and heavy cream! Heavenly!

Creamy Potato Soup with Bacon

ingredients

1 lb bacon, diced

1 Tbs Univer Red Gold Mild

1 tsp Univer Gourmet Garlic Cream

3 stalks celery, sliced

1 onion, chopped

8 Yukon Gold potatoes, cubed

4 cups chicken broth, or enough to cover potatoes

3 Tbs unsalted butter

¼ cup all-purpose flour

1 cup heavy cream

3 tsp fresh thyme, chopped

salt and pepper to taste

shredded cheddar cheese, for garnish

In a large soup pot or Dutch oven, cook the bacon over medium heat until done. Remove bacon from pan and set aside. Drain off all but 2 tablespoons of the bacon grease. Add Red Gold Mild and Garlic Cream. Sauté the celery and onion about 5 minutes. Add potatoes and toss to coat; sauté about 5 minutes. Add chicken stock; cover and simmer until potatoes are tender, about 20 minutes. In a separate pan, melt the butter over medium heat. Whisk in the flour. Cook, stirring constantly, for 1 to 2 minutes. Whisk in the heavy cream and thyme. Bring the cream mixture to a boil, and cook, stirring constantly, until thickened. Stir the cream mixture into the potato mixture. Season with salt and pepper to taste. Garnish with diced bacon and shredded cheese.

Serves 6

Preparation time 30 minutes

Cooking time 30 minutes

Ready in 60 minutes

A ski lodge favorite easily made at home!

Creamy Chicken Stew

ingredients

2 Tbs vegetable oil

1 lb boneless skinless chicken thighs, cut into bite-size chunks

1 lb boneless skinless chicken breasts, cut into bite-size chunks

salt and pepper, to taste

½ lb white mushrooms, sliced

1 Tbs unsalted butter

1 Tbs Univer Red Gold Mild

1 tsp Univer Gourmet Garlic Cream

1 large potato, peeled and cut into ½-inch dice

1 large carrot, cut into ½-inch dice

1 medium onion, cut into ½-inch dice

¼ cup flour

1 cup dry white wine

2 cups low-sodium chicken broth

4 thyme sprigs

1 bay leaf

½ cup heavy cream

1 Tbs parsley, chopped, for garnish

In a large, deep frying pan, heat oil over medium-high heat. Season chicken with salt and pepper; brown in hot oil until golden, about 5 minutes; remove chicken to a platter. Add mushrooms to the pan and cook until lightly browned, about 3 minutes. Remove mushrooms to a small bowl. To the frying pan, add butter, Red Gold Mild, Garlic Cream, potatoes, carrots, and onions. Cook until vegetables are lightly browned, about 5 minutes. Stir in the flour and let cook for 2 to 3 minutes to remove the raw flavor. Add wine and bring to a simmer, scraping up any browned bits. Add broth, thyme, bay leaf, and chicken, along with accumulated juices and bring to a boil. Reduce heat to medium-low, cover and simmer until vegetables are tender and chicken is cooked through, about 10 minutes. Discard the thyme sprigs and bay leaf. Stir in the heavy cream and mushrooms; season with salt and pepper and heat through. Garnish with parsley and serve.

Serves 6

Preparation time 20 minutes

Cooking time 8 hours

Ready in 8 hours, 20 minutes

The king of comfort food! Put it on in the morning and come home to a great smelling kitchen!

Easy Beef Stew

ingredients

3 potatoes, peeled and sliced

3 carrots, sliced

2 celery stalks, sliced

1 small onion, sliced

2 lbs beef stew meat

1 (28 oz) can diced tomatoes, with liquid

½ cup low-sodium beef broth

1 packet dry onion soup mix

1 Tbs Univer Horseradish with Vinegar

1 tsp Univer Gourmet Garlic Cream

Salt and pepper to taste

Layer vegetables in a slow cooker; top with meat. In a medium-size mixing bowl, combine tomatoes with liquid, beef broth, soup packet, Horseradish with Vinegar, and Garlic Cream; pour over meat. Season with salt and pepper. Cover and cook on low for 8 to 10 hours. Adjust salt and pepper to taste. Serve additional Horseradish with Vinegar to garnish.

If you would like to thicken the sauce, combine 2 tablespoons of cornstarch with about ¼ cup of cold water. Turn slow cooker to high and add cornstarch paste, stirring until thickened.

Serves 6
Preparation time 20 minutes
Cooking time 1 hour, 25 minutes
Ready in 1 hour, 45 minutes

No one will be singing the blues when you serve this Louisiana staple!

Hearty Red Beans and Rice Soup

ingredients

6 slices bacon, chopped

2 Tbs Univer Strong Steven, divided

1 Tbs Univer Gourmet Garlic Cream

1 medium onion, chopped

1 green bell pepper, chopped

2 andouille sausage links, sliced

1 cup cooked ham, cubed

6 cups low-sodium chicken broth

1 (15 oz) can kidney beans, with liquid

3 bay leaves

2 cups hot cooked rice

6 Tbs green onions, sliced, including some green tops

In a large stockpot over medium-high heat, brown the bacon until crisp. Remove with a slotted spoon to paper towels. To the bacon drippings, add one tablespoon of Strong Steven, Garlic Cream, onions, and bell peppers; sauté about 3 minutes. Add the sausage and ham; cook for about 5 minutes. Drain stockpot; add the broth, beans, bay leaves and the remaining Strong Steven. Bring to a boil, reduce heat to low and simmer for 1 hour, stirring occasionally. Ladle soup into individual bowls. Top each serving with an equal amount of rice and 1 tablespoon of green onions.

"Our trip to Hungary introduced us to the great food there. Your authentic products allow us to capture the tastes and flavors of that great land. Thank you very much!"

—Delighted Paprika Fan

Strong Seven
A few suggested uses:

- Add a spicy boost to stews, soups and gravies
- Glaze a sizzling steak or chop
- Mix into ground meats
- Add to marinades
- Sauté onions and vegetables
- Create wonderful dips
- Mix into salsa to enhance the flavor
- Add to ranch dressing to make Southwestern dressing with a kick
- Lightly brush onto hot grilled pineapple
- Gluten-free; no trans fats

Serves 8
Preparation time 15 minutes
Cooking time 2 hours, 30 minutes
Ready in 2 hours, 45 minutes

Irish Lamb Stew

A great old-world recipe for fall's cooler days!

ingredients

3 lbs boneless lamb shoulder, trimmed and cut into 1-inch chunks

1 Tbs Univer Goulash Cream Mild

2 tsp Univer Gourmet Garlic Cream

2 Tbs fresh parsley, finely chopped

2 tsp fresh rosemary, finely chopped

6 cups low-sodium chicken broth, divided

4 potatoes, peeled, cut into 1-inch chunks

1 large onion, chopped

3 carrots, sliced

4 celery stalks, sliced

2 Tbs cornstarch

¼ cup cold water

To a large stockpot add the lamb, Goulash Cream Mild, Garlic Cream, parsley, rosemary, and 4 cups of broth. Cover and simmer for about 1½ hours. Add remaining broth, potatoes, onions, carrots, and celery. Cover and simmer 1 hour longer. In a small bowl, whisk together cornstarch and water. Add the cornstarch paste to the stew, mixing in well. Stir until thickened. Serve with crusty bread to mop up the juices.

Leftover soups and stews can be stretched by serving them over rice, mashed potatoes, or hash-brown potatoes.

Serves 6
Preparation time 15 minutes
Cooking time 45 minutes
Ready in 1 hour

Present a delicious European dish at the next football party!

Kielbasa Stew

ingredients

1 Tbs vegetable oil

1 lb kielbasa sausage, sliced on the diagonal into 1-inch pieces

1 onion, chopped

1 cup green bell pepper, chopped

2 (14 oz) cans low-sodium beef broth

1 (28 oz) can diced tomatoes, with juice

1 Tbs Univer Sweet Ann

1 tsp Univer Gourmet Garlic Cream

3 cups cabbage, shredded

2 lbs new potatoes, cut in half

salt and pepper to taste

½ cup sour cream

additional sour cream, for garnish

Heat oil in a large saucepan over medium heat; cook sausage until browned. Add onions and bell peppers; sauté about 5 minutes. Add broth, tomatoes, Sweet Ann, and Garlic Cream into pan with sausage. Add cabbage and potatoes; season with salt and pepper. Bring to a boil; reduce heat and simmer 30 minutes. Stir in sour cream and heat through. Garnish with additional sour cream, if desired.

This recipe easily doubles for a larger crowd!

"I would like to find a stew that will give me heartburn immediately, instead of at three o'clock in the morning."
—John Barrymore

Serves 8

Preparation time 30 minutes

Cooking time 3 hours,15 minutes

Ready in 3 hours, 45 minutes

Truly one of the favorite recipes in our kitchen, and soon to be yours!

Italian Sausage Soup with Tortellini

ingredients

1 lb bulk Italian sausage

1 cup chopped onion

2 Tbs Univer Sweet Ann

2 tsp Univer Gourmet Garlic Cream

5 cups low-sodium beef broth

½ cup water

½ cup red wine

1 (28 oz) can diced tomatoes, with liquid

1 cup carrots, thinly sliced

½ tsp dried oregano

1 (8 oz) can tomato sauce

2 small zucchini squash, sliced

8 oz fresh tortellini pasta

2 Tbs chopped fresh parsley

1 Tbs fresh basil, finely chopped

grated Parmesan cheese, for garnish

In a large stockpot, brown and crumble sausage. Add onions, Sweet Ann, and Garlic Cream; sauté about 5 minutes. Stir in beef broth, water, wine, tomatoes, carrots, oregano, and tomato sauce. Bring to a boil. Reduce heat; simmer uncovered for 45 minutes. Add zucchini, tortellini, and parsley. Cover; simmer 15 minutes. Top with basil and grated Parmesan cheese. Enjoy with a glass of Chianti or Pinot Grigio.

Serves 16

Preparation time 30 minutes

Cooking time 4 hours, 15 minutes

Ready in 4 hour, 45 minutes

A signature dish you'll be proud to serve at your parties.

Patrick's Secret Football Chili

ingredients

2 lbs lean ground beef

1 large onion, chopped

¼ cup Univer Goulash Cream Hot

1 Tbs Univer Gourmet Garlic Cream

1 tsp cayenne pepper

1 tsp dried oregano

½ tsp ground cumin seed

2 (1.25 oz) packages chili seasoning mix

1 (28 oz) can hot chili beans in sauce, with liquid

1 (15 oz) can kidney beans, with liquid

1 (15 oz) can white beans, with liquid

1 (15 oz) can black beans, with liquid

1 (15 oz) can Italian-style tomatoes, with liquid

2 carrots, finely diced

1 cup frozen whole kernel corn

2 large dill pickles, finely chopped

8 oz sour cream

Suggested Garnishes
Additional sour cream
Chopped onions
Sharp cheddar cheese

In a large frying pan over medium heat, brown and crumble ground beef. When about halfway done, drain half of the pan drippings. Add onions and Goulash Cream Hot, Garlic Cream, cayenne, oregano, and cumin. Cook for about 5 minutes, then add chili seasoning mix and amount of water per directions on each package. Let cook until thickened, stirring often. In a separate large stockpot, add all beans, tomatoes, carrots, corn, and pickles; stir to combine. Cook over very low heat, partially covered. When ground beef mixture has thickened, add to bean mixture; stir to combine. Keep partially covered and stir often; cook for about 4 hours. Just before serving, add the sour cream and stir again. Serve with your favorite chili toppings.

Best made the day before so the flavors can marry. Just gently reheat and serve.

Serves 6

Preparation time 10 minutes

Cooking time 8 hours

Ready in 8 hour, 30 minutes

*A very hearty Oktoberfest stew—let's Polka!
Put it together in the morning, it's ready at
the end of the day.*

Pork and Sauerkraut Stew

ingredients

2 onions, chopped

2 lbs boneless pork butt, cut in
   2-inch chunks

3 cups sauerkraut, rinsed and
   drained

1 (12 oz) bottle of your favorite
   German beer

½ cup low-sodium beef broth

2 Tbs Univer Goulash Cream Mild

2 tsp Univer Gourmet Garlic
   Cream

1 tsp caraway seeds

2 cups sour cream plus a dollop
   or two for garnish

Hot cooked rice or noodles
   (6 servings)

Place onions in slow cooker; add meat, top with sauerkraut. In a
small mixing bowl, whisk together beer, broth, Goulash Cream
Mild, Garlic Cream, and caraway seeds. Pour over sauerkraut.
Cover and cook on low 8 to 10 hours. Turn slow cooker to high.
Add sour cream, stirring to
combine. Cook until heated
through. Serve over hot cooked
rice or noodles.

*Sauerkraut benefits from a
light sprinkling of caraway
seeds and absolutely sings
with chopped fried bacon!*

Serves 6

Preparation time 20 minutes

Cooking time 45 minutes

Ready in 1 hour, 5 minutes

This visually stunning dish brings flavor and beautiful color to your table!

Pork and Tricolor Pepper Stew

ingredients

3 Tbs vegetable oil

2 lbs pork tenderloin,
   cut into 1-inch strips

1 onion, sliced

1 tsp dried thyme

2 cups low-sodium beef broth

3 Tbs tomato paste

1 Tbs Univer Strong Steven

1 Tbs Univer Gourmet Garlic Cream

1 green bell pepper, sliced

1 red bell pepper, sliced

1 yellow bell pepper, sliced

1 bay leaf

In a large stockpot, heat oil over medium-high heat. Season the pork and onions with thyme; brown the pork and onions until pork is no longer pink. To the pot, add broth, tomato paste, Strong Steven, Garlic Cream, peppers, and bay leaf. Cover and bring to a boil; reduce heat and simmer 45 minutes, stirring occasionally. Remove bay leaf before serving.

If desired, you can thicken the stew using 2 tablespoons of cornstarch mixed with ¼ cup of cold water. Blend in well to the stew juices, and stir until thickened.

Serves 6
Preparation time 20 minutes
Cooking time 8 hours
Ready in 8 hours, 20 minutes

An updated version of a Depression-era classic! Slow cooker delight.

Pork and Vegetable Stew

ingredients

2 potatoes, peeled and cubed

1 green bell pepper, sliced

1 medium onion, sliced

2 lbs boneless pork shoulder, cut into 1-inch chunks

2 cups low-sodium beef broth

1 (10 oz) can diced tomatoes with green chilies, with liquid

1 Tbs Univer Red Gold Mild

2 tsp Univer Gourmet Garlic Cream

1 (10 oz) package frozen whole kernel corn

1 (10 oz) package frozen cut green beans

Layer potatoes, bell peppers, and onions in a slow cooker; top with pork. In a medium-size mixing bowl, whisk together broth, tomatoes, Red Gold Mild, and Garlic Cream. Pour over meat. Cover and cook on low 8 to 10 hours. Add corn and green beans during final hour of cooking time.

When using a slow cooker, put the vegetables in the bottom of the crock first, then cover with meat.

Serves 4
Preparation time 10 minutes
Cooking time 20 minutes
Ready in 30 minutes

Reuben and Swiss Soup

Enjoy your yummy Reuben sandwich as a soup; your New York friends won't believe how great it tastes.

ingredients

2 cups low-sodium beef broth

1 Tbs Univer Goulash Cream Mild

1 tsp Univer Gourmet Garlic Cream

½ lb deli corned beef, shredded

1 cup sauerkraut, rinsed and squeezed dry

1 small onion, chopped

2 celery stalks, sliced

1 tsp caraway seeds

2 cups half and half cream

1 cup shredded Swiss cheese, divided

Toasted rye bread

In a large stockpot over medium-high heat, combine broth, Goulash Cream Mild, Garlic Cream, corned beef, sauerkraut, onion, celery, and caraway seeds. Cover and bring to a low boil; reduce heat and simmer for 15 minutes. Stir in half and half cream; do not let boil. Add half the Swiss cheese and cook another 5 minutes, until heated through and cheese is mostly melted. Garnish with remaining cheese and serve with toasted rye bread.

Rinse and drain sauerkraut in colander to remove some of the briny taste.

Serves 10
Preparation time 20 minutes
Cooking time 30 minutes
Ready in 50 minutes

Bring the flavors of Barcelona to your dining room!

Spicy Spanish Bean Soup

ingredients

1 lb chorizo sausage, chopped or ground

2 Tbs extra virgin olive oil

1 Tbs Univer Gourmet Garlic Cream

1 Tbs Univer Strong Steven

4 stalks celery, sliced

2 carrots, sliced

1 medium onion, chopped

3 tomatoes, peeled, seeded, and chopped

3 small potatoes, peeled and cubed

1 cup fresh or frozen corn kernels

1 (15 oz) can kidney beans, drained

3 quarts low-sodium beef broth

½ cup tomato paste

salt and pepper to taste

In a large frying pan over medium-high heat, brown and crumble sausage. Drain and set aside. In a stockpot over medium-high heat, heat oil, Garlic Cream, and Strong Steven; sauté celery, carrots, and onions for about 5 minutes. Add tomatoes, potatoes, corn, kidney beans, beef broth, and tomato paste. Bring to a boil; reduce heat, cover and simmer for 20 minutes. Add sausage back in and heat through. Season with salt and pepper to taste. Serve hot.

If chorizo is hard to find, substitute pork sausage.

"Tomatoes and oregano make it Italian; wine and tarragon make it French. Sour cream makes it Russian; lemon and cinnamon make it Greek. Soy sauce makes it Chinese; garlic makes it good.
—Alice May Brock

Serves 8

Preparation time 20 minutes

Cooking time 3 hours,15 minutes

Ready in 3 hours, 35 minutes

Horseradish with Vinegar really pumps in the heat, but without the sting of regular horseradish.

White Chili with Horseradish

ingredients

4 cups cooked chicken thighs, diced or shredded

1 (28 oz) can great northern beans, with liquid

1 (10 oz) package frozen whole kernel corn

1 large white onion, chopped

1 (7 oz) can diced green chilies

3 cups low-sodium chicken broth

2 **Tbs** Univer Horseradish with Vinegar

2 tsp Univer Gourmet Garlic Cream

2 tsp ground white pepper

1 tsp dried oregano

1 tsp ground cumin

Warm flour tortillas

Suggested Garnishes

Chopped onions

Sharp Cheddar cheese

Sour cream

In a large stockpot, combine all ingredients. Cover and bring to a low boil over medium heat; reduce heat and simmer 3 hours. Serve with warmed flour tortillas and your favorite chili condiments.

Use a rotisserie chicken from the supermarket if you want breast meat as well as thighs.

Serves 8

Preparation time 15 minutes

Cooking time 45 minutes

Ready in 1 hour

Spicy Taco Stew

A must-make for the Big Game—and the kids will love it!

ingredients

2 lbs lean ground beef

1 onion, chopped

1 Tbs Univer Goulash Cream Mild

1 tsp Univer Gourmet Garlic Cream

2 (15 oz) cans black beans, drained

1 (10 oz) package frozen whole kernel corn

1 (15 oz) can peeled and diced tomatoes with liquid

1 (10 oz) can diced tomatoes with green chile peppers

1 (1.25 oz) package taco seasoning mix

Shredded Mexican cheese blend, for garnish

In a large frying pan over medium-high heat, brown and crumble beef for about 10 minutes. Add onion and sauté for another 5 minutes; drain excess fat. Add Goulash Cream Mild, Garlic Cream, beans, corn, both cans of tomatoes, and taco seasoning mix. Reduce heat to medium-low and let simmer for about 30 minutes. Ladle into bowls and top with cheese.

Gourmet Garlic Cream

Garlic is revered throughout the world for its flavor-enhancing qualities and is a staple in most kitchens. With Gourmet Garlic Cream, you can do away with messy cleaning and chopping. Just open the jar! Great garlic aroma, pure garlic flavor!

A few suggested uses:

- Add to soups, stews and gravies
- Mix into mashed potatoes for instant Garlic Potatoes
- Make garlic bread in a snap
- Add to sauces, dips and spreads
- Sauté onions and other vegetables
- Toss with hot cooked pasta before dressing with sauce
- Rub onto clean, dry potatoes before baking
- Brush onto pizza crusts before baking

Serves 8

Preparation time 30 minutes

Cooking time 3 hours, 15 minutes

Ready in 3 hours, 45 minutes

Chicken noodle soup, olé-style!

Aspen Chicken Soup

ingredients

6 cups low-sodium chicken broth

1 Tbs Univer Red Gold Mild

1 tsp Univer Gourmet Garlic Cream

½ tsp Univer Red Gold Hot

8 oz vermicelli pasta, broken into 1-inch pieces

2 cups chicken, cooked and diced

1 (4.5 oz) can diced green chilies

⅓ cup prepared salsa

2 tomatoes, peeled, seeded, and chopped

2 avocados, diced

2 green onions, sliced

2 Tbs cilantro, chopped

Bring broth, Red Gold Mild, Garlic Cream and Red Gold Hot to a low boil in a large stockpot. Add pasta and cook about 10 minutes. Add chicken, green chilies, salsa, and tomatoes. Cover and simmer about 10 minutes, or until heated through. Mound avocados and green onions equally in soup bowls. Ladle in soup and garnish with cilantro.

Do not rely on gravy or sauces to reheat your meal at the table. If you want to serve a soup dish first, keep the entrée warm in the kitchen before taking it to the table; otherwise, serve the soup with the entrée.

Serves 4

Preparation time 15 minutes

Cooking time 60 minutes

Ready in 1 hour, 15 minutes

This is a lovely lunch dish and it freezes well.

Hungarian Split Pea Soup

ingredients

4 cups low-sodium chicken broth

1 Tbs Univer Goulash Cream Mild

½ tsp Univer Goulash Cream Hot

1 cup green or yellow split peas, rinsed

1 medium potato, peeled and diced

½ cup onion, chopped

½ cup celery, sliced

½ cup carrots, sliced

1 cup cooked ham, diced

1 bay leaf

salt and pepper to taste

Combine all ingredients in large stockpot. Cover and bring to a boil; reduce heat to low. Simmer, stirring occasionally, until vegetables are tender and soup has thickened, about 50 to 60 minutes. Add salt and pepper to taste. Remove bay leaf before serving.

If you have a leftover hambone in the freezer, cook it with the soup for additional flavor.

Serves 6

Preparation time 20 minutes

Cooking time 55 minutes

Ready in 1 hour, 15 minutes

Meatloaf Soup

Families love meatloaf— now serve it up as a hearty soup!

ingredients

1 lb lean ground beef

1 Tbs Univer Goulash Cream Hot

1 tsp Univer Gourmet Garlic Cream

1 onion, chopped

½ cup seasoned breadcrumbs

1 egg

6 cups low-sodium beef broth

3 carrots, sliced

1 green bell pepper, chopped

2 stalks celery, chopped

1 (15 oz) can diced tomatoes, with liquid

1 small head cabbage, cut into 4 wedges

In a large mixing bowl, mix together the ground beef, Goulash Cream Hot, Garlic Cream, onions, breadcrumbs, and egg. Shape into 1-inch meatballs. Place in bottom of large stockpot and cover with broth. Bring to a low boil; reduce heat and simmer for about 5 minutes. Add carrots, bell peppers, celery, tomatoes, and cabbage. Cover and simmer for about 45 minutes.

Serves 4

Preparation time 10 minutes

Cooking time 30 minutes

Ready in 40 minutes

Make plenty of cornbread for this East Coast classic!

Chicken and Corn Chowder with Thyme

ingredients

6 slices bacon, chopped

1 Tbs Univer Goulash Cream Mild

1 tsp Univer Gourmet Garlic Cream

1 medium onion, chopped

1 (14 oz) can low-sodium chicken broth

2 large potatoes, peeled and cut into 1-inch dice

2 cups corn, fresh or frozen

1 Tbs fresh thyme

8 boneless skinless chicken thighs, cut into 1-inch chunks

1 cup half and half

Cornbread

Cook bacon in a large saucepan over medium-high heat until crisp, about 5 minutes. Using a slotted spoon, transfer bacon to paper towels; discard most of pan drippings. To the pan, add Goulash Cream Mild and Garlic Cream. Add onions and sauté for about 5 minutes. Add broth, potatoes, corn, thyme, and chicken; cover pan and simmer about 20 minutes, until chicken is cooked through and vegetables are tender. Add half and half and cook about 2 minutes longer, until cream is heated through. Season chowder to taste with salt and pepper. Ladle into bowls, sprinkle with cooked bacon, and serve with cornbread.

Clean as you go. Trying to cook with a mess all around you is discouraging.

Serves 6

Preparation time 15 minutes

Cooking time 15 minutes

Ready in 30 minutes

This south-of-the-border special is easy to make and freezes well! Use with any Mexican dish or by itself.

Pork and Green Chile Stew

ingredients

3 Tbs vegetable oil

1 Tbs Univer Goulash Cream Mild

2 tsp Univer Gourmet Garlic Cream

2 lbs lean pork, cubed

1 large onion, coarsely chopped

1 (15 oz) can diced tomatoes, with liquid

1 (14 oz) can low-sodium chicken broth

1 cup prepared salsa verde

1 (4.5 oz) can diced green chilies

2 potatoes, cubed

2 jalapeño peppers, seeded and finely chopped (fresh or pickled)

Heat oil, Goulash Cream Mild, and Garlic Cream over medium-high heat in a large stockpot. Brown pork and onions until pork is no longer pink. Add tomatoes with liquid, broth, salsa verde, green chilies, potatoes, and jalapeño peppers. Cover and bring to a boil; reduce heat. Simmer 1 hour, stirring occasionally, until meat is fork tender. Mash the potatoes slightly to thicken the stew, if desired.

beef entrées

Rib Eye Steaks with Creamy Mushroom Sauce, see page 100

Fancy!

As the saying goes, how lucky can you get? Not only because I got to know Fancy, but because she single-handedly was able to sustain seven, sometimes eight of us, through the dark years after the Second World War—those terrible years of the Russian occupation.

I admired her. I was still a child then. She was tall, I should say big, well-endowed, and beautiful to me, with her red and white coloring in small patches, her big black eyes, long eyelashes, and smart looking face. With her white curlicue, "fufru" we called it, curling downward on her forehead from between her elegant feminine horns, she was the queen of our family and the pride of my grandmother. Right after the bombing and the war ended, Fancy came to us, courtesy of Granma, who purchased her with bartering, I am sure, because money had no value then. Fancy was a cow. She gave us wonderful fresh warm milk, cream, butter, sour cream, and even cheese curd.

When she came to us we concocted a covered place for her, which you couldn't call a barn. It did not have walls; it was more like an open, but covered parking place. After Father came home from the war, he built her a right and proper barn with a door.

Granma would milk her at the crack of dawn. My brother and I were in charge of feeding and watering her and cleaning her stall, which was always a fight, to see who would do that nasty part. I was always trying to talk my younger brother István (Steven) into agreeing that I should do the front chores for Fancy and he should do the back one. Well, he wouldn't go for that, except on occasion when I was able to bribe him with something he wanted.

Fancy and I connected. I liked to take her grazing. Granma's land did not have a grassy area—I had to take Fancy to the roadside in front of the house to let her graze on the banks of the ditches. Granma wanted me to tie her front feet loosely together, like a hobble, so she couldn't go on other peoples' land and eat their crops while I was reading a book.

Books—I loved to read. We didn't have the money to buy any, but we borrowed them from anyone who had them and would share. My favorite books then were the *Count of Monte Cristo* and the *Last of the Mohicans*. I preferred to tie her two horns with a long rope and tell her that she could not go into the cornfield—that would always work with a gentle pull on her tether, and then she would retreat. I know she knew what she could and couldn't do. Basically, all I had to do was tell her not to do something and she obeyed.

She was as smart as my dog Rio, a German Shepherd and Komondor mix. I could talk to her and I knew she understood me. If I'd take her out to the roadside with me to graze Fancy, Rio would stay right by me. She would sound a warning bark if there was a Russian Army vehicle going by; Rio didn't like them either—I told you she was a very smart dog. These were the Russians who took the giant Torontali cheese from us who you will read about in a later section. I was sure Rio would tear them to pieces if they tried to take Fancy from us, too. But still, I always worried if a large enough Russian truck was approaching on the road.

Fancy was a blessing to us, thanks to Granma. She gave us all the milk and all the creations that Mother and Granma could create from her gift, originating from her oversized milk factory. In return, we did everything for her to make her comfortable. She loved to be pampered and the main thing she liked was to have her hide scratched. When she saw the scraper in my hand, which was made of steel with a row of small teeth, she would stretch her neck straight out, because that's where she wanted me to start.

Later on, when my father started to create the greenhouses and gardening on Granma's land, he also seeded almost an acre of alfalfa on Granma's five acres. That became Fancy's winter food, after it was dried by the sun. As I think of all this now, Granma's land and all, I think that her land saved us all from starvation and physically, too, from the bullets of war.

I think of Scarlet in the movie *Gone with the Wind*, which I did not see until I was lucky enough to come to the United States in 1957, when she was totally devastated by the Civil War and had nowhere to turn. "The land, the land," she said, "I will just go back to the land, to Tara and start all over again!" I learned six words of English before coming to America. Thanks to Scarlett, Rhett, and *Gone with the Wind* and the movies *Oklahoma* and *Giant*—my education of the English language expanded.

That's what we were able to do then, despite all the turmoil in those days in our lives, because of the war. Thanks to Granma, I still remember Fancy and Rio affectionately. What else does a boy want, who started his life in the city—space to run and play with animals, pull up fresh vegetables like tomatoes, kohlrabi, green onions, carrots, and eat them raw. Well, and take some to Fancy, the Wonderful Cow.

Many, many others weren't so lucky, especially anyone who lived in the city.

Serves 6
Preparation time 15 minutes
Cooking time 15 minutes
Ready in 3 hour, 30 minutes

Taste the flavors of summer using fresh corn!

Beef and Corn Kebabs

ingredients

⅓ cup vegetable oil

¼ cup red wine vinegar

2 tsp Univer Strong Steven

1 tsp Univer Gourmet Garlic Cream

1 Tbs fresh thyme, chopped

1 Tbs fresh parsley, chopped

2 lbs top sirloin, cut into 2-inch chunks

1 medium onion, sliced into 2-inch squares

2 ears corn, cleaned, sliced into 2-inch rounds

2 red bell peppers, seeded, and sliced into 2-inch squares

Horseradish Butter
(find recipe on page 224)

For the marinade, whisk together the oil, vinegar, Strong Steven, Garlic Cream, thyme, and parsley in a medium bowl and then add the beef and onions. Toss to coat, cover and place in the refrigerator for 3 to 4 hours, or up to 12 hours, to marinate. Stir occasionally. At grill time, remove the beef and onions from the marinade and set the marinade aside. Thread the beef chunks, corn, bell peppers, and onions alternately onto metal skewers, leaving a little space between the pieces. Baste liberally with the marinade.

Grill the kebabs over a medium-hot grill for 15 to 20 minutes for medium doneness. Baste with the marinade occasionally, and turn the skewers periodically. Serve with a crisp green salad and Horseradish Butter for the corn.

Meat MUST rest after cooking, especially off a hot grill. Resist the urge to plunge your knife into hot meats and poultry. Resting will help the juices redistribute for maximum juiciness when sliced.

Serves 6
Preparation time 30 minutes
Cooking time 15 minutes
Ready in 3 hours, 45 minutes

An excellent dish for an outdoor gathering!

Beef and Vegetable Kebabs

ingredients

2 lbs top sirloin, cut into 2-inch inch chunks

1 large onion, sliced into 2-inch squares

24 fresh button mushrooms

2 red bell peppers, sliced into 2-inch squares

2 summer squash, diagonally sliced into 1-inch ovals

2 zucchini squash, diagonally sliced into 1-inch ovals

Marinade

⅔ cup olive oil

½ cup red wine vinegar

1 tsp Univer Gourmet Garlic Cream

1 Tbs fresh cilantro, chopped

1 tsp dried thyme

½ tsp dried sage

½ tsp black pepper

1 tsp Univer Red Gold Hot

Place the beef and vegetables in a large bowl. In a small bowl, whisk together the oil, vinegar, Garlic Cream, cilantro, thyme, sage, pepper, and Red Gold Hot. Pour the marinade over the meat and vegetables, tossing well to coat. Cover and refrigerate for at least 3 hours, stirring occasionally. At grill time, thread the beef and vegetables alternately onto metal skewers and grill on medium-hot grill for 15 minutes, turning the skewers and basting occasionally with any leftover marinade.

Sniff before you season! Check tinned spices and herbs frequently and replace when the aroma is diminished.

Gourmet Garlic Cream

Garlic is revered throughout the world for its flavor-enhancing qualities and is a staple in most kitchens. With Gourmet Garlic Cream, you can do away with messy cleaning and chopping. Just open the jar! Great garlic aroma, pure garlic flavor!

A few suggested uses:

- Add to soups, stews and gravies
- Mix into mashed potatoes for instant Garlic Potatoes
- Make garlic bread in a snap
- Add to sauces, dips and spreads
- Sauté onions and other vegetables
- Toss with hot cooked pasta before dressing with sauce
- Rub onto clean, dry potatoes before baking
- Brush onto pizza crusts before baking

Serves 4

Preparation time 10 minutes

Cooking time 35 minutes

Ready in 45 minutes

These are so crunchy and easy to make, you'll think twice about ordering them again in a restaurant!

Beef Chimichangas

ingredients

1 lb lean ground beef

1 Tbs Univer Gourmet Garlic Cream

1 Tbs Univer Red Gold Hot or Mild

1 green bell pepper, chopped

1 medium onion, chopped

1 (1.62 oz) package burrito seasoning mix

1 cup low-sodium beef broth

¼ cup instant rice

1 cup shredded Mexican cheese blend

8 (8-inch) flour tortillas

Vegetable oil, as needed

Suggested Garnishes
Salsa
Avocados
Lettuce
Tomatoes
Additional Mexican cheese blend
Black olives sliced or diced
Jalapeno peppers sliced or diced
Salsa Verde or green chile sauce

In a large frying pan over medium-high heat, brown and crumble beef; add Garlic Cream and Red Gold. Add bell peppers and onions; cook another 3 to 4 minutes until vegetables have slightly softened. Add burrito seasoning mix, broth, and rice. Bring to a boil; reduce heat to medium and cook, covered, until mixture has thickened, 5 to 6 minutes. Stir in the cheese. Place beef mixture evenly on each tortilla; tightly fold into burritos. Secure ends with wooden toothpicks.

In a second large, deep frying pan, add oil to 1½-inch depth; heat to 375° F. In batches, fry tortillas, turning frequently, 3 to 4 minutes, or until golden brown. Do not crowd pan. Remove with slotted spoon; drain and keep warm. Remove picks before serving. Garnish as desired with your favorite toppings. Enjoy with an ice cold beer in a frosted mug!

Keep beer mugs in the freezer for maximum coldness.

Serves 6

Preparation time 15 minutes

Cooking time 60 minutes

Ready in 1 hour, 15 minutes

An excellent choice for your dinner party.

Beef Stroganoff with Burgundy

ingredients

¼ cup flour

1 tsp dried thyme

½ tsp pepper

2 lbs top sirloin steak, cut into 1-inch cubes

¼ cup extra virgin olive oil

1 medium onion, chopped

1 cup low-sodium beef broth

1 cup Burgundy wine

2 Tbs butter

2 cups sliced white mushrooms

2 cups sour cream

3 Tbs Univer Goulash Cream Mild

1 Tbs Worcestershire sauce

2 tsp Univer Gourmet Garlic Cream

Cooked egg noodles or hot cooked rice (4 servings)

Fresh parsley, chopped, for garnish (optional)

Combine flour, thyme, and pepper in plastic food storage bag. Add meat and shake well to coat. Remove meat, shaking off excess flour. Heat olive oil in large frying pan over medium heat. Add meat and lightly brown, about 5 minutes. Add onion and cook until translucent, about 5 minutes. Pour in broth and wine; reduce heat to medium-low. Simmer until meat is tender, about 45 minutes.

Melt butter in a small frying pan over medium heat. Add mushrooms and sauté until just tender, 3 to 4 minutes. Stir mushrooms into meat mixture. In a medium-size mixing bowl, blend sour cream, Goulash Cream Mild, Worcestershire sauce, and Garlic Cream. Slowly stir into meat; do not allow to boil. Heat through. Serve over cooked egg noodles or hot rice. Garnish with fresh chopped parsley, if desired.

"If you're afraid of butter, use cream."
—**Julia Child**

Serves 4
Preparation time 10 minutes
Cooking time 10 minutes
Ready in 30 minutes

Beef Tenderloin
with Horseradish and Garlic Rub

Once in a while you just have to have a good cut of meat. What better treat than a beautiful tenderloin!

ingredients

3 Tbs Univer Horseradish with Vinegar

1 Tbs Univer Mustard

1 Tbs Univer Gourmet Garlic Cream

1 Tbs Worcestershire sauce

1 Tbs steak seasoning

2 lbs beef tenderloin, trimmed of excess fat

Prepare the grill for medium-high heat. In a small bowl, whisk together the Horseradish with Vinegar, Mustard, Garlic Cream, Worcestershire sauce, and steak seasoning. Rub the tenderloin all over with the mixture. Grill for about 4 to 5 minutes per side for medium, a little less for medium rare. Cover and let stand 10 minutes before carving. Enjoy with a glass of Merlot.

Serves 8
Preparation time 30 minutes
Cooking time 3 hours, 15 minutes
Ready in 3 hours, 45 minutes

Yes, turnips ... just don't tell anyone and they'll clean their plates! This is a tasty way to sneak in those veggies.

Beer-Braised Brisket with Root Vegetables

ingredients

3 Tbs canola oil

2–3 lbs beef brisket

2 medium onions, sliced

6 stalks celery, sliced into 1-inch pieces

3 carrots, sliced into 1-inch pieces

3 turnips, peeled and sliced

3 potatoes, sliced

1 Tbs Univer Red Gold Mild

2 tsp Univer Gourmet Garlic Cream

6 sprigs fresh thyme

2 bay leaves

1 (12 oz) bottle dark beer

2 (14 oz) cans beef broth

2 Tbs tomato paste

Preheat oven to 325° F. Heat oil in a large frying pan over high heat. Brown brisket about 4 to 5 minutes on each side. Transfer to a baking dish. In the same frying pan over medium-high heat, add onions, celery, carrots, turnips, potatoes, Red Gold Mild, Garlic Cream, thyme, and bay leaves; sauté for about 5 minutes. Deglaze pan with beer; simmer to reduce liquid by half.

Add beef broth and tomato paste; stir to combine. Pour vegetable mixture over brisket in the baking dish. Cover and braise for 2 hours.. Uncover and cook 1 hour more, until meat is fork-tender. Discard bay leaves and thyme stems before serving.

Use leftover pan drippings to create a rich gravy.

"Part of the secret of success in life is to eat what you like and let the food fight it out inside."

—Mark Twain

Serves 8

Preparation time 10 minutes

Cooking time 6 minutes

Ready in 3 hours, 16 minutes

An old favorite with exciting new flavors.

Bloody Bill London Broil

ingredients

2 lbs London broil (flank steak)

2 cups tomato juice

¼ cup Worcestershire sauce

3 Tbs dry sherry

2 tsp Univer Gourmet Garlic Cream

2 tsp Univer Goulash Cream Mild

3 Tbs Univer Horseradish with Vinegar

2 tsp dried oregano

1 tsp dried basil

1 tsp black pepper

Vegetable oil cooking spray

To prepare the marinade, whisk together the tomato juice, Worcestershire sauce, sherry, Garlic Cream, Goulash Cream Mild, Horseradish with Vinegar, oregano, basil, and pepper in a small bowl. Place the meat in a separate bowl. Pour the marinade over the meat, spreading to cover. Turn the meat to coat the other side. Cover and refrigerate for at least 3 hours, turning meat occasionally.

At grill time, prepare the grill for medium-high heat. Lightly spray the grill rack with vegetable oil cooking spray. Place the meat on the grill. Grill for about 3 minutes, basting occasionally with the leftover marinade, turn and grill for another 3 minutes for rare, a few minutes longer for medium. Remove from grill, cover and let rest for 10 minutes before slicing against the grain into thin strips. Enjoy with a glass of Pinot Noir.

Try a coarse ground pepper if you really like pepper and like the look of it on your dish.

Serves 4
Preparation time 10 minutes
Cooking time 10 minutes
Ready in 20 minutes

Bleu Cheese Burgers

There's a nice surprise inside these burgers!

ingredients

2 lbs ground sirloin

2 Tbs Univer Red Gold Mild

1 Tbs Univer Gourmet Garlic Cream

2 Tbs fresh parsley, finely chopped

2 green onions, finely chopped with some green tops

2 tsp hamburger or steak seasoning

4 Tbs crumbled bleu cheese

4 crusty rolls, lightly toasted

Suggested Garnishes
Lettuce
Tomato slices
Bleu cheese dressing

In a medium-size mixing bowl, combine beef, Red Gold Mild, Garlic Cream, parsley, green onions, and seasoning. When forming each of the four patties, spoon 1 tablespoon of blue cheese into the center of the meat, and gently form patty around cheese. Grill over medium-high heat for about 5 minutes on each side, or to desired doneness. Serve burgers with lettuce, tomatoes, and bleu cheese dressing.

Remove the meat from the fridge about 30 minutes before grilling so it can get some of the chill off.

Serves 4
Preparation time 20 minutes
Cooking time 2 hours, 10 minutes
Ready in 2 hours, 40 minutes

This may look intimidating, but it's really simple to put together.

Braciole (pronounced bro'zhul)

ingredients

1 cup seasoned breadcrumbs

½ cup grated Parmesan cheese

2 eggs

1 Tbs Univer Goulash Cream Mild

1 tsp Univer Gourmet Garlic Cream

2 Tbs fresh parsley, coarsely chopped

1 Tbs fresh oregano, coarsely chopped

1 tsp fresh rosemary

1 tsp fresh thyme

1½ lbs flank steak, pounded ½-inch thick

2 Tbs extra virgin olive oil, divided

Salt and pepper to taste

1 cup onions, sliced

1 (28 oz) can diced tomatoes, with liquid

1 (10 oz) can diced tomatoes with chilies, with liquid

½ cup dry red wine

Preheat oven to 300° F. In a food processor bowl, mix the breadcrumbs, cheese, eggs, Goulash Cream Mild, Garlic Cream, and herbs until it forms a paste. Brush the flank steak with ½ tablespoon of oil; season with salt and pepper. Spread breadcrumb mixture evenly over steak; roll up tightly and tie with butcher's twine. Heat remaining oil in a large frying pan over medium-high heat; brown meat on all sides.

Place meat in baking dish and top with onions; add tomatoes and wine. Cover and bake for about 2 hours, or until meat is fork-tender. Remove from oven and cover loosely to let rest about 10 minutes. Remove twine and slice into ½-inch slices. Spoon pan juices over slices and serve. Enjoy with a glass of Chianti.

Don't throw out herbs (dried or fresh) or citrus peels; toss them in the garbage disposal to freshen it.

Serves 4
Preparation time 10 minutes
Cooking time 10 minutes
Ready in 4 hours, 10 minutes

The lime and tomato juices will help tenderize this flavorful cut of meat.

Carne Asada Fiesta

ingredients

1½ lbs beef flank steak

2 green bell peppers, thinly sliced

1 large onion, thinly sliced

1 Tbs olive oil

12 (8-inch) flour tortillas

1 Tbs Univer Goulash Cream Hot

2 tsp Univer Gourmet Garlic Cream

¼ cup onion, chopped

2 Tbs fresh cilantro, chopped

1 tsp dried ground cumin seed

Marinade

½ cup lime juice

½ cup tomato juice

Suggested Garnishes

Guacamole
Salsa
Sour cream

For the marinade, whisk together all marinade ingredients. Put the steak in a large plastic food storage bag; pour in marinade. Seal bag, pressing out air; refrigerate for 4 hours. Turn occasionally to distribute marinade. At grill time, cut a large square of heavy-duty foil. Place peppers and onions in center of foil square; drizzle with olive oil. Fold up top and ends to make a packet, leaving a little space for expansion. Remove steak from marinade; reserve marinade.

Place steak in center of grate. Over medium-high heat, grill 5 minutes, turn and grill 5 more minutes for medium. Baste frequently with reserved marinade. Place foil package of vegetables on grate next to steak during the last 5 minutes of grilling. Remove steak, cover and let stand for 10 minutes. Wrap the tortillas in foil and set on grate for 5 minutes, turning once. Slice steak diagonally across the grain into thin slices. Unwrap peppers and onions; serve meat in tortillas with peppers, onions, guacamole, salsa, and sour cream.

Serves 8
Preparation time 15 minutes
Cooking time 2 hours, 10 minutes
Ready in 2 hours, 25 minutes

Garlic Beef over Rice

So nice with a loaf of good bread!

ingredients

4 Tbs vegetable oil

4 lbs lean sirloin steak, cut into bite-sized chunks

1 tsp pepper

1 large onion, sliced

1 (28 oz) can crushed tomatoes

½ cup low-sodium beef broth

2 Tbs Univer Sweet Ann

2 Tbs Univer Gourmet Garlic Cream

2 bay leaves

1 tsp dried oregano

4 cups cooked rice

Preheat oven to 325° F. In a large frying pan, heat vegetable oil over high heat. Season meat with pepper and sear on all sides for about 5 minutes, or until well browned. In a 3-quart baking dish, layer the meat and onions. In a small mixing bowl, combine the tomatoes, beef broth, Sweet Ann, Garlic Cream, bay leaves, and oregano; pour evenly over meat and onions. Cover and bake for about 2 hours, stirring occasionally, until tender. Remove bay leaves. Serve over hot rice with crusty bread and a cold beer.

Serves 4
Preparation time 10 minutes
Cooking time 10 minutes
Ready in 30 minutes

Grilled steak and onions paired up with a delicious red sauce.

Grilled Rib Eyes
with Spicy Red Cream Tomato Relish

ingredients

2 lbs boneless ribeye steaks, about 1-inch thick

2 Tbs Univer Red Gold Mild

1 Tbs Univer Gourmet Garlic Cream

1 tsp freshly ground black pepper

2 Tbs vegetable oil

2 large red onions, sliced ¼-inch thick

Spicy Red Cream Tomato Relish

½ cup sour cream

1 Tbs Univer Strong Steven

1 tsp fresh lime juice

2 tomatoes, seeded and chopped

1 Tbs fresh chives, chopped

1 Tbs fresh cilantro, chopped

Salt and pepper to taste

In a small mixing bowl, whisk together Red Gold Mild, Garlic Cream, and black pepper. Brush the steaks generously with mixture. Place the meat on a hot grill and cook to desired degree of doneness, about 5 minutes on one side and 3 minutes on the other for medium. Cover and let rest 10 minutes, then slice into 1/2-inch strips. Meanwhile, heat oil in a large frying pan over medium-high heat, add the onions and sauté until translucent, about 8 to 10 minutes; keep warm.

In a medium bowl mix together the sour cream, Strong Steven, and lime juice. Stir in tomatoes, chives, cilantro, and salt and pepper to taste. Divide the onions evenly on plates and arrange ¼ of the steak slices over the onions. Top steak slices with a dollop of Spicy Red Cream Tomato Relish.

Don't worry too much about cleaning the stems from soft herbs like parsley and cilantro. They taste as good as the leaves! Just chop and add to your dish.

Serves 4
Preparation time 15 minutes
Cooking time 30 minutes
Ready in 45 minutes

Have a few large zucchini that your neighbor gave you? In this recipe, the bigger the squash the better!

Italian Zucchini Boats

ingredients

1 lb lean ground beef

2 tsp Univer Goulash Cream Mild

1 tsp Univer Gourmet Garlic Cream

½ cup onion, chopped

¼ cup black olives, roughly chopped

1 tsp dried oregano

1 tsp dried thyme

½ tsp black pepper

1 cup tomato sauce

4 large zucchini

½ cup shredded Parmesan cheese

Preheat oven to 350° F. In a large frying pan over medium-high heat, brown and crumble beef. Add Goulash Cream Mild and Garlic Cream and stir into beef; add onions, olives, oregano, thyme, pepper, and tomato sauce. Cover and reduce heat to medium-low. Cut each zucchini in half lengthwise. Scoop out seeds and discard. Scoop out pulp, leaving about ¼-inch zucchini in shells.

Place zucchini halves, cut-side down, in a 13x9-inch microwave-safe baking dish filled with about 1 inch of water; cover and microwave on high power for about 3 minutes. Drain well. Chop the saved zucchini pulp and add to beef mixture. Flip zucchini shells over and fill each with beef mixture, dividing evenly. Bake for 15 to 20 minutes. Remove from oven and top with cheese; return to oven for about 5 minutes, until cheese is melted.

Leftover filling? Use it in omelets or top a side of pasta.

"Ask not what you can do for your country. Ask what's for lunch."

—Orson Welles

Serves 6
Preparation time 30 minutes
Cooking time 3 hours, 30 minutes
Ready in 4 hours

A bacon twist gives this ancient dish a fresh new taste.

Lebanese Lubee

ingredients

6 slices bacon, chopped

½ bone-in leg of lamb
(about 4 pounds)

1 large onion, chopped

8 oz fresh mushrooms, sliced

1 (14 oz) can low-sodium beef
broth

2 (28 oz) cans crushed tomatoes

1 Tbs Univer Goulash Cream Mild

2 tsp Univer Gourmet Garlic
Cream

½ tsp cinnamon, or to taste

2 lbs green beans, trimmed

Hot cooked rice (6 servings)

In a large saucepan, brown the bacon until it is crisp and has rendered its fat. With a slotted spoon, remove the bacon to drain on paper towels. Meanwhile, cut most of the leg meat away from the bone, making 2-inch chunks. Brown the chunks and the leg with the bone in the bacon drippings; remove to a platter. Brown the onions and mushrooms; drain remaining fat. Add lamb back to pot.

Add the broth, tomatoes, Goulash Cream Mild, Garlic Cream, and cinnamon. Cover and bring to a boil; reduce heat and simmer 2 hours. Trim green beans and cut into equal lengths; add to saucepan. Cover and simmer 1 hour longer. Discard bone (or freeze for making stock later); spoon rice into dish, top with Lubee and bacon pieces.

"Our trip to Hungary introduced us to the great food there. Your authentic products allow us to capture the tastes and flavor of that great land. Thank you very much!"
—Delighted Paprika Fan

We've never understood the mushroom/water relationship. If mushrooms will get soggy if we wash them, why don't they get soggy in our sauce? If they are really dirty, we say give them a quick rinse and be done with it!

Serves 6

Preparation time 10 minutes

Cooking time 8 hours

Ready in 8 hours, 10 minutes

This makes the base for a soul-satisfying Mexican meal, and leftover meat freezes well.

Mexican Beef for Burritos and Tacos

ingredients

2 lbs boneless beef chuck

½ cup low-sodium beef broth

½ cup green salsa (salsa verde)

1 tsp Univer Gourmet Garlic Cream

2 tsp Univer Red Gold Hot

3 green onions, chopped

1 jalapeño pepper, seeded, chopped

½ tsp ground cumin

Trim fat from meat and place meat in slow cooker. Whisk together broth, salsa, Garlic Cream, Red Gold Hot, green onions, jalapeño pepper, and cumin. Pour over meat and cover. Cook for 8 hours on low, until meat is very tender. Remove meat from slow cooker and reserve cooking liquid. Shred meat using two forks. Before filling taco shells or tortillas, add about ½ cup of the liquid back to meat. Enjoy with a glass of Sangria.

Sensitive to chopping hot peppers such as jalapeños? Use canned, diced jalapeños.

Serves 8

Preparation time 10 minutes

Cooking time 45 minutes

Ready in about 1 hour

What a kid-friendly dish this is— it's like a taco on top of a meatloaf!

Mexican Meltdown Meatloaf

ingredients

2 lbs lean ground beef

2 (4.5 oz) cans chopped green chilies

1 (1.25 oz) package taco seasoning mix

1 Tbs Univer Goulash Cream Hot

2 tsp Univer Garlic Cream

1 (15 oz) can refried beans

1 cup black beans, drained and rinsed

½ cup green chile sauce

½ cup salsa, drained

1½ cups shredded Mexican cheese blend

Suggested Garnishes
Avocados
Lettuce
Tomatoes
Additional Mexican cheese blend
Black olives sliced or diced
Jalapeño peppers sliced or diced
Sour cream

Preheat oven to 350° F. In a large bowl, mix together ground beef, green chilies, taco seasoning, Goulash Cream Hot and Garlic Cream. Lightly press beef mixture into a 13x9-inch baking pan. Cover and bake for about 30 minutes.

Remove from oven and drain drippings; spread the refried beans on top of the meatloaf, followed by the black beans. Top with green chile sauce and salsa, finishing with the cheese. Bake 15 minutes longer, uncovered, until toppings are heated through and cheese has melted. Slice and garnish each serving with your favorite taco garnishes.

If you are using a recipe, read it thoroughly before you start cooking to make sure you have the ingredients and the time to finish the meal as instructed. If you are rushed and have to cook at too high a heat, your meal will not be the end result you wanted. Be creative if you have to substitute an ingredient. No canned tomatoes? Will a jar of salsa work instead?

"Luckily we found your product online and the feast continues. We have given your web address to several of our friends so that they also can enjoy your wonderful products."
—Delighted Paprika Fan

Serves 4

Preparation time 15 minutes

Cooking time 30 minutes

Ready in 45 minutes

Can also be cut in wedges to serve as an appetizer.

Mexican Pizzas

ingredients

1 lb lean ground beef

1 small onion, chopped

1 tsp Univer Goulash Cream Mild

1 tsp Univer Gourmet Garlic Cream

1 (4 oz) can diced green chilies, drained

1 tsp ground cumin seed

1 Tbs vegetable oil

4 (6-inch) corn tortillas

1 (16 oz) can refried beans

1 (8 oz) package shredded Mexican cheese blend

Suggested Garnishes

Sour cream

Tomatoes, seeded and chopped

Green onions, chopped

Avocado, diced

Black olives, sliced

Jalapeños, sliced or chopped

Preheat oven to 350° F. In a large frying pan, brown and crumble the ground beef. Add the onion and sauté about 3 minutes; drain if necessary. Stir in Goulash Cream Mild, Garlic Cream, green chilies, and cumin. Stir to combine; set aside. In another frying pan, heat oil. Place one tortilla in the hot oil and fry 15 seconds. Flip and fry another 15 seconds. Remove from heat and drain on paper towels. Repeat with remaining tortillas.

Arrange crisp tortillas on a baking sheet. Spread each tortilla with a thin layer of refried beans. Spoon on a layer of the meat mixture, followed by the cheese. Bake for about 15 minutes, or until beans have heated through. Arrange the pizzas on plates and garnish as desired.

"The odds of going to the store for a loaf of bread and coming out with only a loaf of bread are three billion to one."

—Erma Bombeck

Serves 8

Preparation time 10 minutes

Cooking time 8 hours

Ready in 8 hours, 10 minutes

Nicky's Italian Sour Beef

Simple to prepare and these sophisticated flavors will make your family very happy.

ingredients

4 lbs boneless chuck pot roast

2 Tbs capers

1 Tbs Univer Sweet Ann

1 Tbs Univer Gourmet Garlic Cream

1 (16 oz) jar Italian giardiniera, drained, keep the liquid

1 (16 oz) jar sliced pepperoncini peppers, drained, keep the liquid

Place roast in slow cooker. Mix capers, Sweet Ann, and Garlic Cream together; add equal parts of reserved giardiniera liquid and pepperoncini liquid to mixture to make 1 cup. Spoon giardiniera vegetables and peppers over beef; spoon caper mixture over all. Cover and cook on low 8 to 10 hours. Save the juices to serve over the meat, au jus style. Pair with a glass of Cabernet Sauvignon.

Giardiniera and pepperoncini jars are usually found in the olive aisle of the supermarket.

Serves 6

Preparation time 10 minutes

Cooking time 3 hours

Ready in 3 hours, 10 minutes

You won't believe the taste you will coax from these 3 easy ingredients.

Number Three Pot Roast

ingredients

3 lbs chuck roast, cut into 2-inch pieces

3 large onions, sliced

3 Tbs Univer Goulash Cream Mild (or Hot)

Preheat oven to 300° F. Layer onions in the bottom of a roasting pan. Place meat on top of onions. Spread Goulash Cream over the meat. Cover and roast for three hours. Do not add any other liquids to the pan; the onions and Goulash Cream will make a lovely sauce. This recipe is so easy—just remember the number 3!

Serves 4
Preparation time 10 minutes
Cooking time 14 minutes
Ready in 54 minutes

Pepper Jack Chili Burgers

Use jalapeños instead of mild chilies to turn up the heat on these yummy burgers.

ingredients

2 lbs lean ground beef
1 Tbs Univer Goulash Cream Mild
1 Tbs Univer Gourmet Garlic Cream
1 (7 oz) can diced green chilies, drained
1 small onion, chopped or grated
4 slices pepper jack cheese
4 rolls, split and toasted

Prepare the grill for medium to medium-high heat. In a large bowl, mix together beef, Goulash Cream Mild, Garlic Cream, chilies, and onion. Form into 4 patties; cover and let rest 30 minutes. Grill for about 7 minutes on each side, or to desired doneness. Top with cheese during last 3 minutes of grilling. On a cooler part of the grill, toast split rolls until lightly toasted. Serve with your favorite hamburger toppings.

Don't overlook grating onions instead of chopping them. Grate them over a plate and add the onion juices to the ingredients, as well as the onions. The onions themselves almost melt away, leaving great onion flavor without big onion bits. This is a good idea for people who like onion flavor but not onion pieces.

Serves 6
Preparation time 10 minutes
Cooking time 10 hours
Ready in 10 hours, 10 minutes

Pepper lovers, this one's for you

Peppery Pot Roast

ingredients

3 potatoes, washed and sliced
2 medium onions, sliced
2 Tbs Univer Goulash Cream Hot
1 Tbs Univer Mustard
1 Tbs Worcestershire sauce
1 Tbs course ground black pepper

2 tsp Univer Gourmet Garlic Cream
3 lbs boneless chuck pot roast
½ cup low-sodium beef broth

Creamy Green Peas
(find recipe on page 199)

Place potatoes and onions in slow cooker. In a small mixing bowl, combine Goulash Cream Hot, Mustard, Worcestershire sauce, pepper, and Garlic Cream. Spread over meat. Place roast in slow cooker; pour broth around sides of roast. Cover and cook on low 10 to 12 hours, or on high 6 to 8 hours. Serve with a fresh salad and Creamy Green Peas.

White pepper, red pepper, and black pepper have different heat levels and affect the palate in different places. Keep all three in your kitchen for dishes that have complex heat, such as Cajun and Creole recipes.

Serves 4

Preparation time 15 minutes

Cooking time 10 minutes

Ready in 25 minutes

When the family says "steak," there's nothing quite like a ribeye!

Rib Eye Steaks with Creamy Mushroom Sauce

ingredients

2 (1-lb) ribeye steaks, about 1-inch thick

3 Tbs Univer Goulash Cream Mild, divided

Creamy Mushroom Sauce

1 lb fresh mushrooms, sliced

½ cup green onions, sliced, including tops

1 Tbs Univer Goulash Cream Mild

1 tsp Univer Gourmet Garlic Cream

2 Tbs flour

½ cup low-sodium beef broth

½ cup sour cream

Spread 1 tablespoon of Goulash Cream Mild on each steak, both sides. Place the meat on a hot grill and cook to desired degree of doneness, about 5 minutes on one side and 3 minutes on the other for medium. Remove from heat; cover and keep warm.

Meanwhile, in a medium frying pan over medium-high heat, add the mushrooms and sweat until juices are released, about 5 minutes. Add the green onions, remaining Goulash Cream Mild, and Garlic Cream. Cook another 3 minutes. Sprinkle the flour over the vegetables and stir to coat. Let flour cook for a couple of minutes to eliminate the raw flour taste. Reduce heat to medium; add beef broth and sour cream. Cook until mixture is bubbly and thickens. Serve over steaks. Enjoy with a glass of Merlot.

"The only time to eat diet food is while you're waiting for the steak to cook."
—Julia Child

Serves 6

Preparation time 25 minutes

Cooking time 45 minutes

Ready in 1 hour, 10 minutes

A fun surprise when sliced—creamy cheesy filling!

Ricotta Stuffed Meat Loaf

ingredients

¼ cup low-sodium beef broth

2 eggs

1 Tbs Univer Sweet Ann

½ tsp black pepper

2 lbs lean ground beef

¾ cup Italian seasoned breadcrumbs

⅓ cup ketchup

½ cup onions, finely diced

1 (4 oz) can mushrooms, drained and chopped

Ricotta Stuffing

1½ cups ricotta cheese

½ cup grated Parmesan cheese

1 egg, beaten

1 tsp Univer Gourmet Garlic Cream

½ tsp pepper

1 Tbs fresh parsley, chopped

1 Tbs fresh thyme, chopped

Preheat oven to 350° F. In a large mixing bowl, whisk together broth, eggs, Sweet Ann, and pepper. Add beef, breadcrumbs, ketchup, onions, and mushrooms. Mix well to combine all ingredients. Press half of the meat loaf mixture evenly over the bottom of a 13x9-inch baking pan.

For the stuffing, combine ricotta cheese, Parmesan cheese, beaten egg, Garlic Cream, and pepper. Mix well. Add parsley and thyme. Spread the ricotta mixture evenly over the meat, but not touching the sides of the pan. Top with the other half of the meat, pressing the edges of the meat together to form an envelope around the ricotta mixture. Cover and bake for 30 minutes. Uncover and bake another 15 minutes, or until done. Remove from oven, cover and let stand for 10 minutes before slicing. Enjoy with a glass of Chianti.

"I come from a home where gravy is a beverage."

—Erma Bombeck

Serves 6
Preparation time 15 minutes
Cooking time 8 hours, 15 minutes
Ready in 8 hours, 30 minutes

Coffee enhances the flavor of most savory sauces and gravies, and also helps tenderize meats.

Rump Roast in Java Sauce

ingredients

1 medium onion, sliced

⅓ cup flour

1 tsp dried thyme

½ tsp dried rubbed sage

½ tsp black pepper

3 lbs beef rump roast

1 Tbs olive oil

½ cup strong black coffee, cooled

½ cup low-sodium beef broth

1 Tbs Univer Sweet Ann

1 Tbs Univer Goulash Cream Mild

1 tsp Univer Gourmet Garlic Cream

Arrange sliced onions in bottom of slow cooker. Mix flour, thyme, sage, and pepper together on a platter. Dredge roast in flour mixture. In a large, deep frying pan, heat oil over medium-high heat; brown meat on all sides. Place meat in slow cooker on top of onions. In a small bowl, whisk together coffee, broth, Sweet Ann, Goulash Cream Mild, and Garlic Cream. Pour evenly over meat. Cover and cook on low for 8 to 10 hours. Pan drippings can be served au jus.

For recipes calling for coffee, keep a small jar of instant on hand.

Serves 4
Preparation time 15 minutes
Cooking time 10 minutes
Ready in 55 minutes

These little red chilies are hot, so reduce the amount if you would like less heat. The chilies can be found in the spice aisle at the supermarket.

Spicy Mongolian Beef

ingredients

½ cup low-sodium soy sauce

3 Tbs cornstarch

2 Tbs low-sodium beef broth

2 Tbs brown sugar

1 Tbs Univer Gourmet Garlic Cream

2 tsp sesame oil

2 tsp Univer Red Gold Hot

4 small whole dried red chile peppers

2 lbs boneless sirloin tip roast, sliced into thin strips

¼ cup vegetable oil, divided

3 bunches green onions, sliced into 2-inch pieces, including tops

Hot cooked rice (4 servings)

In a large bowl, combine soy sauce, cornstarch, broth, brown sugar, Garlic Cream, sesame oil, Red Gold Hot, and whole chile peppers. Place beef in the marinade and toss to coat evenly. Cover and refrigerate for 30 to 60 minutes. Heat 2 tablespoons of the oil in a large frying pan or wok over medium heat. Sauté green onions for about 5 minutes, or until tender. Remove green onions and set aside.

In the same frying pan or wok, heat remaining 2 tablespoons of oil over medium-high heat. Add beef and marinade and sauté for about 5 minutes, or until the beef is to desired doneness. (You may have to sauté beef in batches.) Return green onions to the pan and cook for 30 seconds more, or until heated through. Serve over hot rice.

Freeze the roast for about 20 minutes to allow easier slicing.

If you leave the chilies in the dish, it will continue to add spicy heat to the dish. Remove them if the dish is hot enough for your taste.

Red Gold Hot
A few suggested uses:

- Add a spicy boost to stews, soups and gravies
- Glaze a sizzling steak or chop
- Mix into ground meats
- Add to marinades
- Sauté onions and vegetables
- Create wonderful dips
- Mix into salsa to enhance the flavor
- Add to ranch dressing to make Southwestern dressing with a kick
- Lightly brush onto hot grilled pineapple
- Gluten-free; no trans fats

Serves 6

Preparation time 15 minutes

Cooking time 50 minutes

Ready in 1 hour, 5 minutes

Use a colorful combination of bell peppers for a beautiful dish!

Stuffed Bell Peppers

ingredients

6 large sweet bell peppers

2 lbs lean ground beef

1 cup uncooked long-grain rice

¼ cup Univer Goulash Cream Mild or Hot

1 tsp dried leaf marjoram

1 tsp dried coriander seed

1 Tbs vegetable oil

1 tsp Univer Red Gold Mild

1 tsp Univer Gourmet Garlic Cream

1 medium onion, chopped

⅓ cup low-sodium beef broth

½ cup ketchup

1 Tbs Univer Red Gold Hot

½ Tbs Univer Gourmet Garlic Cream

1 Tbs fresh thyme, chopped

1 cup shredded Italian cheese blend

Preheat oven to 350° F. Cut a slice off top of each pepper; reserve tops. Remove core and seeds from peppers; place in a baking dish and set aside. In a medium-size mixing bowl, combine ground beef, rice, Goulash Cream, marjoram, and coriander seed. In a medium frying pan, heat oil, Red Gold Mild, and Garlic Cream over medium heat. Add onion and sauté until translucent, about 5 minutes. Add onions to beef mixture and stir to combine.

Lightly stuff the beef mixture into the peppers, mounding over the tops. (Stuffing will shrink slightly during cooking.) Put the reserved pepper tops in the same baking dish, to the side. Pour broth into dish. Cover and bake for about 30 minutes. Meanwhile, in a small mixing bowl, combine ketchup, Red Gold Hot, Garlic Cream, and thyme. Uncover baking dish and pour sauce over the tops of each stuffed pepper. Cover and continue baking another 20 minutes, until beef is cooked through. Remove from oven, uncover, and top with cheese. Place pepper tops on top of stuffed peppers and serve hot.

"I am pleased I found you and excited to try your products."
—**Delighted Paprika Fan**

Serves 6

Preparation time 15 minutes

Cooking time 8 hours, 30 minutes

Ready in 8 hours, 45 minutes

This chili-like stew is just the dish for a cold night.

Taco and Bean Stew with Beef

ingredients

1 onion, sliced

2 lbs rump roast, cut into 2-inch chunks

1 (14.5 oz) can diced tomatoes with jalapeños

1 (8 oz) can tomato sauce

2 Tbs Univer Red Gold Hot

1 (1.25 oz) package taco seasoning mix

1 (4.5 oz) can chopped green chilies, with liquid

2 (15 oz) cans red kidney beans, drained

Shredded Mexican cheese blend, for garnish

Green onions, chopped, for garnish

Add onions to the slow cooker; top with meat. In a small mixing bowl, stir together tomatoes, tomato sauce, Red Gold Hot, taco seasoning, and green chilies. Cover and cook on low 8 to 10 hours, until meat is tender. Add beans; cover and cook 30 minutes longer or until beans are heated through. Garnish with cheese and green onions. Enjoy with a glass of Sangria.

Serves 4
Preparation time 10 minutes
Cooking time 25 minutes
Ready in 35 minutes

A tasty, simple taco-style salad.

Vera Cruz Salad

ingredients

1 lb lean ground beef

1 Tbs Univer Goulash Cream Mild

1 tsp Univer Gourmet Garlic Cream

1 small onion, chopped

1 (15 oz) can black beans, drained

1 (10 oz) package frozen whole kernel corn, thawed

1 Tbs chile powder

1 head iceberg lettuce, shredded

Suggested Garnishes
1 avocado, chopped
1 cup shredded Mexican cheese blend

1 cup **Spicy Red Mayonnaise** (see recipe on page 230)

In a large frying pan over medium-high heat, brown and crumble the ground beef until no longer pink. Add the Goulash Cream Mild, Garlic Cream, and onions and cook for another 5 minutes, until onions are wilted. Drain the pan of fat; add beans, corn, and chile powder, blending well. Cook for another 10 minutes, or until heated through. Serve over lettuce and top evenly with garnishes.

You may substitute ground chicken or turkey, as well.

Serves 4

Preparation time 10 minutes

Cooking time 3 hours, 10 minutes

Ready in 3 hours, 20 minutes

A tropical feast with pineapple and fresh ginger.

Braised Pineapple Short Ribs

ingredients

4 lbs beef short ribs

½ cup Univer Red Gold Mild

1 (20 oz) can pineapple tidbits, with juice

1 cup beef broth

3 Tbs Univer Mustard

2 Tbs Univer Horseradish with Vinegar

½ cup brown sugar

1 Tbs Univer Gourmet Garlic Cream

2 tsp fresh ginger, minced

Preheat oven to 300° F. Prepare grill for high heat. Rub Red Gold Mild on ribs; sear the ribs on the grill for about 10 minutes, turning once. Place ribs on a rack in an oven-proof dish. In a medium-size mixing bowl, whisk together pineapple with juice, broth, Mustard, Horseradish with Vinegar, brown sugar, Garlic Cream, and ginger. Baste ribs liberally and cover. Cook about 3 hours, basting frequently. Let rest for about 10 minutes before serving. Enjoy with a glass of Cabernet Sauvignon.

You can buy small jars of minced ginger, usually in the produce section of the supermarket.

Serves 4

Preparation time 10 minutes

Cooking time 10 minutes

Ready in 25 minutes

Horseradish-Garlic Burgers

So easy and fast to whip up on a weekday night! Adjust the amount of Horseradish with Vinegar to suit your taste.

ingredients

2 lbs lean ground beef

2–3 Tbs Univer Horseradish with Vinegar

2 Tbs Univer Gourmet Garlic Cream

2 tsp fresh thyme, chopped

2 tsp fresh chives, chopped

Salt and pepper to taste

2 Tbs butter, softened

4 onion rolls

4 slices extra sharp Cheddar cheese or Pepper Jack cheese

Combine beef, Horseradish with Vinegar, Garlic Cream, thyme, and chives. Form into 4 patties, and season with salt and pepper. Place on medium-hot grill and cook 5 minutes per side, or to desired doneness. Butter inside of buns and toast on a cooler part of the grill. Remove meat from grill; top each burger with a slice of cheese. Cover loosely and let rest 5 minutes. Enjoy with a cold beer!

Univer Horseradish with Vinegar is perfect for those who love the taste of horseradish, but don't like the "sinusy" bite it has.

Chicken Enchiladas with Green Chile Sauce, see page 123

The Killing of the Chicken!

What is a child to do when his mother hands him a deep bowl and tells him to go catch the big yellow, cut her throat, gather the blood in the bowl and bring it all into the kitchen? Well, he would say, "Yes, Mother, I'll do it." Of course, she was not ordering me, a ten-year-old boy, to murder someone. It was simply Sunday, and she was serving chicken for lunch and dinner for seven people that day. And if I wanted dessert, I wouldn't dare to argue with her.

There were my three siblings and me, Mother, Father, and Granma, the matriarch of the family. I always thought of Granma as the matriarch because she was the one who brought home all the cash each day from the Farmer's Market, and she set the agenda for the work to be performed. (I learned the word matriarch from a nature movie showing elephants; the narrator referred to the large, aggressive female as the matriarch.) Granma would sell all the flowers and vegetables that we, my siblings and I and Mother and Father worked all day to grow. There was very little credit given by her for our efforts in creating that money. She did not count the fact that we as children often had to get up at five in the morning, go down to the garden where Father grew carnations and other flowers, and pick them in their early morning state—loaded with water from the nightly dew. Then we would load up her bicycle truck so she could push it to the market, sell them, and bring home the cash.

And very often, the flower slaves were just me, my brother, and mother. That was because my older sister had excuses. She was going to be a concert pianist and she had to either save her hands from work or practice piano. She had good excuses and they always worked. My younger sister was too little to work, so it was my brother and I who slaved before breakfast and got Granma's bicycle truck on her way, ate breakfast quickly, and ran to school.

Well, it was also my duty to kill the chicken for the family kitchen. My brother would help to catch it, but I was the executioner and I was told by my mother to not give up that position to my brother. He was not old enough. Actually I felt grown up when I received that duty. I would take the chicken, hold the two legs and the two wings together, put her neck on a log and, with my handy little axe, chop her head off. Then I quickly let the blood flow into the deep bowl. This blood was always put into the hot chicken soup where it would cook and harden into a cake on the surface of the soup. Mother would divide it up among the family members. I would always take it out of the soup plate, put a lot of salt on my portion and eat it that way. Granma told us it enriched our blood and made us healthy.

My other favorite chore was making crêpes (palacsinta) for dessert. My mother would make up the mixture and I would stand at the wood-burning stove, create the proper heat in it, then bake the crêpe on the stove top in a pan. I was a genius at flipping the crêpe. They all called me "the juggler." Whenever I wanted to eat some, I had to ruin one by flipping it wrong, then my mother would let me eat it. But she was watching and she was onto me if I did that too often. After I stacked up a considerable number, enough for everyone, Mother would put cottage cheese, jam, or walnut shavings with a lot of sugar in it and rolled it up like a burrito. That was a common, but delicious dessert. I loved it in my childhood, and still do.

My mother was an incredible person. Like my father, she always worked. She cooked breakfast, lunch, and dinner, and washed clothes for all seven of us. She made our clothes on her Singer sewing machine with a foot paddle, which was a wedding gift for her in 1932. She would take my

older sister's clothes that she had outgrown and if the color and the material were adaptable for a boy, namely me, she would create something out of it. Nothing was ever wasted. So it was when I grew out of something, my brother would get a new garment out of that, for sure. But as busy as she was, she always found time to foot race with us at sundown in the summers.

Mother was the ultimate working machine. She worked in the garden and greenhouses with the flowers and the vegetables that we grew for our own use. The vegetables were saved in an earthen bunker that was dug and built by Father during the war, which we used many times during air raids when the sirens went off. After the Second World War, it became a root cellar for vegetables and other things for the winter. She cleaned the house and worked with us on school problems. She fixed my older sister's hair. She had no recreation at all, but I can also say that for all of us.

She loved the theatre, however, and she would take us to see a musical or an operetta, which was her favorite, every once in a while. She was very proud to tell everyone that she volunteered me in my first-grade opening celebration to recite a poem to all the parents and school kids at the ceremony, and how good I was. She started working with me on this a month before school started. This was entirely her idea, but I didn't mind. I actually loved it. She knew I loved the theatre, too. Yet she would always tell me not to grow up to be an actor, because they led very immoral lives.

But she was so proud of me, nevertheless, when I brought her to visit me in Los Angeles and took her to the studio, where I was acting in a Gomer Pyle Show. My name was printed on a director's chair, where I sat until I had to go in front of the camera. She looked at my name many times while I worked there, and she was proud. I reminded her of what she had said about actors when I was a child, that they are immoral. Yes, she said, but this is different, this is filming!

The kitchen where we lived in the 1940s and '50s was about twelve by twelve feet. We had a large table in the middle that would seat all seven of us. On one side we had the old woodstove; it would burn coal, too, but that was hard to come by. And it was awful smelly and dangerous for carbon monoxide emissions. The other side of the kitchen was a large credenza with all the plates, dishes, baking equipment—baking was all done by hand—forks, knives, etc. Behind and to the side there was a door to the pantry. That's where we kept all the food that didn't have to be in the bunker for the winter—flour, sugar, lard, smoked meat, bacon slabs, sausages, honey, and everything else that was food. Left and right of the kitchen were the bedrooms. Very small for seven people, eight when my favorite Granpa, my father's father, would come and stay with us. I was and still am very proud to have his first name.

My mother would do practically all the housework, besides working outside in the green house and the garden, which was our livelihood. Besides being in charge of the killing of the chickens, I was also responsible for the feeding and care of our beautiful German Shepherd, Rex; bringing in wood for the stove, rain or shine; and helping Father in the greenhouse, where he sometimes worked sixteen hours a day. He was also an amateur beekeeper as he called it. Of course, it was his hobby, but it was done for the family. We always had honey year round. He held an eight-hour a day job with the railroad and worked constantly at home. Among everything else I had to do, I had to study for school, which was not my favorite thing to do.

As I mentioned, the vegetables were stored in the root cellar that was an air raid bunker that was used many times during the raids when the sirens went off. I remember those times as if they were happening now. In the late summer of 1944, the sirens started up, and that meant one should find a shelter from possible bombing, for there were enemy aircraft in the area. At such a time it was always sheer panic. The family dropped everything—whatever we all were doing—with Mother screaming to Father, "Get the children and run for the bunker."

The sirens were still sounding when my father picked up my brother in his arms—he was four years old at the time—grabbed my hand, and off we went running to the bunker, except I could not keep up with Father. He let go of my hand and ran ahead of me with my brother, all the while yelling "Run, run, run!" I also hear my mother's voice in the distance behind us, "Run, run—airplanes are coming!"

Mother would always be the last to start running. She had to make sure we were all on the way to safety, that everything was off the stove, and the doors to the house were locked so no one could come in and steal something. We heard stories from the neighbors that this was always happening.

My older sister was always first in the bunker, which was pretty far away from the big house on purpose; if they wanted to bomb the big house, we would be relatively safe in the earthen bunker.

I liked it there because it was nice and cool in the summer, but it was tight with the entire family present. It was about twenty-four feet long, five feet wide, and about seven feet deep. It was covered with railroad ties and then covered with a layer of earth on top of the ties.

One time, fighter planes could be heard above us going at each other at low altitude, trying to out-maneuver each other, all the while shooting. I heard Father's voice saying, "Drop down, lay down and don't move." I threw myself down in the field of carnations, and I saw my father ahead of me doing the same, covering my brother with his body.

Then I saw puffs of dirt in a series going by me toward my father as one of the fighter planes went by, maybe about thirty feet above us. I could clearly see the red star on its tail as he shot back up, high

above us, engaging again in the fight. My gaze followed the plane as it was maneuvering around in his battle with his enemies. I turned on my back in the midst of the carnations to watch the battle.

There must have been about fifteen or twenty of them. It was fascinating how these wondrous machines were flying in every direction, with their slick bodies shining in the sun. I thought to myself, I'd like to do that some day. Every once in a while one would burst into flames or start smoking. Suddenly they would disengage and disappear in the clear blue sky. Then the sirens sounded again, signaling the end of the danger.

Then I heard my mother screaming in the distance. "Are you okay, where are you, I can't see you. Oh, thank God," she said, when my father stood up with my brother in his arms, crying. "I didn't see you because of the flowers." Then she screamed hysterically again, "Where is Johnny? Oh, my God. I can't see him!" I was there, lying on my back, contemplating what I had just seen, when my mother yanked me up from among the carnations. "Oh, thank God, you are alright!"

As we gathered and hugged each other, Mother kept saying, "Next time we hear the sirens we'll have to run right away. Do you understand?" Then she cried out, "Oh, my God, look at your pants," pointing to my father's trouser leg. "Are you hurt? Are you bleeding?" He looked at her, thinking, What is she talking about?

"Look at your pant leg, there are holes in it." We all looked; there were three evenly placed holes in his pant leg, right above each other. They were made by that low-flying Russian fighter plane that caused us to throw ourselves down into the carnations. As my father went down, his pant leg lay flat on the ground next to his leg and the airplane's bullets made holes in it. Otherwise he had no injuries at all. That was one day we did not make it to the bunker except for, of course, my sister.

My brother and I dug for those bullets throughout the war; it now seems we searched for years. We never found them.

Serves 4

Preparation time 20 minutes

Cooking time 55 minutes

Ready in 1 hour, 20 minutes

Juicy, tender chicken thighs get a flavor boost from Goulash Cream and white wine.

Baked Chicken with Artichoke Hearts

ingredients

2 Tbs olive oil

8 boneless skinless chicken thighs

1 cup seasoned breadcrumbs

1 (12 oz) jar marinated artichoke hearts, drained, halved, marinade reserved

1 small yellow onion, chopped

½ lb fresh mushrooms, sliced

1 Tbs Univer Goulash Cream Mild

1 tsp Univer Gourmet Garlic Cream

½ tsp dried oregano

½ tsp dried rosemary

½ cup white wine

Freshly ground black pepper, to taste

Delicious served with
Creamy Mashed Potatoes
(find recipe on page 200)

Chicken breast and thighs are generally interchangeable in most recipes; just keep the meat weight/pieces in balance. You may have to add a thigh if the thighs are small, or a breast if the breasts are small. Just keep in mind the appetites of your family or guests.

Preheat oven to 350° F. In large frying pan, heat oil over medium-high heat. Dredge chicken in breadcrumbs. Fry in batches until lightly browned, turning once. Do not crowd pan. Transfer to baking dish. Add reserved artichoke marinade to frying pan; cook 5 minutes over medium heat, scraping up any browned bits, until liquid turns syrupy. Add onions, mushrooms, Goulash Cream Mild, Garlic Cream, oregano, and rosemary; sauté 5 minutes, until onion is translucent. Stir in artichoke hearts and wine. Season with pepper and bring to a low boil. Remove from heat.

Pour mixture over chicken, cover and bake for about 25 minutes, or until chicken is done. Remove from oven and let rest, covered, for about 5 minutes. Transfer to a serving platter and pour any remaining pan juices over chicken. Serve with Creamy Mashed Potatoes.

Serves 6
Preparation time 10 minutes
Cooking time 45 minutes
Ready in 1 hour, 5 minutes

UniverRed Gold Mild lends beautiful color and flavor to this crispy bird.

Beer Can Garlic Chicken

ingredients

1 (3 lb) whole fryer chicken

¼ cup Univer Gourmet Garlic Cream

¼ cup Univer Red Gold Mild

Salt and pepper to taste

1 (12 oz) can beer, opened

Wash chicken and pat dry. Season inside with salt and pepper. Place chicken butt over open beer can and insert can into chicken. Make sure the chicken is stable on the can and will stand up without aid. In a small bowl, mix together the Garlic Cream and Red Gold Mild. Rub the mixture over the bird, spreading evenly to coat. Season with salt and pepper. Tuck wings in so they don't stick out. Place chicken upright on medium-hot grill.

Grill about 45 minutes, or until a meat thermometer reads about 170°F. (Chicken will continue to cook a few minutes more.) Remove from heat to a cutting board. Cover loosely with foil and let stand on beer can for about 10 minutes before removing from can. Caution: can will be hot. Discard beer can and beer, but enjoy with a fresh, ice-cold brew.

For a spicy version, use Red Gold Hot instead of Mild.

Serves 4

Preparation time 15 minutes

Cooking time 20 minutes

Ready in 35 minutes

Small portions, like sliced pinwheels, are so appealing to kids!

Bleu Cheese Chicken Pinwheels

ingredients

4 boneless skinless chicken breasts

freshly ground black pepper, to taste

1 (3 oz) package cream cheese, softened

1 Tbs Univer Goulash Cream Mild

¼ cup crumbled bleu cheese

½ cup chopped pecans, toasted

2 Tbs butter, melted

1 tsp Univer Gourmet Garlic Cream

Preheat oven to 350° F. Place each chicken breast between two pieces of plastic wrap. Working from center to edges, lightly pound with the flat side of a meat mallet to ¼-inch thickness. Remove plastic wrap and season with pepper. In a small mixing bowl, combine cream cheese, Goulash Cream Mild, and bleu cheese. Add pecans. Spoon mixture evenly over each breast; spread nearly to edges. Fold in the sides and roll up, jelly-roll style, using toothpicks to secure.

Place chicken breasts in a 2-quart baking dish. In a small mixing bowl, combine melted butter and Garlic Cream. Pour over chicken. Bake uncovered for 20 minutes, or until done. Remove to a serving platter and pour any pan juices over chicken. Remove toothpicks before serving; slice into pinwheels. This dish pairs well with a Caesar salad and hot crusty bread.

For a little more color, broil briefly in a broiler-safe pan at the end of baking time.

Serves 6
Preparation time 15 minutes
Cooking time 1 hour
Ready in 5 hours, 15 minutes

Slightly spicy, tender chicken pieces marinated in buttermilk. Buttermilk is a natural tenderizer and will add moisture to the finished dish.

Buttermilk Fried Chicken

ingredients

2 cups buttermilk
1 Tbs Univer Sweet Ann
1 Tbs onion powder
1 tsp Univer Gourmet Garlic Cream
1 tsp Univer Strong Steven
⅓ cup fresh parsley, chopped
⅓ cup fresh thyme, chopped

1 (3 lb) fryer chicken, cut into pieces
1 cup flour
1 cup seasoned breadcrumbs
½ tsp cayenne pepper
1 quart canola oil, for frying

Horseradish Butter
(find recipe on page 224)

In a large mixing bowl, whisk together buttermilk, Sweet Ann, onion powder, Garlic Cream, and Strong Steven. Add herbs and chicken; stir to coat. Cover and refrigerate for 4 hours or overnight. Drain but do not rinse chicken, leaving some herbs on skin. Discard marinade. On a large platter or in a large paper bag, combine flour with breadcrumbs and cayenne pepper.

Heat oil in a large frying pan to 350° F. Dredge chicken in flour mixture and shake to remove excess. Fry in batches on one side for about 20 minutes, flip and fry another 10 minutes, or until done. Do not crowd pan. Drain on paper towels and serve with hot corn on the cob with Horseradish Butter. Enjoy with a glass of Zinfandel.

Don't play with your food when cooking! Leave it alone and let the heat do its job. Breaded chicken that loses its breading when flipped is a sign you are flipping too early. Food like steaks and chops won't stick to the pan if they are ready to turn.

Serves 4
Preparation time 20 minutes
Cooking time 30 minutes
Ready in 1 hour

Butterflied Grilled Game Hens with Herbs

There's something special about having your own little chicken.

ingredients

4 Cornish game hens (about 1¼ lbs each)
¼ cup Univer Mustard
2 Tbs Univer Red Gold Mild
1 Tbs extra virgin olive oil
1 tsp Univer Gourmet Garlic Cream
1 tsp Worcestershire sauce
1 tsp rubbed sage
1 tsp dried thyme
½ tsp freshly ground black pepper

To butterfly hens, use poultry shears or a sharp knife to split the hens lengthwise along one side of the backbone. With the breast side up, pull the body open, pressing down firmly on the breast until the rib bones crack and the hens lay reasonably flat. In a small bowl stir together the Mustard, Red Gold Mild, olive oil, Garlic Cream, Worcestershire sauce, sage, thyme, and pepper.

Place hens, breast side up, on medium grill. Baste liberally with sauce during cooking. Grill for about 30 minutes, or until juices run clear. Transfer hens to a platter and cover loosely with foil; let rest 10 minutes before serving.

Serves 4
Preparation time 10 minutes
Cooking time 25 minutes
Ready in 35 minutes

Chicken Alfredo with Mushrooms and Broccoli

Use your favorite Alfredo sauce in this dish; customize it further by substituting peas or your preferred vegetables.

ingredients

1 Tbs oil

2 Tbs butter, divided

1 Tbs Univer Goulash Cream Mild

4 boneless skinless chicken breasts

1 cup seasoned breadcrumbs

8 oz mushrooms, sliced

1 cup broccoli florets

½ – ¾ cup prepared Alfredo sauce

In a large frying pan, heat oil, 1 tablespoon of butter, and Goulash Cream Mild. Dredge chicken in breadcrumbs; cook until browned on all sides and done, about 15 to 20 minutes. Remove from pan; cover and keep warm. Add remaining butter; sauté mushrooms and broccoli for about 5 minutes. Stir in Alfredo sauce; warm through. Serve over chicken.

Serves 4
Preparation time 10 minutes
Cooking time 15 minutes
Ready in 25 minutes

Here's an inventive way to use up leftover chicken.

Chicken and Mushroom Sauce with Fettuccine

ingredients

8 oz fettuccine pasta

2 Tbs olive oil

1 lb fresh white mushrooms, sliced

½ cup green onions, sliced

1 Tbs Univer Goulash Cream Mild

1 tsp Univer Gourmet Garlic Cream

½ cup low-fat ricotta cheese

¼ cup reserved pasta liquid

1 cup cooked chicken, diced

1 cup tomato, seeded and chopped

¼ cup fresh basil, chopped

Cook pasta according to package directions; drain, reserving ¼ cup of cooking liquid; return pasta to pot and keep warm. Meanwhile, in a large frying pan, heat oil until hot. Add mushrooms, green onions, Goulash Cream Mild, and Garlic Cream; cook, stirring frequently, until mushrooms are tender, about 5 minutes. Add ricotta and reserved pasta liquid to make a creamy sauce. Stir in chicken; toss to coat and heat through. Add tomato and basil; cook 1 minute longer. Serve over pasta with lightly toasted garlic bread. Enjoy with a glass of Chardonnay or white Burgundy.

Seeding tomatoes removes excess liquid that may break a sauce (cause it to separate). To seed, cut tomato into wedges and remove seeds and loose pulp with your fingers or a spoon. Chop as usual.

"Food is our common ground, a universal experience."

—James Beard

Serves 6

Preparation time 15 minutes

Cooking time 35 minutes

Ready in 50 minutes

This dish is so good on a chilly evening and makes a nice entrée for company.

Chicken and Artichokes with Creamy White Sauce

ingredients

2 Tbs extra virgin olive oil

6 boneless skinless chicken breast halves

1 (14 oz) jar marinated artichoke hearts, drained, marinade reserved

1 (8 oz) package cream cheese, softened

⅓ cup sour cream

2 Tbs Univer Mayonnaise

2 Tbs reserved artichoke marinade

1 Tbs Univer Mustard

1 tsp Worcestershire sauce

1 tsp Univer Gourmet Garlic Cream

½ tsp Univer Red Gold Hot

¼ cup grated Parmesan cheese

½ cup green onions, chopped with tops

½ cup shredded mozzarella cheese

Preheat oven to 350° F. In a large frying pan, heat oil over medium-high heat. Brown chicken breasts on both sides until evenly browned, about 10 minutes. Place in broiler-proof casserole dish; set aside. Drain artichoke hearts, reserving marinade for the sauce. Quarter the hearts and place them over the chicken. In a food processor, blend cream cheese, sour cream, Mayonnaise, reserved artichoke marinade, Mustard, Worcestershire sauce, Garlic Cream, and Red Gold Hot until smooth. Mix in Parmesan cheese.

Spoon cream cheese mixture over the chicken and artichokes. Cover and bake about 20 minutes, or until chicken is done. Uncover, turn on broiler, and top with green onions and mozzarella cheese. Place under broiler until cheese bubbles and begins to brown, about 5 minutes or less.

Clean as you go. Trying to cook with a mess all around you is discouraging and can lead to accidents.

Serves 4

Preparation time 20 minutes

Cooking time 55 minutes

Ready in 1 hour, 20 minutes

Enjoy a great Southern-style entrée with the big game on TV. This recipe will easily double.

Chicken and Sausage Jambalaya

ingredients

¼ cup vegetable oil

1½ cups onion, chopped, divided

1 cup green bell peppers, chopped, divided

1 Tbs Univer Strong Steven

2 tsp Univer Goulash Cream Hot

2 tsp Univer Gourmet Garlic Cream

2 Andouille sausage links, sliced on the diagonal

1 lb boneless skinless chicken breasts, cut into ¾-inch chunks

2 bay leaves

1½ cups long grain rice

3 cups low-sodium chicken broth

½ cup green onions, chopped with tops

2 avocados, sliced

Heat oil in a large heavy pot over medium-high heat. Add half the onions and half the bell peppers. Add the Strong Steven, Goulash Cream Hot, and Garlic Cream and stir. Sauté for about 15 minutes, until vegetables are browned. Add the sausage, chicken, the remaining onions and bell peppers, and the bay leaves. Cook another 10 minutes, scraping up any browned bits often.

Add rice and cook several minutes, stirring often to coat and lightly brown the rice. Add the broth, stir, and cover. Cook on medium-low heat for 30 minutes or until liquid is nearly absorbed. Remove from heat, add green onions, stir, cover, and let stand 5 minutes. Remove bay leaves before serving. Top with avocado slices.

The rice will continue to pull moisture from the other ingredients, so serve as soon as possible.

By sautéing the onions and green pepper in stages instead of all at once, you will create a slightly different texture to the dish.

Serves 6

Preparation time 15 minutes

Cooking time 45 minutes

Ready in 1 hour

Coating the pasta with Goulash Cream Hot makes for a pretty spicy dish, perfect for those who love their pasta "kicked up."

Chicken and Sausage Penne

ingredients

½ lb Italian sausage, hot or sweet

1 lb boneless skinless chicken thighs, cut into 1-inch chunks

1 Tbs Univer Gourmet Garlic Cream

1 medium onion, chopped

1 green bell pepper, chopped

1 (26 oz) jar of your favorite prepared pasta sauce

1 (14.5 oz) can diced tomatoes, with liquid

¼ cup grated Parmesan cheese

1 (16 oz) package penne pasta, cooked according to directions

2 Tbs Univer Goulash Cream Hot

¼ cup green onions, chopped, including tops, for garnish

Grated Parmesan cheese, for garnish

Brown sausage in a large frying pan over medium-high heat. When the sausage begins to render its fat, add the chicken; brown on all sides for about 5 to 7 minutes. Drain pan drippings, reserving 1 tablespoon of fat. Add Garlic Cream, onion, and green pepper; sauté another 5 minutes. Add pasta sauce, tomatoes, and cheese. Reduce heat; simmer for 30 minutes. Prepare pasta according to package directions; drain well. Toss with Goulash Cream Hot to coat. Serve sauce over pasta, garnished with green onions and cheese. Chianti is a nice wine choice.

Leftover shrimp? Add peeled and deveined shrimp near the end of cooking time.

Serves 6
Preparation time 10 minutes
Cooking time 30 minutes
Ready in 2 hours, 45 minutes

Chicken Blanco

Sometimes made with mayonnaise, this Blanco recipe calls on yogurt to reduce the calories.

ingredients

1 (3 lb) frying chicken, cut into 8 pieces

Marinade
1 cup plain yogurt
1 Tbs Univer Gourmet Garlic Cream
½ Tbs Univer Sweet Ann
¼ cup extra virgin olive oil
1 lemon

In a small mixing bowl, whisk together yogurt, Garlic Cream, Sweet Ann, and olive oil. Zest and juice the lemon and add to marinade. Place the marinade in a large food storage bag and add chicken. Squeeze air out of bag, seal, and turn chicken to coat thoroughly. Refrigerate for about 2 hours, turning occasionally.

At grill time, remove chicken from marinade and discard marinade. Place chicken on grill over medium heat and grill for about 15 minutes on each side, or until juices run clear. Remove from heat, cover loosely with foil and let rest 5 minutes before serving.

Mix Gourmet Garlic Cream with mashed potatoes for instant Garlic Potatoes.

Serves 4
Preparation time 15 minutes
Cooking time 1 hour, 30 minutes
Ready in 1 hours, 45 minutes

A favorite Italian dish doubled up with the flavor of fresh paprika Red Gold Mild and Goulash Cream Mild.

Chicken Cacciatore

ingredients

¼ cup vegetable oil
1 Tbs Univer Red Gold Mild
½ Tbs Univer Gourmet Garlic Cream
1 egg
½ cup flour
½ cup seasoned breadcrumbs
8 bone-in, skin-on chicken thighs
1 medium onion, chopped

8 oz fresh mushrooms, sliced
2 (28 oz) cans crushed tomatoes
½ cup red wine
2 Tbs Univer Goulash Cream Mild
½ cup fresh parsley, finely chopped
2 cups shredded Italian cheese blend

Hot cooked pasta of your choice

Preheat oven to 350° F. In a large frying pan, heat oil, Red Gold Mild, and Garlic Cream over medium-high heat. Beat egg in a shallow dish. Combine flour and breadcrumbs in another shallow dish. Dip chicken in egg, then dredge in flour mixture. In the frying pan, brown chicken on both sides and place in a baking dish. To the frying pan add onions and mushrooms; sauté for about 5 minutes. Add tomatoes, wine, and Goulash Cream Mild. Blend well and pour over chicken.

Bake for 1 hour, covered. Uncover and sprinkle with parsley. Top with cheese and return to oven, uncovered, and bake 15 minutes longer, until cheese is bubbly and slightly browned. Serve over hot pasta. A glass of Pinot Noir is a lovely touch.

Don't be shy about combining Univer paprika products to produce lovely new flavors.

Serves 6

Preparation time 20 minutes

Cooking time 8 hours

Ready in 8 hour, 20 minutes

Nice, clean flavors with a spicy finish.

Chicken Creole

3 stalks celery, washed and sliced including leafy tops

1 green bell pepper, chopped

1 onion, chopped

8 oz fresh mushrooms, sliced

2 fresh jalapeño peppers, seeded and chopped

3 lbs boneless skinless chicken breasts and thighs

1 (14.5 oz) can diced tomatoes, with liquid

1 cup low-sodium chicken broth

2 Tbs Univer Strong Steven

1 Tbs Univer Gourmet Garlic Cream

Hot cooked rice (6 servings)

Place vegetables in slow cooker. Place chicken pieces on top of vegetables. Add tomatoes. In small mixing bowl, whisk together broth, Strong Steven, and Garlic Cream. Pour mixture into slow cooker. Cook on low for 8 to 10 hours or on high for 5 to 6 hours. Serve over hot cooked rice.

Chop and slice foods with love, not speed. Chop only at the pace at which you are comfortable—no need to keep up with TV chefs! That's just an accident waiting to happen.

Serves 4
Preparation time 15 minutes
Cooking time 15 minutes
Ready in 30 minutes

Cutlets are often overlooked in the meat aisle. They are usually well priced and offer a quick alternative to regular chicken.

Chicken Cutlets with Ham and Swiss

ingredients

8 chicken cutlets, lightly pounded

8 slices deli ham, thinly sliced

8 slices Swiss cheese, thinly sliced

⅓ cup seasoned breadcrumbs

¼ cup grated Parmesan cheese

½ tsp dried rubbed sage

Salt and pepper to taste

2 Tbs vegetable oil

1 Tbs butter

1 tsp Univer Red Gold Mild

1 tsp Univer Gourmet Garlic Cream

1 Tbs flour

1 cup low-sodium chicken broth

Hot cooked rice or mashed potatoes (4 servings)

Place a slice of ham on each cutlet, topped with a slice of cheese. Fold in the sides of the cutlets; beginning at the bottom, roll up tight and secure each with a toothpick. In a shallow pan, combine breadcrumbs, Parmesan cheese, sage, and salt and pepper. Roll cutlets in breadcrumbs to coat. Heat oil in large frying pan over medium-high heat; brown chicken on both sides, about 10 minutes.

Transfer to a serving platter and keep warm. Add butter, Red Gold Mild, and Garlic Cream to frying pan and pull up browned bits. Add flour to melted butter mixture; cook for 1 to 2 minutes, stirring; add broth and stir until gravy has thickened. Serve with hot rice or mashed potatoes.

Substitute turkey or pork cutlets when on sale.

Serves 5

Preparation time 30 minutes

Cooking time 25 minutes

Ready in 55 minutes

Soon to be a family favorite, this creamy filling is so light and delicious. Substitute diced pork for "carne" enchiladas!

Chicken Enchiladas with Green Chile Sauce

ingredients

1 (8 oz) package cream cheese, softened

½ cup half and half cream

1 Tbs Univer Red Gold Hot

1 tsp Univer Goulash Cream Mild

2 cups cooked chicken, shredded

1 (4.5 oz) can chopped green chilies

1 medium onion, chopped

10 (10-inch) flour tortillas

2 (15 oz) cans green chile sauce with pork

1½ cups shredded Mexican cheese blend

Suggested Garnishes
Avocados, chopped
Tomatoes, chopped
Lettuce, shredded
Sour Cream
Salsa

Preheat oven to 350° F. In a large mixing bowl, beat together cream cheese, half and half, Red Gold Hot, and Goulash Cream until smooth. Add chicken, green chilies, and onion; stir to combine. Spoon a thin layer of green chile sauce in the bottom of a large baking pan. Spread each tortilla with a thin layer of green chile sauce. Place about ¼ cup of chicken mixture in center of each tortilla. Roll tortillas and place seam-side down in pan. Spoon some additional sauce over top of tortillas.

Cover and bake about 20 minutes. Uncover and sprinkle on cheese. Bake uncovered about 5 to 7 minutes longer, until cheese is bubbly and slightly browned. Heat remaining sauce and serve with enchiladas. Garnish as desired. A cold Mexican beer is a must!

If you prefer, you may sauté the onions before adding them to the cream cheese mixture. The raw onions add a bit of crunch and have a stronger flavor.

Serves 8

Preparation time 15 minutes

Cooking time 20 minutes

Ready in 35 minutes

This is a wonderful buffet dish because you can keep the shells at room temperature in a basket next to the chicken, then fill as needed.

Chicken in Pastry Shells

ingredients

2 Tbs butter or margarine

2 tsp Univer Red Gold Mild

1 tsp Univer Gourmet Garlic Cream

1 large onion, chopped

2 large carrots, peeled and sliced

2 medium potatoes, peeled, cut into ½-inch dice

1 tsp dried oregano

1 tsp dried thyme

1¾ cups low-sodium chicken broth

1 (10.75 oz) can cream of chicken soup

½ cup heavy cream

3 cups cooked chicken, diced

1 cup green peas, fresh or frozen

Salt and pepper

8 pastry shells, baked according to package directions

In a large saucepan, melt butter, Red Gold Mild, and Garlic Cream over medium heat. Add onions, carrots, potatoes and herbs. Sauté for 5 minutes or until vegetables begin to soften. Add chicken broth; bring to a boil. Cover, reduce heat and simmer until vegetables are tender, about 10 minutes. In a small bowl, mix together cream of chicken soup and heavy cream; add to vegetables. Add chicken and peas; cook until heated through, adding more broth if needed to maintain desired consistency. Season with salt and pepper to taste. Spoon mixture into and around warm pastry shells.

To save time, use fresh herbed rotisserie chicken from the market.

"I encountered Univer's Eros Pista during business trips to Hungary—and LOVED it from the first taste! I would amaze my Hungarian colleagues by spreading it like butter or jam on bread and eating a whole side dish of it BEFORE the entrée arrived."

—Delighted Paprika Fan

Serves 6
Preparation time 30 minutes
Cooking time 25 minutes
Ready in 55 minutes

The supermarket offerings of various new cooking cream cheeses make short work of many recipes usually reserved for a weekend.

Chicken Manicotti with Herb White Sauce

ingredients

12 manicotti pasta shells

2 Tbs Univer Goulash Cream Mild

2 (8 oz) tubs whipped cream cheese with garlic and herbs

⅔–1 cup milk

½ cup grated Parmesan cheese, divided

2 cups cooked chicken, chopped

1 (10 oz) package frozen chopped broccoli, thawed and dried

1 (4 oz) jar chopped pimientos, drained

½ tsp pepper

1 cup shredded mozzarella cheese

Preheat oven to 350° F. Cook pasta shells according to package directions. Drain well; toss gently with Goulash Cream Mild; set aside. While pasta is cooking, blend cream cheese and milk in saucepan over medium-low heat until melted. Use additional milk to thin if the sauce is too thick. Do not boil. Mix in ¼ cup Parmesan cheese. Set aside 1 cup of sauce.

Combine rest of sauce, chicken, broccoli, pimientos, and pepper in a bowl; mix well. Stuff each pasta shell with about 2 tablespoons of the chicken mixture. Arrange in nonstick 9x13-inch baking pan. Spoon remaining sauce over pasta; top with mozzarella cheese. Bake covered for 25 to 30 minutes, or until heated through. Remove from oven and sprinkle with remaining Parmesan cheese.

Leftovers? Freeze them! This dish comes back well, topped with a little Alfredo sauce and baked covered at 350° F until heated through.

Serves 6
Preparation time 10 minutes
Cooking time 8 hours
Ready in 8 hours, 10 minutes

Mexican Chicken for Burritos and Tacos

For another layer of flavor, use skin-on, bone-in thighs. Remove the skin and debone the chicken before shredding.

ingredients

2 lbs boneless, skinless chicken thighs

½ cup low-sodium chicken broth

¼ cup green salsa

1 tsp Univer Gourmet Garlic Cream

2 tsp Univer Red Gold Hot

3 green onions, chopped

1 jalapeño pepper, seeded, chopped

½ tsp ground cumin

Place chicken in slow cooker. Whisk together broth, salsa, Garlic Cream, Red Gold Hot, green onions, jalapeño pepper, and cumin. Pour over chicken and cover. Cook for 8 hours on low, until chicken is very tender. Remove chicken from slow cooker and reserve cooking liquid. Shred meat using two forks. Before filling taco shells or tortillas, add ½ cup of the liquid back to meat.

Serves 4

Preparation time 15 minutes

Cooking time 45 minutes

Ready in 1 hour

A Hungarian mainstay—prepared in your kitchen with authentic Hungarian Sweet Ann Paprika!

Chicken Paprikash

ingredients

8 slices bacon, chopped

1 small onion, chopped

1 cup flour, divided

1 tsp dried thyme

1 tsp dried oregano

½ tsp black pepper

2 lbs boneless skinless chicken breasts, cut into thirds

4 cups low-sodium chicken broth, divided

4 Tbs butter

1⅓ cups half and half cream

3 Tbs Univer Sweet Ann

3 cups sour cream

Egg Dumplings
(find recipe on page 204)

For a variation, serve over hot cooked rice.

In a large frying pan over medium-high heat, cook bacon until crisp and fat is rendered. Remove bacon to paper towels to drain. Add onions to bacon drippings and cook until translucent, about 5 minutes. Transfer onions to a small bowl. In a large dish or large plastic storage bag, mix together ¾ cup of flour, thyme, oregano, and pepper. Place chicken in dish or bag and coat with flour mixture. Brown chicken in bacon drippings (may add a little oil if needed) until golden on all sides, about 10 minutes. Reduce heat to medium and add 2 cups of broth. Cover and cook for 10 minutes. Uncover and cook 10 minutes longer, until broth is reduced and thickened.

Meanwhile, in a large saucepan over medium heat, melt butter. Blend in remaining ¼ cup of flour. Stirring constantly, cook until mixture begins to bubble. Add 2 cups of broth, cream, and Sweet Ann. Do not boil. Lower heat to medium-low and slowly add sour cream, whisking constantly. When blended, add bacon and onions to the sauce. Add chicken and reduced broth from frying pan. Heat about 5 minutes. Serve with Egg Dumplings (Spaetzels). Pair with a bottle of Riesling.

Serves 4

Preparation time 15 minutes

Cooking time 45 minutes

Ready in 1 hour

One of our most-requested chicken recipes! Enjoy!

Chicken Parmesan

ingredients

1 egg

2 tsp Univer Red Gold Mild

1 tsp Univer Gourmet Garlic Cream

1 cup seasoned breadcrumbs

½ tsp dried thyme

½ tsp dried oregano

½ tsp pepper

2 Tbs vegetable oil

4 boneless skinless chicken breasts

2 cups prepared pasta sauce, divided

1 cup shredded mozzarella cheese

½ cup shredded Parmesan cheese

1 lb spaghetti, cooked according to package directions

Preheat oven to 350° F. In a shallow bowl, beat egg with Red Gold Mild and Garlic Cream. In dish or large paper plate, mix together the breadcrumbs, thyme, oregano, and pepper. Heat oil in a large frying pan over medium-high heat. Dip chicken pieces in egg mixture, then coat with breadcrumbs. Brown chicken in hot oil until golden on both sides, about 10 minutes. Remove to a broiler-proof baking dish.

Spread one cup of pasta sauce over top of chicken and cover. Bake for about 20 minutes. Uncover and top with mozzarella cheese. Bake uncovered another 10 minutes. Turn on broiler. Top with shredded Parmesan and broil until lightly browned. Heat remaining pasta sauce. Serve chicken over hot cooked pasta, topped with remaining sauce. Pair with a glass of Chianti for the finishing touch.

Choose a cutting board that has enough room to easily hold all the food that you are chopping.

Serves 4–8

Preparation time 15 minutes

Cooking time 1 hour

Ready in 1 hour, 25 minutes

Spicy Orange Hens

Hot paprika relish or paste works magically with fruits, intensifying the sweet flavors.

ingredients

4 Cornish hens, about 1 pound each

¼ cup Univer Goulash Cream Mild

¼ cup orange marmalade

2 tsp orange zest

⅔ cup orange juice

¼ cup Univer Strong Steven

1 tsp Univer Sweet Ann

Preheat oven to 350° F. Rinse hens under cold water and pat dry. Rub Goulash Cream Mild evenly over each hen. Place hens on rack in roasting pan. Roast hens uncovered for 30 minutes. Meanwhile, put orange marmalade, orange zest, and orange juice in a small bowl. Whisk until combined, then add Strong Steven and Sweet Ann, whisking again. Remove hens from oven and baste liberally, using all the sauce. Return to oven and bake another 30 minutes or until done, basting periodically with drippings in the pan. Let stand 10 minutes before carving.

Serves 6

Preparation time 10 minutes

Cooking time 20 minutes

Ready in 30 minutes

Capers add a yummy tang to this meal— add more if you're a big fan.

Chicken with Tomatoes and Capers

ingredients

3 Tbs olive oil, divided

1 Tbs Univer Goulash Cream Mild

4 lbs boneless skinless chicken breasts

2 tsp Univer Red Gold Mild

1 tsp Univer Gourmet Garlic Cream

6 green onions, sliced

2 small tomatoes, seeded and chopped

2 tsp flour

¾ cup low-sodium chicken broth

2 Tbs capers, drained and rinsed

salt and pepper to taste

Hot cooked rice or mashed potatoes (6 servings)

Heat 2 tablespoons of oil and Goulash Cream Mild in a large frying pan over medium-high heat. Cook chicken until done, about 5 to 6 minutes per side. Transfer to a plate; cover and keep warm. Add remaining 1 tablespoon oil, Red Gold Mild, Garlic Cream, and green onions to same frying pan. Cook 5 minutes, until onion is tender. Add tomatoes, sprinkle in flour, and cook 1 to 2 minutes. Add broth and capers; simmer until slightly thickened, about 5 minutes. Season with salt and pepper. Return chicken and accumulated juices to frying pan and coat with sauce. Serve with hot rice or over a bed of mashed potatoes.

Rinsing the capers helps remove the excess salt.

Serves 6

Preparation time 20 minutes

Cooking time 15 minutes

Ready in 25 minutes

An easy, quick meal for lunch or dinner.

Chicken Wraps with Green Chile Sauce

ingredients

2 Tbs vegetable oil, divided

1½ lbs boneless skinless chicken breasts, sliced into thin strips

1 Tbs Univer Red Gold Mild or Hot

1 Tbs Univer Gourmet Garlic Cream

2 green bell peppers, sliced into thin strips

1 medium onion, sliced

1 (4.5 oz) can chopped green chilies

1 (15 oz) can green chile sauce with chicken

1 Tbs lime juice

1 cup shredded Mexican cheese blend

6 (8-inch) flour tortillas, warmed

Suggested Garnishes

Salsa
Avocados
Lettuce
Tomatoes
Additional Mexican cheese blend
Black olives sliced or diced
Jalapeño peppers sliced or diced
Sour Cream

In a large frying pan, heat 1 tablespoon of oil over medium-high heat and brown chicken strips about 5 minutes, or until pink no longer shows. Remove and set aside. In same pan, heat remaining oil, Red Gold, and Garlic Cream over medium heat and cook bell peppers and onions about 8 minutes or just until tender.

Return chicken to pan and add chopped green chilies. Pour green chile sauce over chicken mixture; stir to blend. Stir in lime juice and cheese; heat through until sauce is hot. Warm tortillas in microwave oven about 15 seconds. Place 1 tortilla on each dish and spoon on chicken mixture. Roll up and top with your favorite garnishes. A glass of Sangria completes the meal.

Check out your local ethnic markets for less expensive produce and make friends with some unfamiliar veggies. The produce manager will be happy to answer questions and provide cooking tips.

Serves 4

Preparation time 30 minutes

Cooking time 20 minutes

Ready in 1 hour

Grilled Chicken with Summer Salsa

Seeding the tomatoes will help keep your salsa from becoming too runny.

ingredients

4 boneless skinless chicken breasts

1 Tbs Univer Red Gold Mild

1 tsp dried thyme

Salsa

2 lbs tomatoes, seeded and finely chopped

1 yellow pepper, finely chopped

1 green pepper, finely chopped

1 red onion, finely chopped

2 stalks celery, finely chopped

2 tsp Univer Red Gold Hot

1 tsp Univer Gourmet Garlic Cream

¼ cup extra virgin olive oil

2 Tbs balsamic vinegar

½ cup fresh parsley, chopped

Salt and pepper to taste

Brush Red Gold Mild onto chicken breasts; season with thyme. Grill over medium-high heat for about 10 minutes per side, or until juices run clear. Remove from heat, cover loosely with foil and let rest about 10 minutes. To make the salsa, mix all salsa ingredients together in a large bowl. Cover and chill until very cold. Serve salsa over chicken.

Goulash Cream Mild

A few suggested uses:

- Add a spicy boost to stews, soups and gravies
- Glaze a sizzling steak or chop
- Mix into ground meats
- Add to marinades
- Sauté onions and vegetables
- Create wonderful dips
- Mix into salsa to enhance the flavor
- Add to ranch dressing to make Southwestern dressing with a kick
- Lightly brush onto hot grilled pineapple
- Gluten-free; no trans fats

Serves 4

Preparation time 15 minutes

Cooking time 35 minutes

Ready in 50 minutes

This dish looks complex, but it is really easy to prepare and worth the "longish" list of ingredients. If you're pressed for time, buy cut up veggies from the supermarket.

Country Captain Chicken

ingredients

- 8 boneless skinless chicken breasts and thighs
- Salt and pepper to taste
- ¼ cup flour
- ¼ cup seasoned breadcrumbs
- 2 Tbs extra virgin olive oil
- 2 Tbs butter
- 1 Tbs Univer Goulash Cream Mild
- 1 tsp Univer Gourmet Garlic Cream
- 1 green bell pepper, seeded, chopped
- 1 red bell pepper, seeded, chopped
- 1 medium onion, chopped
- 1 Tbs curry powder
- 1 cup low-sodium chicken broth
- 1 (14.5 oz) can diced tomatoes, with liquid
- ¼ cup raisins
- ¼ cup slivered almonds, lightly toasted
- 4 cups hot cooked rice
- 2 green onions, chopped, for garnish

Cut each piece of chicken in half; season with salt and pepper. Combine flour and breadcrumbs in a shallow dish; dredge chicken in flour mixture. In a large frying pan over medium-high heat, add oil and butter. Brown chicken on all sides until golden, about 15 minutes. Transfer chicken to a platter.

To the frying pan, add Goulash Cream Mild and Garlic Cream; add the bell pepper and onion; sauté about 5 minutes. Add curry, broth, tomatoes, and raisins; stir. Put chicken back in pan; reduce heat to medium-low and simmer for 15 minutes. Transfer to a serving dish and garnish with almonds. Serve over hot rice topped with green onions.

Leftover soups and stews can be stretched by serving them over rice, mashed potatoes, or hash-brown potatoes.

Serves 6
Preparation time 10 minutes
Cooking time 30 minutes
Ready in 3 hours, 40 minutes

A tropical holiday for your senses, combining orange, peach, and ginger! If you don't have fresh peaches, we suggest frozen.

Fried Chicken with Peach Relish

ingredients

3 lbs boneless skinless chicken thighs

⅔ cup orange marmalade, divided

⅓ cup orange juice

2 Tbs soy sauce

1½ tsp Univer Mustard

1 tsp Univer Gourmet Garlic Cream

1½ tsp fresh ginger, finely chopped, divided

1 cup plain breadcrumbs

¼ cup vegetable oil

Peach Relish

3 fresh peaches, chopped

½ cup green onions, thinly sliced

1 Tbs Univer Strong Steven

Reserved orange marmalade

Reserved ginger

Place chicken in a large bowl or plastic storage bag. For the marinade, combine ⅓ cup marmalade, orange juice, soy sauce, Mustard, Garlic Cream, and 1 teaspoon ginger in a small bowl. Pour marinade over chicken to coat; cover bowl or close bag securely. Refrigerate 3 hours. Remove chicken from marinade and discard marinade. Coat chicken in breadcrumbs. Heat oil in a large frying pan over medium-high heat; brown chicken until golden on one side, about 10 minutes. Turn chicken over and brown the other side, about 10 minutes longer. Reduce heat to medium, cover and cook until juices run clear, about 10 to 15 minutes more.

For the Peach Relish, combine peaches, green onions, Strong Steven, remaining marmalade, and remaining ginger in a medium bowl. Cover and refrigerate until ready to use. To serve, spoon relish over hot chicken.

The sweetness of the peaches is really enhanced by the heat of the Strong Steven.

Serves 4
Preparation time 10 minutes
Cooking time 1 hour
Ready in 1 hour, 20 minutes

Garlic-Rubbed Rosemary Hens

Easy to prepare and pretty enough for company.

ingredients

4 Cornish hens

Salt and pepper

2 lemons

8 rosemary sprigs

2 Tbs Univer Gourmet Garlic Cream

¼ cup chicken broth

¼ cup dry white wine

Preheat oven to 350° F. Rinse and pat dry the game hens; season cavities with salt and pepper. Cut lemons in half and place one-half in each hen, along with 2 rosemary sprigs. Rub Garlic Cream all over hens; season lightly with salt and pepper. Pour broth and wine in pan with a wire rack. Place hens on rack; roast about 1 hour, basting frequently, until juices run clear. Remove from oven, cover loosely with foil. Let hens rest about 10 minutes before serving.

Brine those birds! A simple ⅔ kosher salt to ⅓ sugar dissolved in water, with some added herbs for flavor, will make your meat much tastier. If you don't rinse, remember to add additional salt very sparingly.

Serves 4

Preparation time 15 minutes

Cooking time 10 minutes

Ready in 25 minutes

A nice summery dish done outside on the grill.

Grilled Chicken Florentine

ingredients

1 (10 oz) package chopped frozen spinach, thawed and squeezed dry

¼ cup onion, chopped

¼ cup Univer Mayonnaise

3 Tbs grated Parmesan cheese

3 Tbs extra virgin olive oil, divided

1 Tbs lemon juice

2 tsp Univer Gourmet Garlic Cream

½ tsp Univer Red Gold Hot

6 fresh basil leaves, roughly chopped

1 cup fresh breadcrumbs

8 chicken cutlets, lightly pounded

Salt and pepper to taste

In a food processor bowl, place the spinach, onion, Mayonnaise, Parmesan cheese, 1 tablespoon olive oil, lemon juice, Garlic Cream, Red Gold Hot, and basil leaves. Pulse until combined. Add the breadcrumbs and stir to combine. Place an equal amount of stuffing in the center of each cutlet. Fold in the sides of the cutlets; beginning at the bottom, roll up tight and secure each with a toothpick. Baste the cutlets with some of the remaining oil; season with salt and pepper. Grill over medium heat about 4 to 5 minutes per side, basting occasionally with any remaining oil. Zinfandel goes well with most grilled foods.

"Our trip to Hungary introduced us to the great food there. Your authentic products allow us to capture the tastes and flavor of that great land. Thank you very much!"

—Satisfied Paprika Fan

Serves 4

Preparation time 10 minutes

Cooking time 10 minutes

Ready in 20 minutes

Make your own butter blends (compounds) and store in the freezer until needed.

Grilled Chicken Thighs with Hungarian Butter

ingredients

8 chicken thighs, skin on

8 Tbs **Hungarian Butter,** softened (find recipe on page 225)

1 Tbs olive oil

1 Tbs poultry seasoning

Salt and pepper to taste

Loosen skin on chicken thighs. Stuff one tablespoon of Hungarian Butter under skin of each thigh. Brush chicken thighs with olive oil; dust with poultry seasoning. Season to taste with salt and pepper. Grill over medium heat for 5 minutes on each side or until done.

Open a drawer to temporarily hold a baking sheet if you are short on counter space, but be careful if there are children running about.

Serves 6
Preparation time 20 minutes
Cooking time 45 minutes
Ready in 1 hours, 15 minutes

Grilled Citrus Chicken

A fresh, delightful chicken with citrus overtones and a beautiful red Goulash Cream color.

ingredients

1 (3 lb) whole frying chicken

3 limes, juice reserved

2 lemons, juice reserved

1 medium orange, juice reserved

¼ cup Univer Goulash Cream Mild

Citrus zest

Garlic Butter with Parsley and Cilantro (find recipe on page 223)

Wash and pat dry the chicken. Using a grater or microplane, zest all the fruits; reserve zest in a small bowl. Juice the fruits and combine with zest. Stuff fruit pulp into the chicken cavity. Rub Goulash Cream Mild all over chicken. Grill over medium heat for about 45 to 55 minutes, basting often, until juices run clear. Turn occasionally.

Garlic Butter Baste

For the baste, melt Garlic Butter with Parsley and Cilantro. Whisk in zest and reserved juices. Baste chicken frequently. When chicken is done, remove from heat; cover loosely with foil and let rest about 10 minutes. Enjoy with a glass of Chardonnay.

Serves 8
Preparation time 30 minutes
Cooking time 45 minutes
Ready in 1 hour, 15 minutes

Gently inserting herbs under the skin of the chicken will provide a moist, flavorful bird and it's really easy to do. Try not to tear the skin, but if that happens, it's still going to taste great!

Herb-Rubbed Grilled Chicken

ingredients

1 (4 lb) whole frying chicken, butterflied

½ cup green onions, coarsely chopped

¼ cup flat leaf parsley, coarsely chopped

1 Tbs fresh lemon juice

1 Tbs Univer Sweet Ann

1 tsp Univer Gourmet Garlic Cream

1 tsp dried rosemary leaves

1 tsp dried thyme

1 tsp dried sage

3 Tbs olive oil, divided

Salt and pepper to taste

Remove excess fat from chicken. Rinse and pat dry. To butterfly chicken, use poultry shears or a sharp knife to split the chicken lengthwise along one side of the backbone. With the breast side up, pull the body open, pressing down firmly on the breast until the rib bones crack and the chicken lays reasonably flat.

In a food processor bowl, combine onions, parsley, lemon juice, Sweet Ann, Garlic Cream, and herbs. Pulse to coarsely combine, then add 2 tablespoons of olive oil in a thin stream until herb mixture is moistened.

Place fingers between the skin and meat of the chicken to separate and make space for the herb mixture. Place herb mixture under chicken skin, pushing it in gently under skin until all parts of meat are covered. Gently massage the chicken to evenly distribute herb mixture. Brush chicken skin lightly with remaining oil; season with salt and pepper to taste. Place breast side up in center of cooking surface and grill over medium-high heat for 45 to 55 minutes or until the juices run clear and the skin is crisp. It is not necessary to turn chicken.

If you are not comfortable butterflying the chicken, your butcher will be happy to do it for you.

Serves 6

Preparation time 20 minutes

Cooking time 30 minutes

Ready in 50 minutes

Hearty sausage paired with sliced chicken in a lovely white sauce.

Linguine with Andouille & Chicken

ingredients

2 Tbs extra virgin olive oil

½ lb Andouille sausage, diced

2 boneless skinless chicken breast halves, cut into thin strips

1 green bell pepper, sliced into thin strips

1 red bell pepper, sliced into thin strips

1 medium onion, sliced into thin strips

8 oz fresh mushrooms, sliced

3 Tbs Univer Goulash Cream Hot

2 tsp Univer Gourmet Garlic Cream

1 (14 oz) low-sodium chicken broth

1 cup half and half cream

¼ cup cornstarch

½ cup cold water

1 (16 oz) package linguine, prepared according to package directions

Grated Parmesan cheese, for garnish

Heat oil in a large frying pan over medium-high heat; add sausage and chicken and cook until chicken is nearly done. Add bell peppers, onion, and mushrooms; stir in Goulash Cream Hot and Garlic Cream. Reduce heat to medium; sauté about 8 to 10 minutes. Stir in broth and cream. In a small bowl, mix together cornstarch and water until well combined. Add to frying pan; stir until sauce is thickened. Serve hot over cooked pasta. Top with grated Parmesan cheese and serve with a fresh green salad.

If your mushrooms just need a spot cleaning, use a dampened paper towel.

Serves 4

Preparation time 10 minutes

Cooking time 45 minutes

Ready in 55 minutes

A clever way to serve chicken at your next outing, complete with its own bread!

Picnic Chicken

ingredients

8 boneless skinless chicken thighs

Salt and pepper to taste

1 egg

1 Tbs Univer Red Gold Hot

1 tsp Univer Gourmet Garlic Cream

½ cup seasoned breadcrumbs

2 Tbs olive oil

1 large loaf of French bread

Green Onion and Cilantro Butter, melted (find recipe on page 223)

Preheat oven to 350° F. Season chicken with salt and pepper. In a shallow bowl, beat egg with Red Gold Hot and Garlic Cream. In another shallow bowl, place breadcrumbs. Dip thighs in egg mixture, then dredge in breadcrumbs. Heat oil in a large frying pan over medium-high heat. Brown chicken until golden, about 15 minutes. Transfer chicken to baking dish, cover, and bake 15 minutes.

Slice top off of French bread. Scrape out inside of loaf, leaving about ½-inch of bread. Generously brush inside of bread and inside of bread top with melted Green Onion and Cilantro Butter. Place loaf and bread top on baking sheet. Remove chicken from baking dish and arrange pieces in loaf. Return to oven and bake, uncovered, 15 minutes longer. Remove loaf from oven, replace top and wrap in several layers of foil to keep warm. Iced tea or fresh lemonade makes a perfect drink.

Wrap several layers of news- paper around the foil-wrapped loaf to keep very warm for hours.

Serves 4
Preparation time 10 minutes
Cooking time 20 minutes
Ready in 30 minutes

A good pizza is never hard to find in your kitchen! Try this zippy dish!

Rio Grande Chicken Pizza

ingredients

1 Tbs vegetable oil

1 lb boneless skinless chicken, diced

1 (1.25 oz) package taco seasoning mix

1 (4.5 oz) can chopped green chilies

1 Tbs Univer Red Gold Hot

⅔ cup taco sauce, divided

2 (12-inch) flour tortillas

1 cup refried beans

½–1 cup shredded Mexican cheese blend

Suggested Garnishes
Lettuce, shredded
Avocados, seeded, peeled and diced
Tomato, diced
Black olives
Sour cream

Preheat oven to 375° F. Heat oil in a large frying pan; stir in chicken, taco seasoning mix, chilies, and Red Gold Hot; cook until chicken is no longer pink. Stir in ⅓ cup of taco sauce and remove from the heat. Place the tortillas on a large baking sheet. Spread with refried beans, covering the entire tortilla. Top with chicken mixture; spoon on remaining taco sauce. Top with shredded cheese. Bake until cheese is bubbly and slightly browned, about 10 minutes. Remove from oven and let stand a few minutes. Cut into wedges and serve with garnishes.

If you are short on time, leftover chicken or supermarket rotisserie chicken will work just fine.

Gourmet Garlic Cream

Garlic is revered throughout the world for its flavor-enhancing qualities and is a staple in most kitchens. With Gourmet Garlic Cream, you can do away with messy cleaning and chopping. Just open the jar! Great garlic aroma, pure garlic flavor!

A few suggested uses:

- Add to soups, stews and gravies
- Mix into mashed potatoes for instant Garlic Potatoes
- Make garlic bread in a snap
- Add to sauces, dips and spreads
- Sauté onions and other vegetables
- Toss with hot cooked pasta before dressing with sauce
- Rub onto clean, dry potatoes before baking
- Brush onto pizza crusts before baking

Serves 6
Preparation time 15 minutes
Cooking time 6 hours, 45 minutes
Ready in 7 hours

A creamy mild sauce tops this chicken. Serve with potatoes or rice.

Slow Cooker Chicken with White Sauce

ingredients

1 large onion, sliced

3 lbs chicken pieces

½ cup water

3 Tbs unsalted butter or margarine, melted

1 Tbs Univer Goulash Cream Mild

2 tsp dried Italian herb seasoning

Salt and pepper to taste

1 (10.5 oz) can condensed cream of mushroom soup

2 (3 oz) packages cream cheese, softened and cubed

½ cup low-sodium chicken broth

1 tsp Univer Gourmet Garlic Cream

Place onions in bottom of slow cooker, topped with chicken pieces. Add water. Melt butter and Goulash Cream Mild; add Italian herb seasoning. Pour butter mixture over chicken pieces. Sprinkle with salt and pepper. Cover and cook on low for 6 to 8 hours. About 45 minutes before serving, mix soup, cream cheese, broth, and Garlic Cream in small saucepan over medium-low heat. Stir until smooth. Pour over chicken. Turn slow cooker to high; cover and cook for 45 minutes, or until heated through.

Forgot to take the cream cheese out to soften? Just cut into small pieces and it will soften fast.

ingredients

Serves 6
Preparation time 15 minutes
Cooking time 15 minutes
Ready in 2 hours, 30 minutes

A spicy flavor boost to fat chicken pieces nestled with plump vegetables!

Zesty Chicken Kebabs

⅓ cup vegetable oil

¼ cup red wine vinegar

2 tsp Univer Strong Steven

1 tsp Univer Gourmet Garlic Cream

1 Tbs fresh thyme, chopped

1 Tbs fresh parsley, chopped

2 lbs boneless skinless chicken breasts, cut into 2-inch chunks

1 medium onion, sliced into 2-inch squares

2 red bell peppers, seeded, and sliced into 2-inch squares

2 ears corn, cleaned, sliced into 2-inch rounds

Hot and Spicy Butter
(find recipe on page 224)

For the marinade, whisk together the oil, vinegar, Strong Steven, Garlic Cream, thyme, and parsley in a medium bowl and add the chicken, onions, and bell peppers. Toss to coat, cover and place in refrigerator for about 2 hours; stir occasionally. At grill time, remove the chicken and vegetables from the marinade and discard marinade.

Thread the chicken, onions, bell peppers, and corn alternately onto metal skewers, leaving a little space between the pieces. Grill the kebabs over a medium-hot grill for 15 to 20 minutes, turning occasionally, until done. Serve with a crisp green salad and Hot and Spicy Butter for the corn. Great with an ice cold beer!

"Thank you, I really love this paste and will be giving it as gifts!"
—**Delighted Paprika Fan**

Serves 4
Preparation time 15 minutes
Cooking time 20 minutes
Ready in 35 minutes

St. Louis Chicken Chowder

A welcoming bowl of hearty chowder made with chicken and topped with crisp bacon.

ingredients

6 strips bacon, chopped

1 small onion, chopped

3 celery stalks, chopped

2 cups low-sodium chicken broth

2 Tbs Univer Red Gold Mild

1 (10 oz) package frozen corn

2 large potatoes, diced

2 cups cooked chicken, diced

¼ cup cornstarch

2 cups half and half cream

Cook bacon in a medium stockpot until crisp; remove with a slotted spoon and drain on paper towels. To the drippings add onions and celery; sauté about 5 minutes. Add broth, Red Gold Mild, corn, and potatoes. Bring to a boil, cover, and reduce heat to simmer. Cook for 10 to 15 minutes, until potatoes are cooked through. Add chicken. In a medium-size bowl, combine cornstarch and half and half. Stir into soup and cook until thickened, stirring often. Top with chopped bacon for garnish.

1 slice of bacon equals about 1 Tbs crumbled.

pork entrées

Pork Medallions with Creamy Mustard Sauce, see page 157

Piggy the War Hero!

It is incredible, when I look back to my childhood during and after the Second World War, what I did not know then. My grandmother and parents were no slouches. I can easily compare them to Churchill, Eisenhower, Marshall, and a few other great men and women strategists against the enemies of that era. They were heroes within our family and legendary to the community we lived in on the outskirts of Debrecen, a city of 300,000 in the eastern section of Hungary.

The mission of our family was to survive against all odds. My parents and Granma had previous experience fighting for survival through the First World War. Mother was only a little girl then, but nevertheless she suffered through it, and it made her stronger. She remembered it well.

Food was always paramount for all of us. They had four kids to feed beside themselves. How do you accomplish that when there was no visible possibility? The Germans and the Russians were like locusts—their armies devastated the country and the people living in it. There was no food.

Here came the Strategists. Who were they? My parents and beloved Granma. Of course, us being small kids were not involved in it—the strategy of it all. We just did what we were told, not understanding what was happening. But now, looking back all those years ago, I marvel at the Strategists; the leaders of my family who kept us alive.

Slowly but surely, the war subsided. Even though the Russians were all over the place, to my surprise, our animal ownership made progress, which meant meat. All of a sudden, we had chickens. Not just one to slaughter and eat, but several young ones who could then multiply. Out of this first batch of chickens King Steven was born. I don't know who gave him his name, but my brother is named Steven and St. Steven was our first Christian King over 1,000 years ago. King Steven grew up very quickly to rule

his flock. He was a beautiful large red rooster with gorgeous big black tail feathers. Then suddenly we had a bunch of small yellow geese. They very soon turned into large white birds—about twenty of them. The noise they generated was unbelievable!

One day, a Russian horse-drawn wagon came into our yard and stopped where the geese were kept. Two soldiers jumped out of the wagon into their bin, drew their swords and proceeded to slice off the heads of all our geese. We kids were in shock. Two of the other soldiers held us at gunpoint so we wouldn't interfere with their geese genocide, except to scream and cuss at them—*we were great mimickers of what our parents said.* They threw the dead geese into the wagon and off they went. A whole Russian regiment must have had a nice goose dinner at their camp. Soon our Strategists, who never seemed to give up, managed to get a replacement yellow geese flock; how and with what money, and from where, I never found out.

Then one day I saw a brand new spinning wheel in the house. I could tell it was handmade, because it was rough in places. It was an ingenious device; you made it spin by pedaling it. "What is it for?" I asked. "We will make sweaters with it." "But how?" I asked again. I soon found out.

The whole family was ordered to gather any kind of old wood material and mesh wire; we even took some wood planks from our fence. Pretty soon there was a row of three small cubicles with mesh wire doors on them. Three days later Mother came home with a basket full of cute little white rabbits. "They are Angora rabbits," she said authoritatively. "They grow fast, and then we will cut their fur, spin the fur into yarn, and make sweaters for us. We will sell the sweaters, too. Oh yes, and we might have a feast or two out of them." Enterprising, wasn't she?

Around 1946, the social and political order was established in the country; the Russian army was somewhat controlled and had permanent bases established. They were enmeshed in our community.

One day, a Hungarian peasant driving a one-horse wagon came into Granma's yard. The wagon was covered with planks and some hay on top. I heard the noises of a pig. The wagon backed up to the old pig house; it used to house pigs a long time ago before the war. It was big enough for one or two pigs. We opened the door to the pig house and the wagon backed up to it. The man who brought the pig took the cover off of the wagon, opened up the back, and we saw this magnificent animal just staring at us and looking into her future home. She was making some noise, seemingly asking us, "What now?" We instantly started to call her Piggy. She was Piggy until the end of her life.

Piggy was coaxed off the wagon and all of us guided her into the Piggy Palace prepared for her arrival.

We had hay for her to lie on, water in her trough, and some dry corn on the cob that she devoured instantly. She was the longest pig I ever saw, with very short blond hair and she was about to have babies. "It would be nice if she would have about twelve piglets," Mother said. "We will keep some and trade off the rest. We need glass and other materials for the greenhouses your father wants to build."

We pampered her with every bit of food we could give her; we could hardly wait to see the baby piglets when they arrived. Piggy really liked her Piggy Palace. A few times we wanted to let her out, but she didn't even want to leave her place. She was content.

One morning at dawn, we were all awakened by Rio, our dog. She was making incredible noises that came from around the Piggy Palace. We all ran there. Mother quickly saw the reason for the noise—a soldier was surveying our precious Piggy. Right away, Mother tried to send us back to the house, but we didn't move. We were going to defend Piggy with every ounce of strength we had. We children and Rio and Mother and Granma made enough noise to make the Russian back out and leave over the back fence, which he must have climbed to get into our yard in the first place. That was the way back to their temporary base, where it seemed there were thousands of Russian soldiers. All of us were happy that we were able to persuade the soldier to leave. That was short lived.

About eleven the next morning, four soldiers showed up on a horse-drawn wagon. They backed up to the Piggy Palace and proceeded to try to put Piggy on the wagon. We were all screaming and cussing at them, to no avail. They were yelling back at us in Russian. They had guns. I remember that my sister started to cry, and my brother and I were looking for rocks, anything to throw at the thieves, but Mother stopped us from attacking them. The Grand Red Army, who was supposed to free us from the German occupation, had just now in broad daylight, with guns, stolen our Piggy. We hated them.

Then a miracle happened! About mid-afternoon the same day we heard Rio barking, not in anger but in a happy, playful manner around the Piggy Palace. I rushed there to see what was happening. Lo and behold, there was Piggy in her triumphant glory, trying to get back into her Piggy Palace and waiting for somebody to open the door for her. She had escaped from her captors and came home! We fed her, scratched her back and washed her, which she loved. The word got out to some nearby neighbors about what had happened and they came to see if it was really true.

Our happiness lasted for about three days, when the four Russians showed up again with their wagon to take her. This time Piggy put up a real fight. It took the soldiers about half an hour to get her on the wagon, while my family stood by at gunpoint in utter shock and amazement. Piggy fought hard and she bit one of them, who cried out in pain. We were happy about that. Off they went with Piggy crying her heart out, with her legs tied this time.

Again that same afternoon, Piggy created an encore! She was back at the entrance of her Piggy Palace, waiting for her servants to open the door. Rio was ecstatic and wanted to play with her, but her Royal Highness,

the escape artist, Piggy the Hero, did not want to participate. We were sad, even though we were glad to see her back. We knew that this was not the end of the assault by the hungry Russian soldiers. My Granma even went to some of the neighbors to see if one of them would take Piggy and somehow hide her, because we knew that they would come back for her, but this time it would be different. None of the neighbors wanted to cooperate, fearing retaliation by the soldiers. Some of them went through the same ordeal with their animals, too.

Sure enough, the inevitable happened! The soldiers didn't bother looking for her—they knew where she was. We knew, too, that she only had a few hours to live. Again we gave her all the food and water she wanted, scratched her back and bathed her. She was happy, but we were sad—to us it was like the last supper. We knew she would not live long enough to bring her babies to life. We knew but she, by nature, did not. Maybe that was a good thing.

The soldiers showed up again in about two hours and what we had feared came true; we never saw her again.

Serves 6

Preparation time 20 minutes

Cooking time 3 hours

Ready in 3 hours, 20 minutes

Get that black enamel turkey roaster out of storage and use it to make these ribs. They will be tender and juicy.

Braised Pork Ribs

ingredients

6 lbs pork spareribs

2 cups low sodium chicken broth

1 cup barbecue sauce

½ cup Univer Sweet Ann

1 Tbs Univer Gourmet Garlic Cream

2 tsp fresh thyme

2 tsp fresh parsley

1 tsp black pepper

1 onion, chopped

1 carrot, chopped

Preheat grill for high heat. Preheat oven to 300° F. Sear the spareribs on both sides on the grill. Remove the ribs from grill and place in a baking pan. In a medium-size mixing bowl, combine the rest of the ingredients. Pour over ribs, cover and bake for 3 hours, basting with the pan juices and turning ribs occasionally. Serve pan juices on the side. Enjoy with a glass of Beaujolais.

Note that there is no additional salt in this recipe since several of the ingredients contain salt. Feel free to add salt to taste to the finished dish.

Serves 8
Preparation time 10 minutes
Cooking time 3 hours
Ready in 3 hours, 10 minutes

These succulent ribs travel well to picnics. Just wrap roasting pan in foil and wrap again in several layers of newspaper.

Country-Style Ribs

ingredients

3 Tbs Univer Goulash Cream Mild

1 Tbs Univer Gourmet Garlic Cream

1 tsp pepper

1 tsp dried thyme

4 lbs bone-in pork country-style ribs

1 large onion, chopped

1 cup barbecue sauce

½ cup low-sodium beef broth

Preheat oven to 300° F. Prepare grill for high heat. In a small mixing bowl, combine Goulash Cream Mild, Garlic Cream, pepper, and thyme. Rub mixture over ribs to coat. Sear ribs on all sides on the grill for about 3 minutes per side. Remove from grill and place in a roasting pan with onions. Pour barbeque sauce and broth on ribs and onions, turning to coat. Cover and roast for about 3 hours, checking pan hourly to turn ribs in the sauce. An ice cold beer in a frosty mug completes this dish.

Country-style ribs can be fatty or fairly lean, based on how they are trimmed by the butcher. Watch the liquids in the roasting pan and drain excess juices, or add more broth or barbeque sauce if too dry. Do not let the pan go dry. A black enamel turkey roaster is an ideal pan to use.

"I believe that if I ever had to practice cannibalism, I might manage if there were enough tarragon around."
—James Beard

Red Gold Hot
A few suggested uses:

- Add a spicy boost to stews, soups and gravies
- Glaze a sizzling steak or chop
- Mix into ground meats
- Add to marinades
- Sauté onions and vegetables
- Create wonderful dips
- Mix into salsa to enhance the flavor
- Add to ranch dressing to make Southwestern dressing with a kick
- Lightly brush onto hot grilled pineapple
- Gluten-free; no trans fats

Serves 6
Preparation time 10 minutes
Cooking time 8 hours
Ready in 8 hours, 10 minutes

What a treat to step in the kitchen and smell this wonderful aroma!

Mexican Pork for Burritos and Tacos

ingredients

2 lbs pork roast
½ cup low-sodium beef broth
¼ cup green salsa (salsa verde)
1 tsp Univer Gourmet Garlic Cream
2 tsp Univer Red Gold Hot

3 green onions, chopped
1 jalapeño pepper, seeded, chopped
½ tsp ground cumin

Place meat in slow cooker. In a bowl, whisk together the remaining ingredients. Pour over meat and cover. Cook for 8 hours on low, until meat is very tender. Remove meat from slow cooker to a platter; reserve cooking liquid. Shred meat using two forks. Before filling taco shells or tortillas, add about ½ cup of the liquid back to the meat to moisten. A glass of Sangria is a nice touch.

Don't worry too much about cleaning the stems from soft herbs like parsley and cilantro. They taste just as good as the leaves! Just chop and add to your dish. Do trim stems from woody herbs such as rosemary.

Serves 10

Preparation time 10 minutes

Cooking time 1 hour, 30 minutes

Ready in 2 hours

A beautiful holiday presentation!

Cherry-Glazed Ham

ingredients

1 (12 oz) jar cherry jelly or jam

1 (15 oz) can unsweetened pie cherries

¼ cup Univer Horseradish with Vinegar

5 lbs fully cooked ham

Preheat oven to 350° F. In a medium-size mixing bowl, mix together cherry jelly (or jam), pie cherries, and Horseradish with Vinegar. Place ham in baking dish. Brush top and sides of ham with cherry baste. Cover and bake for about 60 minutes. Uncover and bake about 30 minutes longer, basting often, until internal temperature is 160° F. Remove from heat, loosely cover and let set about 20 minutes before carving. Pour remaining cherry baste over ham.

Serves 4

Preparation time 15 minutes

Cooking time 10 minutes

Ready in 2 hours, 25 minutes

The ginger makes this dish so good! You can buy fresh minced ginger in a small jar, usually found in the produce department of the supermarket.

Grilled Pork Skewers with Ginger

ingredients

2 lbs pork loin, cut in 1½-inch chunks

1 large red onion, cut into 2-inch squares

2 green bell peppers, cut into 2-inch squares

Marinade

2 Tbs orange juice

1 Tbs rice wine vinegar

1 Tbs Univer Gourmet Garlic Cream

1 Tbs Univer Sweet Ann

2 Tbs fresh ginger, minced

½ tsp dried rosemary

½ tsp black pepper

In a large mixing bowl, whisk together all marinade ingredients; add meat, onion, and peppers. Toss to coat, cover and refrigerate for about 2 hours. Remove the meat from the marinade; set marinade aside. Alternately thread the pork, onions, and peppers on metal skewers. Grill over medium heat about 5 minutes on each side, basting occasionally with the marinade. Discard unused marinade. Enjoy with a glass of Merlot.

I am VERRRRRRY impressed. :)"
—**Delighted Paprika Fan**

Serves 4

Preparation time 10 minutes

Cooking time 25 minutes

Ready in 40 minutes

Here's your go-to recipe when you want a good chop! Slather on some white gravy and pair with mashed potatoes. Comfort food at its best!

Marie's Old-Fashioned Breaded Pork Chops

ingredients

4 boneless pork loin chops, 1-inch thick

1 egg, beaten

1 Tbs Univer Goulash Cream Hot

1 tsp Univer Gourmet Garlic Cream

½ cup seasoned breadcrumbs

½ cup panko (Japanese-style breadcrumbs)

2 Tbs dried parsley

½ tsp dried oregano

½ tsp dried thyme

½ tsp coarsely ground black pepper

2 Tbs vegetable oil

In a shallow baking dish, beat egg, Goulash Cream Hot, and Garlic Cream. In another shallow dish, combine breadcrumbs, panko, parsley, oregano, thyme, and pepper. In a large frying pan, heat oil over high heat. Dip each chop into egg mixture, and then dredge in breadcrumb mixture. Fry chops until well browned on one side, then flip to brown other side. Reduce heat to medium and cover. Cook until meat thermometer reads 160° F and juices run clear, about 20 to 25 minutes. Remove from heat. Let rest about 5 minutes before serving.

Buy pork loin roast when it's on sale and slice into thin or thick chops. Portion them out and freeze them until you need them.

Serves 4

Preparation time 10 minutes

Cooking time 6–8 minutes

Ready in about 2 hours, 20 minutes

Tender slices grill up quickly for a mid-week dinner.

Marinated Grilled Pork Loin Slices

ingredients

2 lbs pork loin, cut into ½-inch slices

Marinade

⅓ cup low-sodium beef broth

3 Tbs Univer Red Gold Mild

1 Tbs Univer Horseradish with Vinegar

1 tsp Univer Gourmet Garlic Cream

1 tsp dried oregano

1 tsp onion powder

½ tsp black pepper

Place pork in a large shallow dish or a large plastic storage bag. In a small mixing bowl, whisk together the marinade ingredients. Pour marinade over pork and coat all sides thoroughly. Cover dish or seal bag and refrigerate at least 2 hours, turning meat occasionally.

At grill time, grill the meat slices over medium high heat for about 3–4 minutes per side, basting frequently with the remaining marinade. Serve with a crisp green salad or wrapped in a warmed tortilla. Enjoy with a glass of Pinot Noir.

Dried herbs and spices have a pretty short shelf life. Buy the smallest tins or jars of the herbs you use least and write on the cap the date that you opened it.

Serves 6
Preparation time 10 minutes
Cooking time 8 hours
Ready in 8 hours, 10 minutes

Make this great dish tonight—your family will love it!

Peppercorn Pork Roast

ingredients

1 large onion, sliced

3 Tbs brined green peppercorns, drained

3 Tbs Univer Mustard

2 Tbs Univer Horseradish with Vinegar

1 Tbs Univer Gourmet Garlic Cream

½ tsp salt

3 lbs pork roast

1 cup low-sodium beef broth

Cornstarch

Cold water

Place sliced onions in a slow cooker. In small mixing bowl, combine peppercorns, Mustard, Horseradish with Vinegar, Garlic Cream, and salt; spread on top and sides of pork roast. Place roast on top of onions; pour broth around sides of roast. Cover and cook on low 8 to 10 hours. Remove pork and onions; cover and keep warm. Drain juices from slow cooker into a small saucepan. Make a paste of the cornstarch and a little water; add gradually to pan juices and bring to a boil. Reduce heat and simmer until thickened. Slice roast and serve with pan sauce. Enjoy with a glass of Merlot.

Warming dinner plates and chilling salad bowls will elevate your meal presentation to a professional level.

"We have used your products three times for dinners that we served friends. The results were outstanding. One couple reported that they had goulash at a famous restaurant in nearby Milwaukee, Wisconsin, and that it was not nearly as good as the meal they had with us. Since we make no great claims as cooks, we must give the majority of the credit to the wonderful products from Univer Foods."

—Delighted Paprika Fan

Serves 6

Preparation time 15 minutes

Cooking time 5 minutes

Ready in 20 minutes

Keep the heat out of the kitchen with this easy summer salad.

Medallions of Pork Salad

ingredients

½ cup Univer Sweet Ann

1 tsp Univer Gourmet Garlic Cream

½ tsp dried sage

½ tsp freshly ground black pepper

1½ lbs pork tenderloin, trimmed, sliced into ½-inch medallions

2 heads romaine lettuce, chopped

3 avocados, sliced

1 (15 oz) can Mandarin oranges, drained

½ cup red onion, thinly sliced

¼ cup fresh parsley, chopped

Sweet Ann Dressing
(find recipe on page 230).

In a small mixing bowl, mix Sweet Ann, Garlic Cream, sage, and pepper. Put in a large food storage bag, along with the meat. Turn to coat, seal, and let marinate for 30 minutes. (Refrigerate if not using within 30 minutes.) Place medallions on a grill-safe pan and grill meat over-medium high heat for 3 to 5 minutes, or until done. Remove from heat, cover and keep warm. On a serving platter, prepare a bed of lettuce and top with avocados, orange slices, onions, and parsley. Place medallions on top of the salad. Top with Sweet Ann Dressing.

Don't throw out herbs (dried or fresh) or citrus peels; toss them in the garbage disposal to freshen it.

Serves 8

Preparation time 10 minutes

Cooking time 25 minutes

Ready in 35 minutes

This colorful dish can also be a hearty dip.

Picadillo Stew

ingredients

2 lbs ground pork

1 medium onion, chopped

1 green pepper, chopped

2 Tbs Univer Red Gold Hot

1 tsp Univer Gourmet Garlic Cream

1 (15 oz) can diced tomatoes

½ cup raisins

½ cup pimiento-stuffed olives, chopped

2 Tbs slivered almonds

Hot biscuits

Heat a large frying pan over medium-high heat; add pork and brown and crumble, about 10 minutes. Add onions, green peppers, Red Gold Hot, and Garlic Cream. Cook about 5 minutes; stir in tomatoes, raisins, olives, and almonds. Reduce heat to medium-low; cover and simmer for 10 minutes. Serve piping hot over fresh biscuits.

Golden raisins add a pretty touch of color, but the black are just fine, too.

Serves 6
Preparation time 10 minutes
Cooking time 15 minutes
Ready in 25 minutes

For a change of pace, try these with your favorite green chile sauce instead of salsa.

Pork & Pepper Tortillas

ingredients

2 Tbs vegetable oil, divided

1 lb boneless pork loin, halved and sliced into thin strips

1 Tbs Univer Red Gold Mild or Hot

1 Tbs Univer Gourmet Garlic Cream

2 green bell peppers, sliced into thin strips

1 medium onion, sliced

1 (16 oz) jar salsa, any heat

1 Tbs lime juice

6 (6-inch) flour tortillas, warmed

1 cup shredded Mexican cheese blend

Suggested Garnishes
Black olives, chopped
Jalapeño peppers, sliced
Lettuce, shredded
Tomatoes, chopped

In a large frying pan, heat 1 tablespoon of oil over medium-high heat and brown pork about 5 minutes, or until pink no longer shows. Remove and set aside. In the same pan, heat remaining oil, Red Gold, and Garlic Cream over medium heat and cook bell peppers and onion about 8 minutes or until just tender. Return pork to pan and pour salsa over pork and vegetables; stir to coat. Stir in lime juice. Cover and heat through. Warm tortillas in the microwave oven for about 15 seconds. Place 1 tortilla on each dish and spoon on pork mixture; top with cheese and your favorite garnishes. Pour a hearty beer and enjoy!

"My kids are eating all the vegetables, and even the fish dishes are eaten until it's all gone. I worked in a gourmet Hungarian restaurant and can tell you that I can make dishes as good as they did."
—Delighted Paprika Fan

Serves 4
Preparation time 10 minutes
Cooking time 40 minutes
Ready in 50 minutes

You'll love this hearty sauce with tender pork chops.

Pork Chops with Beer and Onions

ingredients

2 Tbs olive oil
⅓ cup flour
1 tsp dried thyme
1 tsp dried sage
½ tsp pepper
4 bone-in pork chops, about 1-inch thick

1 medium onion, sliced
½ cup low sodium beef broth
1 cup beer
1 Tbs Univer Sweet Ann or Strong Steven
2 tsp Univer Gourmet Garlic Cream

Heat oil in a large frying pan over medium-high heat. In a shallow dish, mix flour, thyme, sage, and pepper. Dredge pork chops and brown in oil until golden on both sides, about 10 minutes. Add onions and cook 5 minutes longer.

In a small mixing bowl, blend the broth, beer, Sweet Ann or Strong Steven, and Garlic Cream. Pour over chops and onions; reduce heat to medium. Cover and simmer for about 15 minutes; uncover and cook about 10 minutes longer to reduce and thicken sauce.

Bone-in chops will be more moist, but boneless will be very good, too.

"A nickel's worth of goulash beats a five dollar can of vitamins."
—Martin H. Fischer

Serves 6
Preparation time 10 minutes
Cooking time 30 minutes
Ready in 40 minutes

Pork Chops with Country Gravy

Cool fall evenings and country gravy! Anything better?

ingredients

2 Tbs vegetable oil
6 boneless pork chops, about 1-inch thick
1 (14.5 oz) jar of your favorite country-style gravy
1 Tbs Univer Goulash Cream Mild
½ tsp Univer Goulash Cream Hot
1 Tbs dried parsley
½ tsp dried sage

Rice or mashed potatoes (6 servings)

Heat oil in a large frying pan over medium-high heat; brown chops on both sides, about 10 minutes. In a medium-size mixing bowl, combine gravy, Goulash Cream Mild, Goulash Cream Hot, parsley, and sage. Pour over chops; reduce heat to medium-low, cover and let simmer for about 20 minutes, or until chops are done. Serve with rice or mashed potatoes.

Serves 4

Preparation time 10 minutes

Cooking time 25 minutes

Ready in 35 minutes

Some folks enjoy thin, crispy chops. If you're one of them, add a couple more chops to the pan.

Pork Chops with Mustard and Horseradish

ingredients

2 Tbs extra virgin olive oil

1 egg

3 Tbs Univer Mustard

2 Tbs Univer Horseradish with Vinegar

1 tsp Univer Gourmet Garlic Cream

1 cup seasoned breadcrumbs

4 boneless pork chops, 1-inch thick

Heat oil in a large frying pan over medium-high heat. In a shallow bowl, mix egg, Mustard, Horseradish with Vinegar, and Garlic Cream. Place breadcrumbs in another shallow bowl or paper plate. Coat chops in egg mixture, then dredge in breadcrumbs. Brown chops on both sides, about 10 minutes; cover and reduce heat to medium. Fry for about 15 minutes or until done in center. Remove from heat and let rest a few minutes before serving. Great served with a full-bodied ice cold beer.

Don't overcrowd the pan when frying or deep-frying foods. You will lose the heat needed to really sear the outside of the food and instead the food will steam.

Serves 4

Preparation time 10 minutes

Cooking time 25 minutes

Ready in 35 minutes

A lovely presentation suitable for dinner guests.

Pork Medallions with Creamy Mustard Sauce

ingredients

3 Tbs extra virgin olive oil

2 lb whole pork tenderloin, sliced into 1-inch thick medallions

1 Tbs Univer Goulash Cream Mild or Hot

1 tsp Univer Gourmet Garlic Cream

½ cup low-sodium chicken broth

½ cup sour cream

2 Tbs Univer Mustard

1 tsp black pepper

2 Tbs fresh dill, chopped

Jicama and Mandarin Orange Salad (find recipe on page 206)

Heat oil in a large frying pan over medium-high heat. In batches, add pork medallions and cook until browned, 5 minutes per side. Remove pork from skillet; cover meat and keep warm. To the pan, add Goulash Cream, Garlic Cream, and chicken broth, scraping up any browned bits. Cook liquid 2 to 3 minutes to reduce. Remove frying pan from heat and slowly whisk in sour cream and Mustard. Return pork to frying pan, along with any meat juices that have accumulated. Cook pork over medium low heat 2 to 3 minutes to warm through. Transfer to a serving dish and pour sauce over pork; garnish with black pepper and dill. Serve with Jicama and Mandarin Orange Salad.

If you need softened butter, grate it instead of using the microwave. The consistency is better and it will soften quickly.

Serves 6
Preparation time 15 minutes
Cooking time 3 hours
Ready in 3 hours, 15 minutes

Pork Spareribs with Red Currant Sauce

A sweet-sour flavor and pretty color appeal for the kids.

ingredients

- 3 lbs pork spareribs
- 1 cup red currant jelly
- ¼ cup low-sodium soy sauce
- ¼ cup white wine vinegar
- 1 Tbs Univer Goulash Cream Hot
- 1 tsp Univer Gourmet Garlic Cream
- 1 large onion, chopped

Preheat oven to 300° F. Place ribs in a single layer in a baking dish. Combine jelly, soy sauce, vinegar, Goulash Cream Hot, and Garlic Cream. Add onions and stir well. Pour sauce over ribs. Cover and "bake for about 3 hours, checking occasionally and basting with sauce. If needed, sauce may be thinned with a little beef broth or water.

Serves 4
Preparation time 15 minutes
Cooking time 15 minutes
Ready in 2 hours, 30 minutes

Food on a stick! Who doesn't love juicy pieces of hot tenderloin with sweet grilled veggies?

Pork Skewers

ingredients

- 2 Tbs extra virgin olive oil
- 2 Tbs Univer Red Gold Mild
- 1 Tbs red wine vinegar
- 1 Tbs Univer Gourmet Garlic Cream
- 1 tsp dried thyme
- 1 tsp dried parsley
- 2 lbs pork tenderloin, cut into 1½-inch chunks
- 2 green bell peppers, sliced into 2-inch pieces
- 1 large onion, sliced into 2-inch pieces
- pepper to taste

In a large mixing bowl, whisk together the oil, Red Gold Mild, vinegar, Garlic Cream, thyme, and parsley; add the pork and vegetables. Toss to coat, cover and place in refrigerator for about 2 hours; stir occasionally. At grill time, remove the pork and vegetables from the marinade; set marinade aside. Thread the pork, bell peppers, and onions alternately onto metal skewers, leaving a little space between the pieces. Baste liberally with the marinade; season with pepper.

Grill the skewers over a medium-hot grill for about 15 minutes, or until meat is done. Baste with the marinade occasionally; turn the skewers periodically. Great with a glass of Zinfandel.

For a spicy version, use Red Gold Hot instead of Mild.

Serves 6

Preparation time 20 minutes

Cooking time 8 hours

Ready in 8 hours, 20 minutes

If you are short on time in the mornings, you can buy precut vegetables in most supermarkets in the produce section.

Pork Stew with Tomatoes

ingredients

4 carrots, sliced into 1-inch pieces

3 medium potatoes, unpeeled, cut into 2-inch cubes

3 stalks celery, sliced into 1-inch pieces

1 large onion, sliced

1 large zucchini, sliced into 1-inch pieces

2 lb pork sirloin roast, cut into 1-inch cubes

1 (28 oz) can diced tomatoes, with juice

2 cups low-sodium beef broth

1 Tbs Univer Goulash Cream Hot

1 Tbs Univer Sweet Ann

1 tsp Univer Gourmet Garlic Cream

½ tsp salt

½ tsp pepper

3 Tbs cornstarch

2 Tbs water

Place cut vegetables in a slow cooker. Add meat and tomatoes. In a medium-size mixing bowl, whisk together broth, Goulash Cream Hot, Sweet Ann, Garlic Cream, salt, and pepper. Cover and cook at low setting for 8 to 10 hours or at high for 5 to 6 hours. Increase heat to high. Combine cornstarch and water. Stir slowly into stew mixture and cook until thickened. Enjoy with a glass of Pinot Noir.

Choose a cutting board that has enough room to easily hold all the food that you are chopping.

Sweet Ann

A few suggested uses:

- Add a spicy boost to stews, soups and gravies
- Glaze a sizzling steak or chop
- Mix into ground meats
- Add to marinades
- Sauté onions and vegetables
- Create wonderful dips
- Mix into salsa to enhance the flavor
- Add to ranch dressing to make Southwestern dressing with a kick
- Lightly brush onto hot grilled pineapple
- Gluten-free; no trans fats

Serves **4**
Preparation time 15 minutes
Cooking time 40 minutes
Ready in 55 minutes

The green olives add a tangy flavor, add more if you like the taste.

Pork Tenderloin with Tomatoes and Olives

ingredients

1 Tbs olive oil

1½ lbs pork tenderloin

½ cup dry white wine

2 tsp Univer Sweet Ann

2 tsp Univer Gourmet Garlic Cream

1 tsp Univer Red Gold Hot

2 tomatoes, seeded and chopped

½ cup green onions, chopped, including green tops

⅓ cup green olives, chopped

1 tsp fresh rosemary, chopped

½ tsp pepper

½ cup heavy cream

Preheat oven to 350° F. Heat the oil in a frying pan over medium-high heat. Brown pork on all sides, about 10 minutes, and transfer to a baking dish; reserve frying pan. In a mixing bowl, whisk together the wine, Sweet Ann, Garlic Cream, and Red Gold Hot. Add the tomatoes, green onions, olives, rosemary, and pepper. Pour over the pork. Bake uncovered for about 20 minutes, or until done. Remove pork from baking dish; cover and keep warm.

Add tomato mixture and pan juices back to the frying pan, scraping up browned bits. Over medium heat, gradually stir in the cream. Stirring constantly, bring to a boil. Reduce heat to low and continue cooking about 5 minutes, or until thickened. Slice pork, and spoon on the sauce to serve.

A trusty meat thermometer is an essential in every kitchen; whatever is the easiest for you to read is the right one for you

All Univer paprika products contain vitamin C. One teaspoon of Red Gold has 2 percent of vitamin C, based on a 2,000 calorie diet. By actual weight, paprika contains more vitamin C than lemon juice!

Serves 10

Preparation time 10 minutes

Cooking time 4 hours

Ready in 4 hours, 10 minutes

Don't be afraid to let this pork cook gently for a long time. It will absorb the liquids and be "pull apart" tender.

Pulled Pork for Sandwiches

ingredients

5 lbs pork shoulder, bone in, excess fat trimmed

1 Tbs Univer Gourmet Garlic Cream

2 cups tomato juice

1 (28 oz) can diced tomatoes, with liquid

½ cup white vinegar, divided

1 bay leaf

2 Tbs Univer Goulash Cream Mild

1 Tbs Worcestershire sauce

1 tsp Univer Goulash Cream Hot

2 Tbs brown sugar

1 medium onion, finely chopped

Toasted Buns or Bread

Rub the pork all over with Garlic Cream. Place meat in a heavy, large stockpot; add the tomato juice, tomatoes, ¼ cup of vinegar, and the bay leaf. Bring to a boil over medium-high heat; reduce the heat to a simmer. Cover and cook, turning meat occasionally, until it is very tender, about 3 hours. Add the remaining ¼ cup vinegar, Goulash Cream Mild, Worcestershire sauce, Goulash Cream Hot, brown sugar, and onions. Stir to combine.

Cook uncovered over medium-low heat until the pork shreds easily and has absorbed most of the liquid, about 1 more hour. Stir the pork often to break up large pieces of meat and to prevent sticking to the pan. Remove and discard the bone and bay leaf. Shred the meat using two forks to pull it apart; serve the pork over toasted buns or bread with a cold dark ale.

Here's a great recipe when you've got a lot of baking to do. This is cooked on the top of the stove, so when you know you're going to be in the kitchen for awhile, make this for dinner. It's easy to prepare, and cooks all afternoon with occasional stirring.

Serves 8

Preparation time 15 minutes

Cooking time 8 hours

Ready in 8 hours, 15 minutes

Savory Pork Roast with Herbs

Use your favorite herbs to put your own signature on this dish.

ingredients

1 large onion, sliced

2 large carrots, sliced

1 Tbs Univer Gourmet Garlic Cream

1 Tbs Univer Sweet Ann

¼ cup parsley, finely chopped

1 tsp dried thyme

1 tsp dried rubbed sage

1 tsp dried rosemary leaves

½ tsp freshly ground black pepper

4 lbs boneless pork loin roast

1 cup low-sodium beef broth

Mashed Potatoes with Garlic and Horseradish (find recipe on page 207)

Place sliced onions and carrots in a slow cooker. In a small mixing bowl, whisk together Garlic Cream, Sweet Ann, parsley, thyme, sage, rosemary leaves, and pepper. Rub mixture all over roast and place roast on top of onions and carrots. Add broth to the slow cooker, pouring down the sides and not over the top of the roast. Cook on low 8 to 10 hours, or on high 6 to 8 hours. Serve with Mashed Potatoes with Garlic and Horseradish. A glass of Cabernet Sauvignon is a nice accompaniment.

Serves 8

Preparation time 15 minutes

Cooking time 45 minutes

Ready in 1 hour, 15 minutes

Add any of your favorite vegetables, like chopped bell peppers or sliced mushrooms.

Sausage and Onion Pie

ingredients

1 (16 oz) package bulk pork sausage

2 tsp Univer Red Gold Mild

1 tsp Univer Gourmet Garlic Cream

1 small onion, chopped

1½ cups shredded Mexican cheese blend

¾ cup cottage cheese

4 oz cream cheese, softened and cubed

1–2 eggs

1 Tbs fresh parsley, chopped

2 (9-inch) prepared pie crusts

1 egg, beaten for wash

Preheat oven to 350° F. Lightly grease or spray a 9-inch deep-dish pie pan. In a large frying pan, brown and crumble sausage, about 10 minutes; drain and place in large bowl. Add Red Gold Mild, Garlic Cream, and onions to the frying pan. Sauté about 5 minutes. Add onion mixture to the sausage and stir. Add shredded cheese, cottage cheese, cream cheese, egg, and parsley. Stir to combine. (If mixture seems too dry, add another egg.)

Place one, 9-inch crust in the pie pan. Spoon in the sausage mixture. Cover with remaining crust and seal edges of top crust to bottom crust. Cut 3 slits in top crust and brush with egg wash. Bake about 45 minutes or until golden brown. Let stand uncovered for about 15 minutes before slicing. Enjoy with a glass of Syrah.

If you forgot to take the cream cheese out to soften, just cut into small pieces and it will soften quickly.

Serves 6
Preparation time 30 minutes
Cooking time 50 minutes
Ready in 1 hour, 20 minutes

Once you've mastered this stuffing, it will be your go-to recipe for lasagna and manicotti shells, as well.

Sausage and Spinach Stuffed Jumbo Shells

ingredients

1 (12 oz) box jumbo shells

1 lb bulk Italian sausage

1 Tbs Univer Goulash Cream Mild

2 tsp Univer Gourmet Garlic Cream

1 medium onion, finely chopped

8 oz white mushrooms, finely chopped

2 eggs

¼ cup seasoned breadcrumbs

2 cups ricotta cheese

2 cups shredded mozzarella cheese, divided

1 cup grated Parmesan cheese, divided

1 (10 oz) package frozen chopped spinach, thawed and squeezed dry

1 tsp dried oregano

1 tsp dried basil

1 (28 oz) jar prepared spaghetti sauce, or your own

Preheat oven to 350° F. Cook shells according to package directions, drain. Cool in a single layer on wax paper to keep shells from sticking together. Brown sausage in a frying pan, crumbling it very small as it cooks, about 10 minutes. Remove and put in a medium-size mixing bowl. To the frying pan, add the Goulash Cream Mild, Garlic Cream, onions, and mushrooms and sauté for 5 minutes. Add onions and mushrooms to sausage in the bowl. In another bowl or food processor, combine eggs, breadcrumbs, ricotta cheese, 1 cup of mozzarella cheese, ½ cup Parmesan cheese, spinach, oregano, and basil. Mix thoroughly by hand or pulse several times to combine. Add this mixture to the meat mixture and stir to combine.

Spread a thin layer of spaghetti sauce on the bottom of a 13x9-inch baking pan. Fill each shell with about 2 tablespoons of the meat filling and place in pan. Generously spoon sauce over stuffed shells. Cover with foil and bake for about 30 minutes. Remove from oven, uncover and top with remaining 1 cup of mozzarella cheese and ½ cup of Parmesan cheese. Return to oven and bake uncovered for about 5 minutes, or until the cheese melts and browns slightly. Serve with a crisp green salad and a crusty slice of garlic bread. Pair with a glass of hearty Chianti.

Leftovers? This filling is great in scrambled eggs, and it also freezes well.

Serves 6

Preparation time 15 minutes

Cooking time 45 minutes

Ready in 1 hour

It seems you can't go wrong with Italian! No ziti? Use whatever pasta you have on hand.

Spicy Baked Ziti with Sausage

ingredients

1 (16 oz) package ziti pasta

3 Tbs Univer Goulash Cream Hot

1 lb bulk Italian sausage

1 small onion, chopped

1 (26 oz) jar pasta sauce

1 (15 oz) can diced Italian-style tomatoes, with liquid

1 egg

1 (15 oz) container ricotta cheese

⅓ cup grated Parmesan cheese

¼ cup fresh parsley, finely chopped

1 Tbs Univer Gourmet Garlic Cream

2 cups shredded Italian cheese blend, divided

Preheat oven to 350° F. Grease or lightly spray a large baking dish. Cook pasta according to package directions; drain well. To the pasta, add Goulash Cream Hot; toss lightly. Meanwhile, in a large frying pan, brown and crumble the sausage, about 10 minutes. Add the onions and sauté another 5 minutes; drain. Add sausage mixture, pasta sauce, and tomatoes to pasta; mix well.

Spread ½ of pasta mixture in prepared baking dish. In a small bowl, mix egg, ricotta, Parmesan, parsley, and Garlic Cream; spoon evenly over pasta. Sprinkle half of the Italian cheese blend over top. Spread remaining pasta mixture over cheese and top with remaining cheese. Cover and bake about 20 minutes; uncover and bake 10 minutes longer, until heated through and cheese is bubbly. Serve with a robust Chianti, garlic bread, and a Caesar salad.

Fresh garlic bread is a snap. Mix Garlic Cream with butter, spread on bread and top with Parmesan cheese. Broil until lightly browned.

Serves 4
Preparation time 10 minutes
Cooking time 16 minutes
Ready in 2 hours, 26 minutes

Grilled pineapple with Strong Steven is a real treat. Spicy hot and sweet at the same time—it's a crowd pleaser!

Zesty Grilled Pork Tenderloin and Pineapple

ingredients

2 lb pork tenderloin

1 ripe pineapple, rind and core removed

Marinade

1 cup fresh orange juice

¼ cup white vinegar

2 Tbs fresh lime juice

2 Tbs Univer Strong Steven

1 Tbs Univer Gourmet Garlic Cream

½ tsp ground nutmeg

½ cup green onions, thinly sliced, including green tops

In a medium-size bowl, combine all marinade ingredients; add pork. Cut pineapple into wedges and add to marinade. Cover and refrigerate for about 2 hours. At grill time, remove pork and pineapple; reserve marinade. Grill pork and pineapple over medium-high heat for about 8 to 10 minutes on each side, or until done, basting frequently with reserved marinade. Remove from heat, cover and let rest about 10 minutes before slicing. Pair with a glass of Zinfandel.

"My son fell in love with "Strong Steven," so I'm giving him twelve jars of it for Christmas this year. I also ordered twelve jars for myself ..."
—Delighted Paprika Fan

Serves 4
Preparation time 35 minutes
Cooking time 16 minutes
Ready in 1 hour

Spicy Pork Tenderloin
with Red Gold Hot

Moist pork with a zesty kick—sure to please.

ingredients

2 Tbs Univer Red Gold Hot

1 tsp Univer Gourmet Garlic Cream

1 tsp dried rubbed sage

1 tsp dried thyme

1 tsp onion powder

1½ lbs pork tenderloin

Salt and pepper to taste

Creamy Horseradish Sauce for Meat
(find recipe on page 231)

In a small bowl, mix together Red Gold Hot, Garlic Cream, sage, thyme, and onion powder. Generously rub all over the tenderloin. Set aside for 30 minutes, or cover and refrigerate up to 4 hours. Grill over medium-high heat for about 8 to 10 minutes per side, or until done. Remove from grill, cover and let stand about 10 minutes before slicing. Salt and pepper to taste. Serve with a dollop of Creamy Horseradish Sauce for Meat.

seafood entrées

Orange-Glazed Grilled Salmon, see page 177

Fish Story

On the Great Plains of Hungary, where I grew up, there are few rivers and lakes, and fishing was not a popular pastime. There was a small, shallow creek fairly close to our house but it had no fish. Several other kinds of aquatic animals lived in it ... several kinds of frogs, salamanders, and even some harmless water snakes. Of course, this small aquatic environment was a wonder for me and my neighborhood friends, especially in the spring when life was reborn around the creek and an ocean of aquatic flowers would also spring up in and around it.

There was a beautiful yellow flower that started in the early spring in the wetlands around the creek. It was called "gólya hir" or "stork news." This ocean of yellow flowers was called that because it announced the return of the storks.

We would see many of them as they began arriving for their summer vacation in Hungary around the wetlands, feasting on the frogs after their long journey from the continent to the south—Africa. They would return to their same nests, season after season, to bring up their young in nests perched on chimney tops in villages around the lakes, rivers, and wetlands, like my little aquatic world. Spring was an exciting time for me and my friends, especially because our mothers would allow us to go barefoot. I often thought of Huckleberry Finn at those times.

My hometown Debrecen was far from our two large and famous rivers—the Danube and the Tisza. These two rivers slice Hungary in two, flowing parallel in the middle of the country, north to south, eventually joining forces, merging to flow together into the Black Sea. Just think of the history that surrounds their existence in Europe. Nothing could stop them as they happily flow—unopposed—in unison down to the sea.

They and the other rivers and lakes in Hungary are rich with all the different river species, and all kinds of wonderful food dishes are made with them. My favorite of all is Fisherman's Soup. Absolutely delicious, naturally, it is made with lots of paprika, using carp, catfish, or other species singly or in combination. The main ingredients are fish, red onions, green peppers, tomatoes, and, of course, paprika paste. When I travel to Hungary, my first trip within Hungary is to a city on the bank of the Tisza River called Tokaj. Tokaj not only has the best Fisherman's Soup in the world, it has the best wines, too. The other city for the best dishes is Szeged, also on the Tisza River.

My fishing experience was limited when I was growing up. In our entire family, I knew of only one person who was an ardent fisherman—my uncle Ferenc. He and his family lived in Miskolc in the northeastern part of the country. I would visit them in the summertime for two or three weeks at a time.

He was a real fisherman! He worked in a large machine manufacturing company and would go fishing almost every day before work, leaving at early dawn except when it was raining, and even on the weekends.

Rising as early as three a.m., he would dress for work, get his fishing gear together, and bicycle down to the Sajo River not far from his home. There he would fish for a couple of hours and bring the fish home on the way to work which started at seven a.m. When I first visited my aunt and uncle, he got me up with him in the pitch dark to go to the river and fish. He even made me fishing gear sized for a child.

At first I didn't want to go, or even get up for that matter, that early. He said to me, "Come on kid, fishing is a manly thing to do. I'll show you a thing or two about it. I'll make a fisherman out of you." Then he put me up on the cross bar of his bicycle and off we went to the river, his bicycle's headlight showing the way. He would head for a special spot where he always camped for fishing. Getting there on the narrow passage along the bank of the river scared me to death. We could easily have fallen in the river if he lost his balance.

The first time we arrived at his fishing spot, I was amazed. He had it all set up in a practical manner. First he hung the storm lamp on a particularly designed, carved wood branch. It lit up the little area of the fishing site. He had his seat carved from a tree trunk. There was a place for the fishing poles to lean on, a flat area for the bucket with the worms in it, a little table made of wood for his coffee thermos, and a handy place where he would hang the fishing net by the handle—the net used to lift the fish out of the water after reeling them in.

It was totally dark when he demonstrated how to put a live worm on the hook. Then he said, "You do it!" Well, I did not mind handling the slimy little bodies of the worms with my bare hands, but I couldn't make myself pierce their slimy little bodies with the hook. Thankfully, he did it for me. "Don't worry kid, you'll get the hang of it when you're older," he would say. He threw in the lines of his two poles, and then, holding my arms, we tossed in mine.

After that, we waited and waited for the fish to bite. Naively, that first time I thought you threw your hook in and then you pulled it out with a fish on it. No such luck. Every once in awhile, we pulled in the hooks and changed worms, either because we had lost them or they were dead—not moving and no longer attractive to the fish. When we had all our poles in the water, we waited and waited … and waited.

Suddenly I began to hear ever-so-tiny noises every once in awhile from behind us. After a time, I asked Uncle what those tiny noises were. He said they were either some large bugs waking up, a water snake, or the big white mushrooms that grow there, pushing up the loam. He said, "We'll get some of those later before we go home; we'll let them grow a little bit more first."

"But Uncle, I did not know mushrooms make noises."

"They don't. The noise comes from when their large head is pushing up the soil."

"You mean they grow so fast?"

"Sure, they grow overnight. People will start coming soon to pick them. We should get some before they start coming."

Soon the sun was on the horizon and I saw several people in the distance hunting and picking mushrooms.

Well, we actually caught some fish. It was interesting for me to fish for the first time in my life, but I was more fascinated about the mushrooms that made noise. Uncle Ferenc said, "Go find some, and we'll have your aunt make them for breakfast for us. They grow overnight, you know. They will go well with the fish."

I went to look for the big white mushrooms. I only had to go about fifteen feet from where we were, and there one was—a gigantic white mushroom. It must have been about five inches across. I'd never seen anything like that before.

The sun was climbing higher in the clear blue sky when the order came from Uncle Ferenc. "Let's pack up and get a few mushrooms; then I'll have to go to work." By the time we did all that, it was daylight. We started to bicycle back on the riverbank; I looked at the water and could not believe what I saw. It was totally black, so I asked Uncle about it. He said, "Oh yes, there are several factories up-river that use this water, and they make it black, ruining it for the fishermen. The water is pristine coming out of the mountains.

"What kind of factories?" I asked.

"Well, there is a paper factory, a steel mill, and several others." I looked at the color of the water again and decided I would not eat the fish we caught.

But the giant mushrooms intrigued me. And sure enough, they were delicious. Aunty cut two slices horizontally from each one, put them in egg batter and then rolled them in breadcrumbs. Every time I went to visit my uncle and aunt, I begged him to take me fishing … for mushrooms! I sincerely believe that this fish story—this experience—later in life made me an environmentalist—a "tree hugger" they call me.

I'll always remember the black oily color of that river water. Even as a child, I could not fathom that people would catch and eat fish from a sewer like that. Of course, one has to understand that damage to the environment did not count as much sixty-five years ago as it does now. This fact is true, especially then, behind the Iron Curtain: Fish, even from a source like that, was free food. And food was scarce and had a very high value in those days. I realized this truth later in life; there was relatively little food when I was growing up.

And yes, I am a "tree hugger," concerned with our environment and the conservation of our natural resources. With my love of great food and the culinary arts, I founded the company Univer Foods USA, which has a web marketing arm called www.JudisUniverStore.com. Besides that, twenty-two years ago I founded a solar thermal energy company, now called Solargenix Energy.

And a few years ago, we founded Agregy Renewables, an "Aquaculture" facility, meaning we grow fish in an enclosed environment. Nutrient-rich water from fish raised in large tanks is used to grow vegetables without soil. The plant roots clean the water by absorbing the nutrients, and the water is then cycled back to the tanks in a continuous fashion to be used again and again. I think that my first fishing trip growing up, the one that took place in black, oily river water, had a lot to do with all this.

Why am I involved in such an enterprise? Very few people know that the oceans are fished out! We took a three and a half month long, around-the-world trip on the new Queen Elizabeth. We crossed the equator twice, visited forty-eight countries, and at the end of the trip I realized that only in New Zealand, Australia, and the Los Angeles Harbor did we see sea gulls. Why? Because there is nothing for them to eat in the oceans. More than 50 percent of the fish that were in the oceans no longer exist. But the population of the world grows exponentially.

In 1955, there were two billion people on this Earth. Today, its population is approaching eight billion! And the Earth is warming—global warming is now an acknowledged fact. There are tremendous crop failures because of that already. What is the world population going to eat? There are millions of people starving, especially in the Third World countries. If, God forbid, we have another World War, it's going to be over food, water, and energy.

Serves 4
Preparation time 10 minutes
Cooking time 15 minutes
Ready in 25 minutes

Another timeless classic easily served up as an elegant appetizer!

Bacon-Wrapped Scallops

ingredients

8 slices bacon, halved to make 16 pieces

16 sea scallops

1 Tbs Univer Red Gold Mild or Hot

1 Tbs olive oil

1 lemon, cut into wedges

Place bacon in a large frying pan and cook over medium-high heat, turning occasionally, until lightly browned but still pliable, about 5 minutes. Drain the bacon slices on paper towels. Wrap each slice of bacon around one sea scallop and secure with a toothpick. Baste with Red Gold Mild or Hot.

Heat olive oil in a frying pan over medium-high heat; sear scallops until golden and bacon is crisp, 3 to 4 minutes on each side and edges. Squeeze lemon wedges over scallops and serve.

"Now I can order right from my own home. Thank you so much and a special thank you from my family."
—Satisfied Paprika Fan

Serves 4

Preparation time 10 minutes

Cooking time 6 minutes

Ready in about 1 hour, 16 minutes

Catfish Kebabs with Cherry Tomatoes

ingredients

2 lbs catfish (or other white fish of your choice), cut into 2-inch pieces

1 lb cherry tomatoes

Marinade

½ cup canola oil

⅓ cup white vinegar

1 Tbs Univer Goulash Cream Hot (or Mild)

2 tsp Univer Gourmet Garlic Cream

1 Tbs onion powder

Zest of 1 lemon

1 tsp lemon juice

1 tsp salt

½ tsp pepper

Mix all marinade ingredients together in a shallow dish. Place fish pieces and tomatoes in marinade, cover and refrigerate for 1 hour. At grill time, thread fish pieces and tomatoes alternately onto metal skewers, reserving marinade. Place skewers over direct medium-high heat; grill, turning and basting occasionally, for about 3 to 4 minutes per side.

If you want to serve this dish as an appetizer, use wooden skewers that have been soaked in water for about 20 minutes before grill time.

Serves 6

Preparation time 5 minutes

Cooking time 20 minutes

Ready in 25 minutes

Carolina Crab Boil

Enjoy this Southern specialty with family and friends!

ingredients

3 (3 oz) package crab boil mix

2 Tbs Univer Strong Steven

2 Tbs Univer Gourmet Garlic Cream

½ bunch parsley

30 live, hard-shell blue crabs

In a small bowl, blend the crab boil mix with the Strong Steven and Garlic Cream. Pour the mixture into a large stockpot along with the parsley.

Fill the pot ¾ full with water and bring to a full boil. Add the crabs. Cover and boil until all of the shells turn red and the meat is white and no longer translucent, about 20 minutes, stirring occasionally.

You may add your favorite veggies, such as small potatoes, to the pot during the boil.

Serves 6

Preparation time 15 minutes

Cooking time 25 minutes

Ready in 40 minutes

Celebrate the sea with this Italian favorite!

Cioppino (cho-pea-no)

ingredients

3 Tbs extra virgin olive oil

2 tsp Univer Gourmet Garlic Cream

1 tsp Univer Red Gold Hot

1 medium onion, chopped

2 celery stalks, sliced

1 cup dry white wine

1 (14 oz) can low-sodium chicken broth

1 (28 oz) can crushed tomatoes

1 dried bay leaf

¼ cup fresh parsley, chopped

1 Tbs fresh thyme leaves

2 lbs cod, cut into bite-sized chunks

8 large shrimp, peeled and deveined, tails left on

6 large sea scallops, halved

16 raw mussels, cleaned

In a large frying pan over medium heat, combine oil, Garlic Cream, and Red Gold Hot. Add onions and celery. Sauté about 5 minutes; add wine. Reduce for 2 minutes; add broth, tomatoes, bay leaf, parsley, and thyme. Bring sauce to a boil; reduce heat to medium-low. Add cod and simmer 5 minutes, covered. Stir gently once or twice, taking care not to break up the fish. Add shrimp, scallops, and mussels. Cook 10 minutes longer, stirring occasionally. Discard any unopened mussels and bay leaf. Serve with a green salad and crusty bread for dipping.

Reduce a liquid by letting it simmer gently until the desired thickness is achieved. The flavor of a reduction liquid is more intense.

Serves 6
Preparation time 15 minutes
Cooking time 15 minutes
Ready in 30 minutes

Using 1 can of minced clams and 1 can of chopped clams offers a texture and taste that is a bit more complex than just using the same type of clams in this dish.

Serves 4
Preparation time 10 minutes
Cooking time 10 minutes
Ready in 20 minutes

Clams Linguine in Red Wine Sauce

ingredients

2 Tbs canola oil

1 Tbs Univer Goulash Cream Mild or Hot

1 Tbs Univer Gourmet Garlic Cream

1 onion, chopped

8 oz white mushrooms, sliced

1 (28 oz) can diced fire-roasted tomatoes, with liquid

½ cup red wine

2 (6.5 oz) cans clams, 1 minced and 1 chopped, clam juice reserved

½ cup Parmesan cheese, grated

1 (16 oz) package linguine

½ cup fresh parsley, chopped, for garnish

In a large frying pan, heat oil, Goulash Cream, and Garlic Cream over medium-high heat. Add the onions and mushrooms and sauté until soft, about 5 minutes. Add the tomatoes and wine; stir to combine. Add the clams, with their juices. Reduce heat to medium-low and simmer for about 10 minutes. Add cheese and combine.

Meanwhile, prepare pasta as directed on package. Drain thoroughly. Serve pasta topped with sauce; garnish with fresh parsley.

When the pasta is cooked and drained, put it back in the warm pot to dry a little before adding sauce. If not using immediately, dress the pasta with a little sauce or Goulash Cream to prevent clumping. (Or use Gourmet Garlic Cream if you are a serious garlic fan!)

Pecan-Panko Fried Catfish

Toasted pecans mixed with crisp panko breadcrumbs make this a crunchy, fast dinner!

ingredients

¾ cup panko breadcrumbs

½ cup toasted pecans, finely crushed

1 tsp Old Bay seasoning

½ tsp black pepper

3 Tbs canola oil

2 lbs catfish, cut into 6 equal pieces

2 Tbs Goulash Cream Mild or Hot

Lemon wedges, for garnish

In a shallow dish, mix panko crumbs, pecans, Old Bay seasoning, and pepper until combined. In a large frying pan, heat oil over medium-high heat. Rinse catfish and pat dry. Brush catfish with Goulash Cream on both sides. Dredge in panko-pecan crumb mixture and place fish in hot oil, being careful not to crowd pan (fry in 2 batches, if necessary). Fry for 4 to 5 minutes per side, depending on thickness of fish. Serve hot with lemon wedges for garnish.

Toast pecans in a small frying pan over medium-high heat, turning often, for about 5–7 minutes, until toasted and fragrant. Let pecans cool and grind in a spice mill or food processor until finely crushed.

Serves 4
Preparation time 5 minutes
Cooking time 15 minutes
Ready in 20 minutes

Poached Salmon in White Wine and Peppercorns

Poaching is such an easy treatment for fish and results in a creamy texture that almost melts in your mouth.

ingredients

2 cups white wine, such as Pinot Grigio

1 Tbs Univer Goulash Cream Mild

1 Tbs black or green peppercorns

1 Tbs capers

2 lbs fresh salmon

Lemon wedges, for garnish

In a large, deep frying pan, bring wine, Goulash Cream Mild, peppercorns, and capers to a light boil. Add salmon and reduce heat to low. Simmer, covered, until salmon flakes easily, about 15 minutes. Remove from pan and garnish with lemon wedges.

If you prefer not to use wine, we recommend a blend of one cup fish stock or clam juice, and one cup water.

Serves 4
Preparation time 15 minutes
Cooking time 10 minutes
Ready in 25 minutes

This is the creamiest Benedict you will ever eat— it is sensational!

Eggs Benedict with Salmon

ingredients

2 (0.9 oz) packages dry hollandaise sauce mix, prepared according to package directions

1 Tbs Univer Sweet Ann

4 muffins, split and toasted

12 oz honey-smoked salmon

2 avocados, pitted and sliced

8 slices tomatoes

8 eggs, poached

Salt and pepper to taste

To the prepared hollandaise sauce, mix in the tablespoon of Sweet Ann; keep warm.

To assemble, on 4 individual plates, place 2 toasted muffin halves. Top each muffin with 1 tablespoon of hollandaise sauce. Divide the salmon evenly and place on each muffin. Top with sliced avocados, tomatoes, and lastly with an egg. Drizzle each muffin with remaining hollandaise and serve warm.

Hollandaise is easily made at home, but the dry and canned mixes are very good; we use them all the time.

Serves 4

Preparation time 10 minutes

Cooking time 5 minutes

Ready in 15 minutes

Get this to the table fast on those busy weeknights.

Deep-Fried Tilapia

ingredients

1 qt canola oil, for frying

1 egg

1 Tbs water

1 Tbs Red Gold Hot or Mild

1 cup panko breadcrumbs

1 Tbs Old Bay seasoning

4 (6 oz) tilapia fillets

1 (10 oz) Package frozen peas, cooked

1 avocado, peeled and sliced

Heat oil in a deep pot or deep fryer to 375° F. In a shallow bowl, beat egg, water, and Red Gold Hot or Mild. In another shallow bowl, mix breadcrumbs with Old Bay. Dredge fish pieces in egg wash, then coat with breadcrumb mixture. Fry about 4 to 5 minutes, until fish are golden brown. Drain on paper towels and serve hot. Top with peas and avocado slices.

Use a good thermometer to accurately track the oil temperature.

Serves 4

Preparation time 10 minutes

Cooking time 18 minutes

Ready in about 28 minutes

Sea Bass with White Wine Sauce

Sea bass, while not the least expensive of fish, is a special occasion treat for friends and family!

ingredients

2 Tbs extra virgin olive oil

1 Tbs Univer Red Gold Mild

1 Tbs Univer Gourmet Garlic Cream

¼ tsp Univer Red Gold Hot

1 large white onion, thinly sliced

1 (28 oz) can diced tomatoes

2 Tbs capers, drained

1 cup dry white wine

4 (6 oz) sea bass fillets

2 Tbs butter

¼ cup fresh parsley, chopped

Heat oil, Red Gold Mild, Garlic Cream, and Red Gold Hot in a large frying pan over medium heat. Add onions and sauté until soft, about 5 to 7 minutes. Add tomatoes, capers, and wine; reduce heat to low. Place sea bass into the sauce. Cover, and gently simmer for 10 to 12 minutes, or until fish flakes easily with a fork. Transfer fish to a serving plate, and keep warm. Add butter and parsley to pan, heat until butter is melted. Serve sauce over fish.

Serves 6

Preparation time 10 minutes

Cooking time 20 minutes

Ready in 30 minutes

Bring a West Coast favorite to your table in 30 minutes!

Fast and Easy Fish Stew

ingredients

3 Tbs olive oil

1 Tbs Univer Red Gold Mild

2 tsp Univer Gourmet Garlic Cream

1 tsp Univer Red Gold Hot

1 onion, chopped

1 (28 oz) can crushed tomatoes, with liquid

4 cups low-sodium chicken broth

1 (10.5 oz) red clam sauce

¼ cup fresh parsley, chopped

1 Tbs Worcestershire sauce

2 lbs cod, cut into bite-sized pieces

1 dash nutmeg

8 oz linguine, broken into 1-inch pieces

Heat oil, Red Gold Mild, Garlic Cream, and Red Gold Hot in a large stockpot over medium-high heat; add onions and sauté for about 5 minutes. Add the tomatoes, broth, clam sauce, parsley, Worcestershire sauce, cod, and nutmeg. Cover and bring to a boil; reduce heat to medium-low and simmer for 5 minutes. Add pasta and cook 10 minutes longer, or until pasta is al dente.

Red clam sauce is generally found by the canned clams in the supermarket.

Serves 4

Preparation time 10 minutes

Cooking time 10 minutes

Ready in 1 hour, 20 minutes

Some fruits are just natural partners for salmon. Enjoy this orange glaze enriched with balsamic vinegar.

Orange-Glazed Grilled Salmon

ingredients

1½ pounds salmon

Marinade

½ cup orange marmalade

3 Tbs balsamic vinegar

1 Tbs Univer Sweet Ann

1 Tbs low-sodium soy sauce

1 Tbs fresh ginger, minced

1 tsp Univer Gourmet Garlic Cream

2 green onions, thinly sliced

Mix marinade ingredients together in a small bowl. Lay the salmon skin-side down (if it has skin) and pour marinade over salmon, coating evenly. Cover and refrigerate for 1 hour. At grill time, prepare grill for medium heat. Cook salmon (skin-side down), reserving marinade. Baste salmon frequently and flip once at about 5 minutes. Grill until salmon flakes easily, or until done.

This marinade is pretty sweet, so watch your grill to control any flare-ups. Move fish to a cooler spot on the grill if there are too many flames.

Serves 6

Preparation time 20 minutes

Cooking time 1 hour

Ready in 1 hour, 20 minutes

This is such a versatile dish—use with shrimp, toss in leftover chicken, add some white fish or crab! It's a great way to finish up leftovers and everyone will think you slaved for hours!

Seafood Gumbo

ingredients

- 3 Tbs canola oil
- 2 Tbs Univer Strong Steven
- 1 Tbs Univer Gourmet Garlic Cream
- 1 cup green peppers, chopped
- 1 large onion, chopped
- 1 cup celery, sliced
- 1 (10 oz) package frozen okra, thawed
- 2 Tbs Cajun spice seasoning
- 2 bay leaves
- 1 tsp salt
- ½ tsp red pepper
- ½ tsp white pepper
- ½ tsp black pepper
- 2 (28 oz) cans fire-roasted diced tomatoes
- 2 cups clam juice or chicken broth
- 1 lb cooked ham, cut into 2-inch chunks
- 1 lb whitefish (cod, tilapia, swai, or catfish), cut into 2-inch chucks
- 1 lb shrimp (51–60 count), peeled and deveined

Hot cooked rice (6 servings)

In a large stockpot, heat the oil, Strong Steven, and Garlic Cream over medium-high heat. Add green peppers, onions, celery, and okra; sauté for about 5 minutes. Add Cajun seasoning, bay leaves, salt, red pepper, white pepper, and black pepper. Stir to combine the spices into the veggie mixture. Add tomatoes and broth. Reduce heat to a simmer; let simmer gently about 30 minutes. Add ham and whitefish; cook another 10 minutes. Add shrimp and cook 5 minutes longer. Remove bay leaves before serving. Serve over hot rice.

Ham provides a very nice contrast of saltiness in this dish. Remember, taste as you cook and adjust the seasonings accordingly.

Serves 4
Preparation time 20 minutes
Cooking time 4 minutes
Ready in about 1 hour, 24 minutes

An elegant treat for guests and family alike. Nothing can match a well-executed tuna steak!

Seared Ahi Tuna with Mango-Papaya Relish

ingredients

¼ cup extra virgin olive oil

juice of 1 lime

¼ cup cilantro, chopped

¼ cup honey

¼ cup balsamic vinegar

1 Tbs fresh ginger, minced

1 Tbs lime zest

1 Tbs Univer Red Gold Mild

2 tsp Univer Gourmet Garlic Cream

4 (6 oz) ahi tuna steaks

Mango-Papaya Relish

1 mango, diced

1 papaya, diced

⅓ cup red onion, diced

¼ cup cilantro

juice of 1 lime

1 Tbs extra virgin olive oil

1 Tbs honey

1 tsp Univer Gourmet Garlic Cream

Salt and pepper to taste

In a large shallow dish, mix olive oil, lime juice, cilantro, honey, vinegar, ginger, lime zest, Red Gold Mild, and Garlic Cream. Blend until well combined. Lay tuna steaks in dish and coat both sides well with marinade. Cover and refrigerate 1 hour.

For the relish, combine all ingredients in a small bowl and mix well. Cover and refrigerate until ready to serve.

At grill time, prepare the grill for medium-high heat. Remove steaks from marinade; reserve marinade. Place steaks on grill and sear for about 2 minutes, basting with reserved marinade. Flip and sear other side for about 2 minutes more for rare, depending on thickness of steaks. Serve hot with Mango-Papaya Relish.

You can generally find mangos and papayas in the canned fruit or frozen section of the supermarket if you are short on time. You may also substitute canned or fresh pineapple.

Gourmet Garlic Cream

Garlic is revered throughout the world for its flavor-enhancing qualities and is a staple in most kitchens. With Gourmet Garlic Cream, you can do away with messy cleaning and chopping. Just open the jar! Great garlic aroma, pure garlic flavor!

A few suggested uses:

- Add to soups, stews and gravies
- Mix into mashed potatoes for instant Garlic Potatoes
- Make garlic bread in a snap
- Add to sauces, dips and spreads
- Sauté onions and other vegetables
- Toss with hot cooked pasta before dressing with sauce
- Rub onto clean, dry potatoes before baking
- Brush onto pizza crusts before baking

Serves 6

Preparation time 15 minutes

Cooking time 8 minutes

Ready in about 1 hour, 23 minutes

A summertime favorite, but this dish can also make a cold winter day feel tropical!

Shrimp and Pineapple Skewers

ingredients

1½ lbs shrimp, 51–60 count, peeled and deveined

3 cups pineapple, cut into 1-inch cubes

1 lb cherry tomatoes

2 green bell peppers, cut into 2-inch squares

1 onion, cut into 2-inch squares

Marinade

½ cup (packed) light brown sugar

½ cup vegetable oil

⅓ cup white wine vinegar

¼ cup low-sodium soy sauce

1 Tbs fresh ginger, minced

1 Tbs Univer Gourmet Garlic Cream

1 Tbs Univer Sweet Ann

1 Tbs orange zest

1 Tbs orange juice

½ tsp cayenne pepper

Mix together the marinade ingredients in a large, shallow bowl. Add the shrimp, pineapple, tomatoes, peppers, and onions and stir to coat. Cover and refrigerate 1 hour. At grill time, preheat grill to medium-high heat. Thread the shrimp, pineapple, tomatoes, peppers, and onions alternately onto metal skewers, reserving marinade. Grill for about 4 to 5 minutes per side, basting liberally with reserved marinade.

"I have made so many great recipe's that there are never any leftovers after dinner. My kids are eating all the vegetables and even the fish dishes are eaten until it's all gone."

—Satisfied Paprika Fan

Serves 6
Preparation time 20 minutes
Cooking time 20 minutes
Ready in 40 minutes

*A low-country and New Orleans classic;
sounds exotic, and it is!*

Shrimp Étouffée

ingredients

½ cup unsalted butter

½ cup canola oil

2 Tbs Univer Red Gold Hot

1 Tbs Univer Gourmet Garlic
Cream

1 large onion, chopped

1 green bell pepper, chopped

1 cup celery, sliced

8 oz mushrooms, sliced

2 Tbs all-purpose flour

1 (14.5 oz) can fire-roasted diced
tomatoes

1 tsp Worcestershire sauce

1½ lbs fresh shrimp, 51–60
count, peeled and deveined

Salt and pepper, to taste

Cooked rice (6 servings)

In a large frying pan over medium-high heat, melt butter;
add oil, Red Gold Hot, and Garlic Cream. Add onion, bell
pepper, and celery; sauté for about 5 minute, until softened.
Add the mushrooms and sauté another 5 minutes. Sprinkle
flour over vegetables, stir and cook for 2 to 3 minutes.

Add tomatoes and Worcestershire sauce. Stir until slightly
thickened. Add shrimp and cook for 4–5 minutes, until shrimp
are pink. Salt and pepper to taste. Serve with hot cooked rice.

*This great dish can be made with chicken as well!
We recommend thighs because they are so much
juicier than breasts.*

Serves 6

Preparation time 15 minutes

Cooking time 30 minutes

Ready in 45 minutes

This timeless Creole dish is stove-to-table in less than an hour.

Shrimp Jambalaya

ingredients

4 Tbs butter

1 Tbs Univer Strong Steven

½ Tbs Univer Gourmet Garlic Cream

1 onion, chopped

2 celery stalks, chopped

1 green pepper, chopped

3 cups low-sodium chicken broth

1½ cups uncooked long grain rice

1 tsp Worcestershire sauce

1 (14.5 oz) can diced tomatoes, with liquid

1 (10 oz) can tomatoes and green chilies, with liquid

1 lb medium shrimp, peeled and deveined

1 (10 oz) package frozen baby peas

In a large frying pan, melt butter, Strong Steven, and Garlic Cream; add the onion, celery, and green pepper and sauté for about 5 minutes. Add the broth, rice, and Worcestershire sauce. Cover and bring to a boil; reduce heat to low. Simmer, covered, for about 15 to 20 minutes or until rice is tender. Stir in the tomatoes, shrimp, and peas; heat through until the shrimp turn pink.

If you have a little leftover chicken, throw it in the pot to add another layer of flavor.

Serves 4

Preparation time 10 minutes

Cooking time about 5 minutes per quesadilla, or 20 minutes

Ready in about 30 minutes

A mild Mexican dish— with lots of flavor—get it to the table fast using pre-cooked shrimp from the supermarket!

Shrimp Quesadillas with Pineapple

ingredients

1 lb shrimp, cooked

1 (8 oz) can pineapple tidbits, drained

1 (4 oz) can mild green chilies, drained

1 (8 oz) package cream cheese, softened

½ cup shredded mozzarella cheese

1 Tbs Univer Goulash Cream Hot or Mild

8 flour tortillas

2 Tbs canola oil

Roughly chop the shrimp and place in a medium-size bowl. Add pineapple tidbits and chilies. In a small bowl, mix the cream cheese, mozzarella cheese, and Goulash Cream. Add to shrimp mixture and stir to combine.

Spread mixture evenly over 4 tortillas. Warm oil in a large frying pan over medium-high heat. Place 1 tortilla in hot oil and top with another tortilla. Fry on one side until lightly browned, then carefully flip and fry the other side until lightly browned, about 5 to 6 minutes total. Continue with rest of tortillas; cut each into 4 wedges and serve warm.

A griddle will speed up the cooking process.

Forgot to take out the cream cheese? Cut it into little pieces and it will soften quickly.

Serves 4

Preparation time 15 minutes

Cooking time 10 minutes

Ready in 25 minutes

Shrimp Skewers with Andouille and Yellow Bells

These large shrimp can be pricey, so watch for them on sale; freeze them until you need them (thaw before using).

ingredients

1 lb shrimp (16–21 count), peeled and deveined

½ lb andouille sausage, cooked, cut diagonally into 1-inch pieces

2 yellow bell peppers (or any color), cut into 2-inch squares

1 Tbs Univer Gourmet Garlic Cream

1 Tbs Univer Red Gold Hot

Preheat an outdoor grill to medium-high heat. Thread shrimp, sausage, and bell peppers alternately onto metal skewers. Baste with Gourmet Garlic Cream and Red Gold Hot. Place on the preheated grill, and cook for about 3 to 5 minutes per side, until shrimp are pink.

If you can't find andouille sausage, you may substitute any firm sausage of your choice.

Serves 4
Preparation time 10 minutes
Cooking time 8 minutes
Ready in 18 minutes

This is a rich sauce with chunks of fresh, warm avocado brushing against the plump pink shrimp. Don't forget crusty garlic bread and a salad!

Shrimp Scampi with Creamy Avocado

ingredients

¼ lb unsalted butter (1 stick)

2 Tbs Univer Gourmet Garlic Cream

2 Tbs red onion, chopped

1 Tbs fresh parsley, finely chopped

½ tsp freshly ground black pepper

dash white pepper

½ tsp Worcestershire sauce

1 lemon, juiced

1 lb raw jumbo shrimp, 16–20 count, peeled and deveined

2 Tbs Univer Red Gold Mild

1 Tbs white wine

1 large avocado, coarsely chopped

2 Tbs shredded Parmesan cheese

Lemon slices, for garnish

Fresh parsley, for garnish

Hot rice or noodles (4 servings)

In a large frying pan over medium heat, melt the butter. Add Garlic Cream and onions and sauté about 3 minutes. Add parsley, black pepper, white pepper, Worcestershire sauce, and lemon juice. Add shrimp, Red Gold Mild, and wine; cook 3 minutes, until shrimp begin to turn pink. Add avocado and cheese and stir to combine. Cook 2 minutes longer or until shrimp are done. Serve over rice or noodles; garnish with lemon slices and fresh parsley. A lovely glass of Pinot Grigio will put the finishing touch on your meal!

If jumbo shrimp are not available or priced too high, buy smaller shrimp. Do not use cocktail shrimp; they won't stand up to the sauce.

If you have leftovers, make an omelet or stir into a tomato-based soup.

Serves 4

Preparation time 15 minutes

Cooking time 25 minutes

Ready in 40 minutes

An old-fashioned favorite updated with the deliciousness of fresh paprika!

Tuna Broccoli Bake with Noodles

ingredients

1 (12 oz) package home-style egg noodles

2 (10.75 oz) cans condensed cream of mushroom soup

1 (5 oz) can evaporated milk

1 Tbs Univer Goulash Cream Mild

1 (12 oz) can solid albacore tuna, drained

1 (10 oz) box frozen chopped broccoli, thawed and drained

1 small onion, chopped

1 (4 oz) can sliced mushrooms, drained

1 cup cheddar cheese, shredded

¼ cup breadcrumbs

Preheat oven to 350° F. Cook pasta according to package directions. Meanwhile, in an ovenproof baking dish, mix mushroom soup, evaporated milk, and Goulash Cream Mild until blended; add tuna, broccoli, onions, and mushrooms. Mix in the drained noodles. Top with cheese, then breadcrumbs. Bake for about 25 minutes or until heated through and cheese is melted.

Don't be afraid to cook old-fashioned once in awhile. These are the comfort foods that we remember and so will our kids.

Red Gold Mild
A few suggested uses:
- Add a spicy boost to stews, soups and gravies
- Glaze a sizzling steak or chop
- Mix into ground meats
- Add to marinades
- Sauté onions and vegetables
- Create wonderful dips
- Mix into salsa to enhance the flavor
- Add to ranch dressing to make Southwestern dressing with a kick
- Lightly brush onto hot grilled pineapple
- Gluten-free; no trans fats

Serves 4

Preparation time 10 minutes

Cooking time 10 minutes

Ready in 20 minutes

Busy weeknights beg for seafood. It's our go-to quick-fix. Dress it up with fun sauces.

Tacos with Beer-Battered Cod

ingredients

2 lbs fresh cod, cut into 2–3 oz pieces

1 quart canola oil, for frying

Beer Batter

1 cup all-purpose flour

2 Tbs cornstarch

1 tsp baking powder

1 egg

1 (12 oz) beer

1 Tbs Univer Strong Steven

Spicy Red Mayonnaise

(find recipe on page 230)

1 Tbs lime juice

1Tbs jalapeño, finely chopped

2 cups cabbage, finely shredded

1 cup pepper jack cheese, shredded

1 (12 oz) package corn tortillas

Heat oil in deep fryer or deep frying pan to 375° F. Combine flour, cornstarch, and baking powder in a bowl. In another small bowl, mix egg, beer, and Strong Steven; stir into flour mixture. Dip fish pieces in batter, and fry in batches until golden brown, about 3 to 4 minutes. Do not crowd pan. Drain on paper towels and keep warm until all fish is fried.

Meanwhile, combine Spicy Red Mayonnaise with lime juice and jalapeño. To serve, place fish in a tortilla, top with cabbage and cheese, then add a dollop of Spicy Red Mayonnaise. Enjoy with a glass of Sangria!

If you would like to warm the tortillas, place them in the microwave for a few seconds or pop them in the hot oil for a few seconds.

Serves 4
Preparation time 10 minutes
Cooking time 10 minutes
Ready in 20 minutes

Stir-frys are a great way to get a nutritious meal on the table in a hurry!

Shrimp Stir-Fry

ingredients

2 Tbs canola oil

1 Tbs butter

1 Tbs Univer Goulash Cream Mild or Hot

1 Tbs low-sodium soy sauce

2 tsp Univer Gourmet Garlic Cream

2 tsp fresh ginger, minced

1 cup broccoli, chopped

1 cup celery, sliced

1 cup snow peas

½ cup green onions, sliced including tops

1¾ cups chicken broth

3 Tbs cornstarch

1 lb fresh shrimp, 51–60 count, peeled and deveined

Hot cooked rice (4 servings)

In a large frying pan or wok, heat oil, butter, Goulash Cream, soy sauce, Garlic Cream, and ginger. Add broccoli and celery to the pan and sauté for a few minutes before adding snow peas and green onions. While vegetables are cooking, mix cornstarch into the chicken broth, add to pan and stir to blend. Add shrimp and let simmer until shrimp are pink, about 3 minutes.

Use your favorite stir-fry vegetables; if you are short of time, most supermarkets sell packaged stir-fry ingredients in the produce department.

side dishes

Corn Maque Choux (Mock-Shoe) with Bacon, see page 197

The Torontaly Cheese

The Story of Our Giant Wheel of Torontaly Cheese and an Event in Our Life during the Second World War

The time was in the middle of the Second World War. We were starving! We had nothing to eat, and we were in the process of losing the roof over our heads as the bullets came through the walls and where the glass windows once were. The originator of this havoc was the Russian army, and from what we could make out, a tank brigade of eight German soldiers, firing from behind our big house about two hundred meters away from where we were.

We lived in the country just outside the city of Debrecen. Near our home, the one being decimated, was a small structure we called the Gamekeeper's House. It was built halfway into the ground, so that the bottoms of the windows were about a foot above ground level. To enter it we had to go down into it, like going into a basement. That was where we were hiding, just below ground, trying to avoid being killed by the warring Russians and Germans shooting at each other on our property.

I was about seven years old, and I was hungry. I was dreaming of some miracle food stash that my grandmother was being so secretive about, saying it would save us all, once the firing was over and things settled down. If only God would save us until that happens, that is.

It was obvious to her that the Russians would win this battle because there were, as she would say, as many of them as

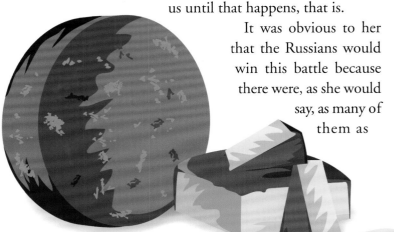

the blades of grass in the fields. When they advanced toward Budapest, Vienna, and then Germany, leaving our area of Hungary, then she would uncover this wondrous stash of food and save us from starvation, but not until then, because the Russian soldiers might come in and take our secret stash of food. Well, the theory was good, in theory. Needless to say, when the Russian soldiers reached our life-saving Gamekeeper's House, which had hardly any roof or attic left, her theory did not work. When Granma kept constant vigilance on the remaining roof and attic, I realized that that's where the miracle food stash must be.

Suddenly six or seven Russian soldiers burst in, lining us all up against the wall while they ransacked what was left of our Gamekeeper's House. We considered it a shrine because it saved our lives, being halfway below ground. When they appeared, we suddenly forgot our hunger. Granma, myself, my five-year-old brother, my sister, and my mother were standing against the wall facing several guns and pistols in the hands of screaming Russian soldiers. Father was somewhere in the war, facing the same Russian guns. My sister and mother were crying; my grandmother, being the hero she was, was screaming at the soldiers to put away the guns, what could children and women do to harm them. Needless to say, the soldiers ate and took everything else that could perhaps be called food and was still edible. They also took clothes and other things that fancied them, even the cheap little ring that was my sister's first-ever piece of jewelry.

Then, a Russian officer ordered the soldiers out to advance toward town, and when they didn't go, he took his pistol out and aimed it at his soldiers. They left! The officer quickly walked through our safe fort, and when he realized we were not a threat, he also left. I remember that he was half in military clothes and half in civilian clothes. With them gone, we breathed a sigh of relief, which, unfortunately, did not stop our hunger. It came back overwhelmingly after the excitement subsided.

I remember looking through the blown-out window and seeing what seemed like millions of Russian soldiers advancing through the fields toward town without any resistance from the enemy. Seeing them, despite their great numbers advancing past us, I thought this was not much of a war compared to what we went through the night before and after four years of bombing by the Russians, English, Americans, and Germans. Seeing all the war activity—tanks, artillery, airplanes—I wasn't hungry anymore. My sister finally yanked me away from the window, fearing I might get shot.

In the next few days more soldiers came in and took whatever food we had left, despite being guarded by my grandmother and mother at the risk of being shot.

After a few days, when the shooting stopped and we could hear the noises of the war going away from us, Granma went outside our citadel to try to go down to the big house to see the damage and to see if she could get some food from there. Noting that the Russian soldiers carried red flags, she took a red scarf, tied it to a broomstick, lifting it high, trying to show that she was not an enemy to them. She returned with some sugar and spices, but no food. My brother and I jumped on the sugar, but we were yanked away from it by my mother, who feared it was poisoned by the Germans.

I asked Granma about her miracle food stash, but she was still secretive about it. I was beginning to wonder whether there really was food hidden somewhere or if she was just trying to keep our hopes up. She kept saying not yet, there are too many Russian soldiers around still.

My grandmother, the war strategist, knew that armies always leave occupational forces behind to keep their captured territories, so there were still a lot of soldiers around securing the area and capturing hiding Hungarian and German soldiers.

But there was no eating from the wondrous stashed food, of which only my grandmother knew the whereabouts. In the meantime, we ate whatever we could scrounge and from whatever my mother and grandmother could concoct from practically nothing.

One day in midmorning I heard screaming and cursing outside. We all rushed out and saw two Russian officers climbing on a ladder to the attic where the good part of the roof still existed. I remember that both of them had on beautiful full-length leather coats that they probably took off some unlucky dead German officers. They just didn't look right on those Russians.

My grandmother screamed at the two Russians to get off the ladder; she even climbed after them to try to pull them off the ladder. Then one of them took out his pistol and was shouting back at her in Russian. When he shot near her into the ground, she climbed back down, but she kept cursing at them. In the meantime, my mother huddled us behind a tree so we wouldn't get shot, and shouted at Granma to stop her attack on the Russians.

That's when I realized that my heroic grandmother was trying to protect our last bite of food, risking her life by trying to pull the Russians off the ladder. Aha, that's where the secret stash of food is, I thought! What could that miracle food be, I wondered, when the two Russians disappeared into the shot-up, but still somewhat intact, part of our savior citadel that hid the food that was to save us all from starvation.

As I was waiting there with my siblings, protected by my mother, with my stomach growling, I was trying to think what the food was. I certainly found out when the two Russians reappeared at the top of the ladder. The first one had his gun pointed at us and my grandmother.

The other Russian had the biggest, the largest, the most beautiful Torontaly cheese I ever saw. It was bigger than a wagon wheel, round and golden. It was beautiful! He could hardly carry it. I thought grudgingly that it would feed half the entire Russian army. But not us!

I will always remember my heroic grandmother and her fight for the Torontaly cheese, so that we, her family, could live. But unfortunately, that personal war of hers was lost to the Russians.

I have never seen a bigger cheese wheel than the one that lived in our attic for a long, long time, hoping to save its owners from starvation during and after the war. But that was not to be, as I reflect on it more than half a century later.

Serves 4
Preparation time 10 minutes
Cooking time 12 minutes
Ready in 22 minutes

All the green hues in this dish make a very pretty side plate!

Artichoke Zucchini Sauté

ingredients

1 Tbs extra virgin olive oil

1 Tbs unsalted butter

1 tsp Univer Gourmet Garlic Cream

1 tsp Univer Sweet Ann

1 (9 oz) package frozen artichoke hearts, thawed, halved

2 cups zucchini, sliced ¼-inch on the diagonal

½ cup green onions, chopped

¼ cup kalamata olives, roughly chopped

¼ cup dry white wine

¾ tsp thyme

1 cup tomatoes, peeled, seeded, and diced

Black pepper, to taste

In a medium frying pan over medium-high heat, add oil, butter, Garlic Cream, and Sweet Ann. Sauté artichokes and zucchini for about 5 minutes. Add green onions, olives, wine, and thyme. Cook another 4 minutes. Add tomatoes and pepper; continue to cook until tomatoes are heated through, about 3 minutes more. Serve hot.

Don't store spices above your stove or other heat source. Keep them in a cool, dark place for maximum shelf life.

Serves 6
Preparation time 5 minutes
Cooking time 6 minutes
Ready in 1 hour, 11 minutes

Asparagus with Dilled Yogurt Sauce

Here's a terrific sauce suitable for most vegetables.

ingredients

2 lbs fresh asparagus, trimmed

½ cup yogurt

½ cup Univer Mayonnaise

1 tsp lemon juice

1 tsp Univer Gourmet Garlic Cream

1 tsp Univer Mustard

½ tsp salt

¼ tsp pepper

2 Tbs fresh parsley, finely chopped

2 tsp fresh dill, finely chopped

About 1 hour before cooking asparagus, prepare sauce. In a small mixing bowl, whisk together yogurt, Mayonnaise, lemon juice, Garlic Cream, Mustard, salt and pepper; add parsley and dill. Stir to blend. Cover and refrigerate 1 hour. At cooking time, bring large pot of water to a boil. Cook asparagus in 2 batches. Blanch each batch for 2 to 3 minutes; drain and pat dry. Spoon sauce over warm asparagus and serve.

Veggies cooked in water or broth will benefit from being put back in the warm pan after draining to dry a bit before serving.

Serves 4

Preparation time 3 minutes

Cooking time 3 minutes

Ready in 6 minutes

Fresh asparagus has a snappy bite when cooked very briefly.

Asparagus with Creamy Garlic Sauce

ingredients

1 lb asparagus, trimmed

2 Tbs Univer Mayonnaise

1½ tsp Univer Gourmet Garlic Cream

1 Tbs grated Parmesan cheese

3 Tbs milk

3 Tbs shredded Parmesan cheese

Salt and pepper to taste

Bring water to a boil in a shallow pan. Place asparagus in boiling water, cover, and cook 2 to 3 minutes. Transfer to a colander and rinse under cold running water to stop the cooking process. Drain well and pat dry. In a small mixing bowl, whisk together the Mayonnaise, Garlic Cream, grated Parmesan, and milk. Add shredded Parmesan. Adjust milk to achieve desired consistency. Spoon over steamed asparagus; season with salt and pepper.

After draining asparagus, return to hot pan for a minute to remove excess moisture. The sauce will adhere better.

Serves 6

Preparation time 5 minutes

Cooking time 6 minutes

Ready in 11 minutes

Serves 6

Preparation time 10 minutes

Cooking time 30 minutes

Ready in 40 minutes

This stuffing is also great in bell peppers.

Baked Tomatoes Florentine

ingredients

6 firm, medium tomatoes

2 Tbs unsalted butter

1 Tbs Univer Goulash Cream Mild

1 tsp Univer Gourmet Garlic Cream

1 small onion, chopped

1 (10 oz) package frozen chopped spinach, thawed, squeezed dry

⅓ cup half and half cream

freshly ground black pepper, to taste

3 Tbs seasoned breadcrumbs

2 Tbs fresh parsley, finely chopped

5 Tbs grated Parmesan cheese

3 Tbs shredded mozzarella cheese, to garnish

Preheat oven to 400° F. Slice the tops off the tomatoes and scoop out the pulp and seeds. Place the tomatoes upright in an ovenproof dish. In a small frying pan, melt the butter. Add the Goulash Cream Mild and Garlic Cream. Add the onions and sauté about 5 minutes, until onions are translucent. In a medium-size mixing bowl, combine the spinach, cream, pepper, breadcrumbs, parsley, and Parmesan cheese. Add the onions and mix well. Spoon the mixture into the prepared tomatoes. Bake for 20 minutes, or until heated through. Top with shredded mozzarella cheese. Return to the oven for 5 more minutes or until the cheese melts.

Easily remove excess moisture from thawed spinach by putting it in cheesecloth and twisting until the liquid is gone.

Asparagus with Wasabi Mayonnaise

This is a nice side dish for the buffet table.

ingredients

2 lbs asparagus, trimmed

1 cup Univer Mayonnaise

4 tsp soy sauce

1 tsp Univer Gourmet Garlic Cream

1½ tsp sugar

2 tsp fresh lemon juice

½ tsp wasabi paste

Blanch asparagus in 2 batches in a large saucepan of boiling water 2 to 3 minutes. Transfer to a colander and rinse under cold running water to stop the cooking process. Drain well and pat dry. In a small mixing bowl, whisk together Mayonnaise, soy sauce, Garlic Cream, sugar, lemon juice, and wasabi paste until sugar is dissolved. Serve asparagus with sauce.

Wasabi is very hot, so add a little at a time and work your way up for more heat.

Serves 4

Preparation time 10 minutes

Cooking time 15 minutes

Ready in 25 minutes

Decadence enhanced with bacon, green onions, and cheese!

Bacon Cheese Mashed Potatoes

ingredients

2 lbs russet potatoes, washed, unpeeled, cut into 1-inch chunks

6 strips bacon, cut in ½-inch dice

1 cup green onions, sliced

½ cup heavy cream

½ cup sour cream

2 tsp Univer Goulash Cream Mild

1 tsp Univer Gourmet Garlic Cream, or to taste

¼ tsp freshly ground black pepper

1 cup shredded sharp cheddar cheese

Place potatoes in a large pot and add enough water to cover potatoes by about 1 inch. Cover and bring to a boil. Remove cover and cook for about 15 minutes, or until the potatoes are fork tender. Meanwhile, in a frying pan over medium-high heat, fry bacon until crisp. Remove bacon from pan and drain on paper towels. Add green onions to the frying pan and sauté for about 2 minutes. Remove from pan and set aside. Drain potatoes well and return to the pot. With a potato masher or mixer, blend in heavy cream, sour cream, Goulash Cream Mild, Garlic Cream, and pepper. Add bacon, green onions, and cheese. Stir to combine. Serve warm.

A long wooden spoon laid over a boiling pot will help prevent the liquid from boiling over. However, if you fear the pot will boil over, you probably have the heat too high.

Serves 4

Preparation time 15 minutes

Cooking time 15 minutes

Ready in 30 minutes

Little bites that look like baby cabbages.

Brussels Sprouts with Bacon and Carrots

ingredients

1 lb fresh Brussels sprouts

1 Tbs extra virgin olive oil

1 Tbs unsalted butter

1 tsp Univer Gourmet Garlic Cream

1 tsp Univer Sweet Ann

½ cup bacon, chopped

3 small carrots, peeled and diced

2 tsp chives, snipped

Trim stem ends off sprouts; remove tough outer leaves. Halve sprouts lengthwise if they are very large. In a large frying pan over medium-high heat, add oil, butter, Garlic Cream, and Sweet Ann. Add bacon and cook until crispy, about 5 minutes. Remove bacon and if necessary, drain some fat. Add Brussels sprouts and carrots and stir to coat with remaining fat. Cook, stirring often, until carrots begin to soften, about 10 minutes. Remove from heat and add bacon back in. Place in a serving dish and garnish with chives.

1 slice of bacon equals about 1 tablespoon crumbled.

Serves 4

Preparation time 10 minutes

Cooking time 10 minutes

Ready in 20 minutes

A beautiful side dish for any holiday and every day.

Cauliflower with Roasted Red Peppers

ingredients

1 small head cauliflower, separated into florets

1 tsp Univer Gourmet Garlic Cream

1 tsp Univer Red Gold Hot

1 (15 oz) jar roasted red peppers, drained and diced

1 (3.8 oz) can sliced black olives

½ cup fresh parsley, finely chopped

Freshly ground black pepper, to taste

2 Tbs grated Parmesan cheese

Cook cauliflower florets in 1 inch of boiling water, covered, 8 to 10 minutes, until tender. Drain. Add Garlic Cream and Red Gold Hot and toss to coat. Add roasted red peppers, olives and parsley. Season with pepper and heat through on gentle heat, stirring to avoid scorching. Garnish with Parmesan cheese and serve warm.

"Tis an ill cook that cannot lick his own fingers."
—William Shakespeare

Serves 6

Preparation time 20 minutes

Cooking time 25 minutes

Ready in 45 minutes

Our interpretation of this creamy corn recipe uses fresh corn shucked from the cob. Use frozen corn, thawed, if fresh corn is out of season.

Corn Maque Choux (Mock-Shoe) with Bacon

ingredients

½ lb bacon, chopped

2 Tbs vegetable oil

1 Tbs Univer Goulash Cream Mild

1 tsp Univer Goulash Cream Hot

1 tsp Univer Gourmet Garlic Cream

4 cups sweet corn (about 6 ears)

1½ cups onions, chopped

1 cup green bell peppers, chopped

2 cups tomatoes, seeded and chopped

1 cup heavy whipping cream

¼ cup green onions, chopped including tops

In a large frying pan over medium heat, fry the bacon until crispy. Drain the bacon on paper towels and set aside. Pour off all of the bacon fat except for 2 tablespoons. Add oil, Goulash Cream Mild, Goulash Cream Hot, and Garlic Cream. Stir to mix with oil and bacon fat. Add the corn, onions, and bell peppers. Cook 8 minutes, stirring occasionally. Add the tomatoes and cook 5 minutes more, until corn is tender. Add the cream and cook another 2 minutes to heat through. Remove from heat and stir in bacon and green onions. Serve hot.

Check out your local ethnic markets for less expensive produce and make friends with some unfamiliar veggies. The produce manager will be happy to answer questions and provide cooking tips.

Serves 6
Preparation time 10 minutes
Cooking time 20 minutes
Ready in 30 minutes

Couscous Provençal

Cans or jars of herbes de Provence can be found in the spice aisle.

ingredients

1 Tbs extra virgin olive oil

1 tsp Red Gold Mild

1 tsp Univer Gourmet Garlic Cream

½ cup onions, finely chopped

1 (14 oz) can low-sodium chicken broth, plus water to make 3 cups liquid

1 tsp herbes de Provence

1½ cups couscous

4 oil-packed dried tomatoes, finely chopped

¼ cup kalamata olives, coarsely chopped

Freshly ground black pepper

In a medium saucepan, heat oil over medium heat. Add Red Gold Mild and Garlic Cream and stir to combine with oil. Add onion and sauté about 5 minutes. Stir in broth, herbs, couscous, dried tomatoes, olives, and pepper to taste. Bring to a boil, stirring well with a fork. Cover; turn off heat. Let sit 10 minutes. Fluff couscous with a fork before serving.

Herbes de Provence is just the French version of Italian seasoning. It contains thyme, rosemary, savory, basil, lavender, and other herbs and spices. Use it as you would any herb blend.

Serves 4
Preparation time 5 minutes
Cooking time 7 minutes
Ready in 12 minutes

A very good side dish that is also great served over meats.

Creamy Parmesan Mushrooms

2 Tbs unsalted butter

1 Tbs extra virgin olive oil

1 lb firm white mushrooms, cleaned and thinly sliced

1 Tbs Univer Goulash Cream Mild

2 Tbs low-sodium chicken broth

¼ cup sour cream

2 Tbs grated Parmesan cheese

Freshly ground black pepper, to taste

Additional Parmesan cheese, for garnish

In a medium-size frying pan, melt butter. Add olive oil and whisk to blend. Add mushrooms and Goulash Cream Mild and sauté 2 minutes. Add broth and sauté another minute. In a small mixing bowl, mix together sour cream, cheese, and pepper. Add mixture to mushrooms and stir. Simmer over low heat until sour cream has heated through; do not let come to a boil. Place mushrooms in a serving dish and garnish with additional Parmesan cheese. Serve warm.

Serves 6
Preparation time 5 minutes
Cooking time 10 minutes
Ready in 15 minutes

Keep a bag of pearl onions in the freezer—they are sweeter than regular onions and make a great accompaniment for meats.

Creamy Green Peas

ingredients

½ cup water

1 (16 oz) bag frozen green peas

1 cup frozen pearl onions

¼ cup butter

½ tsp sugar

Pepper, to taste

1 tsp parsley, finely chopped

1 dash nutmeg

1 cup heavy cream

2 tsp Univer Goulash Cream Mild

2 Tbs flour

Bring water to boil in a medium saucepan; add peas and onions. Cook about 5 minutes; drain. Reduce heat to medium and add butter, sugar, pepper, parsley, and nutmeg to the pan. Meanwhile, in a small mixing bowl, mix cream, Goulash Cream Mild, and flour until smooth. Add to peas and onions; simmer about 5 minutes. Garnish with a sprinkling of paprika. Serve warm.

You may purchase fresh pearl onions in the produce department, but they need to be peeled like any onion before you can use them in your dish. To save time, blanch them briefly in boiling water, place in ice water to stop the cooking, and the peels should slip off easily. Our recommendation—buy them frozen!

"I went to a restaurant that serves 'lunch at any time.' So I ordered bean soup during the Renaissance."
—Stephen Wright

Gourmet Garlic Cream

Garlic is revered throughout the world for its flavor-enhancing qualities and is a staple in most kitchens. With Gourmet Garlic Cream, you can do away with messy cleaning and chopping. Just open the jar! Great garlic aroma, pure garlic flavor!

A few suggested uses:

- Add to soups, stews and gravies
- Mix into mashed potatoes for instant Garlic Potatoes
- Make garlic bread in a snap
- Add to sauces, dips and spreads
- Sauté onions and other vegetables
- Toss with hot cooked pasta before dressing with sauce
- Rub onto clean, dry potatoes before baking
- Brush onto pizza crusts before baking

Serves 4

Preparation time 10 minutes

Cooking time 25 minutes

Ready in 35 minutes

Create wonderful variations by using your favorite Alfredo sauce, such as 4-cheese

Creamy Mashed Potatoes

ingredients

4 medium to large potatoes

4 Tbs butter or margarine

½ cup prepared Alfredo sauce, or more to taste

1½ tsp Univer Gourmet Garlic Cream

Bring water to boil in a large saucepan. Dice peeled or unpeeled potatoes into even-size chucks and place in salted, boiling water. Over medium-high heat, cook potatoes partially covered for 20 minutes or until fork tender. Drain well; return potatoes to hot pan to dry excess moisture. Mash potatoes with the butter or margarine. Mix together the Alfredo sauce and the Garlic Cream. Blend in well to potato mixture. Serve hot.

Keep jarred Alfredo sauce in your pantry. It can be used in so many ways to add creamy and cheesy texture and flavor to your dishes. Use it on veggies, stir into potatoes, even add to cooked rice.

Serves 6

Preparation time 25 minutes

Cooking time 20 minutes

Ready in 45 minutes

Try this as an alternative to French fries sometime!

Deep-Fried Crispy Cauliflower

ingredients

1 large cauliflower head, cut into florets

1 tsp salt

2 large eggs

2 Tbs milk

1 Tbs Univer Goulash Cream Mild

1 tsp Univer Gourmet Garlic Cream

1 cup all-purpose flour

1 quart canola oil, for deep frying

Soak the florets in very cold, salted water for 15 minutes; drain. In a large saucepan, bring 6 cups of water to a boil. Cook the cauliflower florets until just tender, about 5 to 6 minutes. Drain and rinse under cold water to stop the cooking process. Drain again very thoroughly and pat dry. In a medium-size mixing bowl, whisk together the eggs, milk, Goulash Cream Mild, and Garlic Cream. Dip each floret in the egg mixture, then coat in flour. Place on waxed paper or foil to let the excess drip off. In a large, deep frying pan, heat the oil until nearly smoking, about 375° F. Deep-fry the florets in batches until golden brown, about 5 minutes. Do not crowd pan. Remove with a slotted spoon and drain on paper towels. Serve warm.

Don't overcrowd the pan when frying or deep-frying foods. You will lose the heat needed to really sear the outside of the food and instead the food will steam. When frying in batches, let the oil reheat before adding another batch.

Serves 4
Preparation time 10 minutes
Cooking time 35 minutes
Ready in 45 minutes

Dirty Rice

Use ground beef or chicken if you prefer.

ingredients

1 lb spicy bulk pork sausage

1 small onion, finely chopped

2 cups low-sodium chicken broth

1 cup long-grain rice

1 Tbs Univer Goulash Cream Mild

1 tsp Univer Gourmet Garlic Cream

½ tsp Univer Goulash Cream Hot, or to taste

In a large frying pan over medium-high heat, brown and crumble sausage until pink is gone. Add onions and sauté about 5 minutes longer; drain. Add broth, rice, Goulash Cream Mild, Garlic Cream, and Goulash Cream Hot. Cover and bring to a boil; reduce heat to medium-low and simmer, covered, 18 to 20 minutes, until rice is tender and most of the liquid is absorbed.

Chop and slice foods with love, not speed. Chop only at the pace at which you are comfortable—no need to keep up with TV chefs! That's just an accident waiting to happen.

Serves 4
Preparation time 10 minutes
Cooking time 60 minutes
Ready in 1 hour, 10 minutes

Starting from the garlic-crusted skins to the zesty insides, you will love these potatoes!

Tijuana Twice-Baked Potatoes

ingredients

1 Tbs Univer Garlic Cream

1 Tbs canola oil

2 large baking potatoes, scrubbed and dried

½ cup salsa, drained, any heat level

⅓ cup half and half cream

¼ cup sour cream

1 cup cooked black beans, drained

½ cup cooked Mexican corn, drained

½ cup green onions, chopped, including tops

1 Tbs cilantro, finely chopped

1 cup shredded Mexican cheese blend, divided

Salt and pepper, to taste

1 large avocado, diced

Preheat oven to 375° F. In a small mixing bowl, whisk together Garlic Cream and oil. Coat potatoes with mixture. Place on small baking sheet and pierce several times with a fork. Bake potatoes for 40 to 50 minutes, until potatoes give when gently squeezed. Remove from oven and cut in half lengthwise. Scoop pulp into a medium-size mixing bowl. Mash with salsa, half and half, and sour cream. Add the beans, corn, green onions, and cilantro. Add half the cheese and mix well. Spoon the mixture back into the potato skins. Top with remaining cheese. Bake 20 minutes more. Season with salt and pepper and garnish with diced avocado.

Leftover mashed or baked potatoes can go directly into a stew or soup as a thickener—dice the baked potatoes.

Serves 6

Preparation time 10 minutes

Cooking time 15 minutes

Ready in 25 minutes

Does bacon make it better? You bet!!

Fried Spinach with Bacon and Garlic

ingredients

4 slices bacon, chopped

8 oz fresh mushrooms, sliced

1 small onion, chopped

1 Tbs Univer Gourmet Garlic Cream

2 (10 oz) bags fresh baby spinach

Salt and pepper to taste

Fry bacon until crisp in a large frying pan. Remove with a slotted spoon and drain on paper towels. Drain all but 2 tablespoons of bacon drippings. To the pan, add mushrooms, onions, and Garlic Cream. Sauté for about 5 minutes, then add spinach. Cover and continue cooking until spinach has wilted, about 5 to 8 minutes longer. Serve hot, topped with reserved bacon.

Choose a cutting board that has enough room to easily hold all the food that you are chopping.

Serves 4

Preparation time 5 minutes

Cooking time 5 minutes

Ready in 40 minutes

Egg Dumplings (Spaetzle)

Tasty little puffs to go with soups and stews.

ingredients

2 eggs

½ cup water

1 tsp Univer Sweet Ann

1½ cups flour

1 tsp salt

¼ tsp baking powder

Mix together eggs, water, and Sweet Ann; then add flour, salt, and baking powder. Let flour mixture stand for 30 minutes. Drop small spoon-size amounts into boiling broth or soup. Cover and cook for about 5 minutes until dumplings rise to surface of the liquid.

Serves 4

Preparation time 20 minutes

Cooking time 10 minutes

Ready in 30 minutes

Grilling brings out great flavor in vegetables and fruits.

Grilled Vegetables with Dried Tomato and Green Onion Butter

ingredients

2 medium zucchinis, sliced ½-inch on the diagonal

2 medium summer squash, sliced ½-inch on the diagonal

1 large red onion, peeled and sliced

1 lb small new potatoes, halved

Lemon-flavored cooking spray

Salt and pepper to taste

Dried Tomato and Green Onion Butter
(find recipe on page 222)

Place vegetables in a grilling basket and spray lightly with lemon cooking spray. Season with salt and pepper. Place on grill over indirect heat. Grill for about 10 minutes, until crisp-tender. Remove to a serving dish and dot with pats of Dried Tomato and Green Onion Butter.

Compound butter is just butter mixed with other ingredients, such as dried tomatoes and green onions. They are fun to make and fun to serve. It's one of those small details that your family and guests will appreciate.

Serves 4

Preparation time 10 minutes

Cooking time 20 minutes

Ready in 30 minutes

Spicy, oven-roasted potatoes served skin-on for a rustic look.

Herb-Crusted Roasted Potatoes

ingredients

4 medium potatoes, washed, unpeeled, cut into 1½-inch chunks

⅓ cup olive oil

¼ cup Univer Red Gold Hot

1 tsp Univer Gourmet Garlic Cream

1 tsp dried oregano

1 tsp dried rosemary leaves

1 tsp dried parsley

1 tsp dried thyme

Salt and pepper to taste

2 green onions, chopped (optional)

Preheat oven to 400° F. Place potatoes in a large roasting pan. In a small bowl, whisk together olive oil, Red Gold Hot, and Garlic Cream to blend. Pour over potatoes and toss to evenly coat. In another small bowl, mix together oregano, rosemary leaves, parsley, thyme, salt, and pepper. Sprinkle mixture over potatoes and toss again to distribute herbs. Arrange in a single layer. Bake 20 minutes uncovered or until potatoes are fork tender, turning once. Serve hot with chopped green onions as garnish.

Open a drawer to temporarily hold a baking sheet if you are short on counter space. Be careful if there are children running about.

Serves 6
Preparation time 20 minutes
Cooking time 20 minutes
Ready in 40 minutes

Herb-Roasted Corn on the Cob

There are so many creative ways to prepare corn. Roasting brings out the natural sweetness!

ingredients

4 ears corn on the cob, husks and silk removed

2 Tbs unsalted butter, melted

1 green onion, finely chopped

1 tsp fresh dill, finely chopped

½ tsp dried rubbed sage

½ tsp Univer Gourmet Garlic Cream

½ tsp Univer Red Gold Mild

Salt and black pepper to taste

Preheat oven to 425° F. In a small bowl, combine the butter, green onion, dill, sage, Garlic Cream, Red Gold Mild, and salt and pepper; mix well. Brush each ear of corn with butter mixture. Wrap individually in foil and place in baking pan. Roast for about 20 minutes, until the corn is done. Carefully open foil and remove corn. Serve hot.

To easily and quickly shuck corn, cut a little off each end and "unroll" sideways. Most of the silk will come right off in the husk.

Serves 4
Preparation time 20 minutes
Ready in 20 minutes

Jicama is a root vegetable found fresh in the produce department. It tastes like a cross between a potato and an apple. It's very refreshing served raw.

Jicama and Mandarin Orange Salad

ingredients

2 cups jicama, peeled and cut into thin strips (julienne)

1 (15 oz) can Mandarin oranges, juice reserved

1 medium red bell pepper, seeded and cut into thin strips

1 cup shredded lettuce

½ cup yogurt

1 Tbs reserved juice from Mandarin oranges

1 tsp orange zest

1 tsp Univer Sweet Ann

Salt, to taste

Freshly ground black pepper, to taste

In a medium-size mixing bowl, combine the jicama, Mandarin oranges, bell pepper, and lettuce. In a small mixing bowl, whisk together the yogurt, juice, zest, and Sweet Ann. Spoon yogurt mixture over jicama mixture; stir to combine. Season with salt and pepper to taste.

A microplane grater is a great help in the kitchen for zesting and grating. Treat yourself to a nice one, and it will last for years.

Serves 8
Preparation time 20 minutes
Cooking time 20 minutes
Ready in 40 minutes

A hint of horseradish elevates plain potatoes into gourmet potatoes!

Mashed Potatoes with Garlic and Horseradish

ingredients

5 lbs Yukon Gold potatoes, cut into 1-inch chunks

⅔ cup heavy cream

6 Tbs unsalted butter

1 Tbs Univer Gourmet Garlic Cream

1 Tbs Univer Horseradish with Vinegar, or more to taste

Salt and pepper to taste

Place potatoes in a large pot; add enough salted water to cover by 1 inch. Bring to a boil; cook until potatoes are tender when pierced with the tip of knife, about 20 minutes. Drain well, and return to pot. Meanwhile, in a small saucepan over medium-low heat, combine cream, butter, Garlic Cream, and Horseradish with Vinegar. Cook until butter is melted and cream is hot. Add to potatoes. Using a potato masher or mixer, mash potatoes to desired consistency. Season with salt and pepper. For thicker potatoes, use a bit less heavy cream; add more butter at the table for a richer taste. Serve hot.

Leftovers? Fried potato patties make a great hit for breakfast!

Serves 8
Preparation time 5 minutes
Cooking time 25 minutes
Ready in 30 minutes

Mexican Corn

A slightly spicy, creamy corn dish that will please the corn-lovers in your home.

ingredients

1 (8 oz) package cream cheese, softened

¼ cup unsalted butter, softened

2 tsp Univer Strong Steven

1 tsp Univer Gourmet Garlic Cream

1 (4 oz) can mild chilies

1 tsp sugar

¼ cup fresh parsley, chopped

2 (16 oz) packages frozen corn kernels, thawed

Preheat oven to 350° F. Lightly grease or spray a casserole dish. In a medium-size mixing bowl, combine cream cheese, butter, Strong Steven, Garlic Cream, chilies, sugar, and parsley. Add corn and mix well. Spoon into baking dish. Bake for about 25 minutes or until top is lightly browned. Serve hot.

Leftovers? Add some to pancake batter to make savory pancakes!

Serves 4
Preparation time 5 minutes
Cooking time 15 minutes
Ready in 20 minutes

Nutmeg is the secret ingredient in this easy recipe.

Cheesy Creamed Spinach

ingredients

2 Tbs unsalted butter

1 tsp Univer Gourmet Garlic Cream

1 tsp Univer Goulash Cream Mild

½ cup onions, chopped

2 (10 oz) packages frozen chopped spinach, thawed and squeezed dry

½ cup heavy cream

½ tsp freshly ground black pepper

¼ tsp nutmeg

¼ cup grated Parmesan cheese

Melt the butter in a medium frying pan over medium-high heat. Add Garlic Cream and Goulash Cream Mild and stir into butter. Add the onions and sauté for about 3 minutes. Add the spinach and cook, stirring, until spinach is nearly done, about 8 minutes. Add the cream, pepper, and nutmeg, and cook until the cream is reduced by half, about 4 minutes. Remove from heat. Add the Parmesan cheese and stir to blend. Serve hot.

Check the spinach to make sure it's really chopped. If you find many stringy pieces, grab your knife and give the spinach another chop.

Serves 6
Preparation time 20 minutes
Cooking time 10 minutes
Ready in 30 minutes

Add a little meat of your choice and turn this into an entrée.

Mixed Vegetable Medley

ingredients

1 Tbs extra virgin olive oil

1 Tbs butter

2 Tbs Univer Goulash Cream Mild

1 Tbs Univer Sweet Ann

1 tsp Univer Gourmet Garlic Cream

2 zucchinis, split lengthwise and sliced

2 summer squash, split lengthwise and sliced

½ green bell pepper, sliced

½ red bell pepper, sliced

½ yellow bell pepper, sliced

8 oz fresh white mushrooms, sliced

1 red onion, sliced

In a large frying pan, heat olive oil, butter, Goulash Cream Mild, Sweet Ann, and Garlic Cream. Add all vegetables and sauté for about 10 to 12 minutes, until vegetables are crisp-tender. If the pan is getting too dry, add a little water or vegetable broth.

This is a tasty blend of vegetables, but use your own favorites to make it your dish. Just make sure that everything is chopped or sliced roughly the same size so the dish cooks evenly.

Sweet Ann
A few suggested uses:

- Add a spicy boost to stews, soups and gravies
- Glaze a sizzling steak or chop
- Mix into ground meats
- Add to marinades
- Sauté onions and vegetables
- Create wonderful dips
- Mix into salsa to enhance the flavor
- Add to ranch dressing to make Southwestern dressing with a kick
- Lightly brush onto hot grilled pineapple
- Gluten-free; no trans fats

Serves 6
Preparation time 20 minutes
Cooking time 8 hours
Ready in 8 hours, 20 minutes

Mushrooms with Garlic and Bacon

A nice side dish, and also a good topper for steaks and chops!

ingredients

1 Tbs unsalted butter

1½ Tbs Univer Gourmet Garlic Cream

4 slices bacon, diced

1 lb fresh white mushrooms, sliced

¼ cup dry white wine (optional)

⅓ cup fresh parsley, chopped

1 Tbs fresh thyme, chopped

In a large frying pan over medium-high heat, heat the butter. Add the Garlic Cream and bacon and cook until bacon is crispy. Remove bacon with a slotted spoon and drain on paper towels. Raise the heat to high, add the mushrooms and continue to sauté, stirring briskly, until they release their juices and the liquid evaporates, about 5 to 8 minutes. If the mushrooms do not release much liquid, add the wine and cook until the liquid evaporates. Add the parsley, thyme, and the reserved bacon; stir to mix. Serve hot.

Serves 6
Preparation time 20 minutes
Cooking time 11 minutes
Ready in 31 minutes

Louisiana red beans add the spice and protein. They are often found in Cajun-style cooking.

Mixed Vegetables with Louisiana-Style Beans

ingredients

1 large head broccoli, cut into florets

2 Tbs extra virgin olive oil

2 tsp Univer Goulash Cream Mild

1 tsp Univer Gourmet Garlic Cream

1 red bell pepper, seeded and sliced

1 onion, sliced

½ lb white mushrooms, sliced

1 cup Louisiana-style red beans, with liquid

In a medium-size saucepan, cook broccoli in 1 inch of boiling water for 3 minutes, stirring often; drain. In a large frying pan over medium-high heat, heat oil, Goulash Cream Mild, and Garlic Cream. Add bell peppers, onions, and broccoli; sauté 5 minutes. Add mushrooms and beans and sauté another 3 minutes, or until beans are heated through. Serve warm.

"How come when you mix water and flour together you get glue ... and then you add eggs and sugar and you get cake? Where does the glue go?"
—Rita Rudner

Serves 6
Preparation time 10 minutes
Cooking time 10 minutes
Ready in 20 minutes

Like most soufflé-style dishes, this one will settle a bit when removed from the oven. Serve promptly.

Puffed Broccoli with Swiss Cheese

ingredients

2 heads fresh broccoli, cut into florets
2 egg whites, room temperature
¼ tsp salt
½ cup Univer Mayonnaise
½ cup shredded Swiss cheese

Cook broccoli in boiling water until just tender, about 5 minutes. Lightly grease or spray a broiler-proof pan. Arrange broccoli in pan in a single layer. In small bowl with mixer at high speed, beat egg whites and salt until stiff peaks form. Fold in Mayonnaise and cheese; spoon evenly over broccoli. Broil six inches from source of heat about 5 minutes or until golden brown (watch closely).

When adding fresh eggs to a mixture, break the eggs into a little bowl first so you can remove any shell bits before adding to the mixture (especially if your mixture is white, as in pancake or a cake batter).

Serves 4
Preparation time 2 minutes
Cooking time 10 minutes
Ready in 12 minutes

Orzo with Basil and Garlic

When serving with a meat entrée such as chicken or beef, try substituting chicken or beef broth for some or all of the water to prepare the orzo.

ingredients

4 cups water

½ lb orzo (rice-shaped pasta)

2 tsp extra virgin olive oil

1 cup fresh basil, chopped

1½ tsp Univer Garlic Cream

Salt and pepper to taste

In a large saucepan, bring 4 cups water to a hard boil. Add orzo; reduce heat and cook according to package directions. Drain; return to pot. Add oil, basil, Garlic Cream, salt and pepper to taste. Stir to combine and serve.

"… and they [products] are fantastic! Bringing back so many memories."
—Satisfied Paprika Fan

Serves 6
Preparation time 10 minutes
Cooking time 20 minutes
Ready in 40 minutes

This cheesy rice dish has an appealing mix of colors and the pimientos give just the right tang.

Rice Pilaf with Corn, Pimientos, and Cheese

ingredients

2 Tbs vegetable oil

1 small onion, finely chopped

1 cup long-grain white rice

2 cups low-sodium chicken broth

1 Tbs Univer Goulash Cream Mild

1 (4 oz) jar diced pimientos, drained

1 cup fresh or frozen corn kernels, thawed

½ cup shredded mozzarella cheese

½ cup fresh parsley, finely chopped

Heat the oil in a large saucepan over medium heat. Add the onions and rice and cook, stirring frequently, about 5 minutes, until onion is softened. Add the broth and Goulash Cream Mild; bring to a boil. Reduce heat and simmer, covered, about 10 minutes. Add the pimientos and corn; simmer 5 minutes longer, or until the rice is tender. Remove from heat, stir in cheese and let stand, covered, about 10 minutes. Stir in the parsley and fluff with a fork.

Usually jars of pimientos are kept near the pickles and olive section in your supermarket. Also look for them with the canned vegetables.

Serves 6
Preparation time 10 minutes
Cooking time 1 hour, 30 minutes
Ready in 1 hour, 40 minutes

A simple and delicious presentation for family or guests.

Stuffed Potatoes with Horseradish and Garlic

ingredients

6 baking potatoes, rinsed and dried

6 Tbs sour cream

6 Tbs unsalted butter, softened

4 Tbs Univer Horseradish with Vinegar, **divided**

1 Tbs Univer Gourmet Garlic Cream

Salt and pepper to taste

Topping

½ cup sour cream

Remaining Horseradish with Vinegar

2 Tbs fresh chives, chopped

Preheat oven to 400° F. Pierce top of potatoes with a small knife or fork; bake 1 hour. Remove and place on baking sheet. When cool enough to handle, cut off top of each potato lengthwise and scoop out most of pulp, leaving about ¼-inch pulp in each potato. In a mixing bowl, combine pulp, sour cream, butter, 2 tablespoons of Horseradish with Vinegar, Garlic Cream, and salt and pepper to taste. Spoon into potato shells, return to oven and bake 30 minutes longer. For the topping, whisk together sour cream, remaining 2 tablespoons Horseradish with Vinegar, and chives. Cover and chill until potatoes are done. Garnish potatoes with topping mixture.

Use a muffin tin to hold several potatoes for baking at the same time.

Univer Horseradish with Vinegar is perfect for those who love the taste of horseradish, but don't like the "sinusy" bite it has.

Serves 4
Preparation time 10 minutes
Cooking time 15 minutes
Ready in 25 minutes

Green Bean Sauté

Fresh green beans can usually be found year-round in the produce department of the supermarket. If you can't find them, use frozen; thaw before using.

ingredients

6 slices bacon

1 Tbs Univer Goulash Cream Mild

1 lb green beans, trimmed

1 small red bell pepper, seeded and roughly chopped

¼ cup bean sprouts

Salt and pepper to taste

In a large frying pan, cook the bacon until crisp. Remove from pan and drain on paper towels; crumble when cool. Into the bacon drippings, add the Goulash Cream Mild, green beans, and peppers. Sauté for about 8 minutes, until vegetables are just tender. Stir in the bean sprouts and bacon. Season with salt and pepper; serve warm.

Taste as you cook—for example, if you like more pepper, add more pepper. Recipes are merely tools to get you started!

Serves 4
Preparation time 15 minutes
Cooking time 25 minutes
Ready in 40 minutes

This side dish can easily serve as a nice lunch or light dinner.

Sausage-Stuffed Portobello Mushrooms

ingredients

4 portobello mushrooms, stems removed and chopped

½ lb Italian sausage, bulk

½ cup seasoned breadcrumbs

½ cup fresh parsley, chopped

½ cup cream cheese, softened

2 tsp Univer Gourmet Garlic Cream

1 tsp Univer Red Gold Hot

¼ cup grated Parmesan cheese

Extra virgin olive oil, for drizzling

Preheat oven to 375° F. Remove stems from portobello mushrooms. Arrange the mushroom caps, bottoms up, on a medium baking sheet. Chop the stems and set aside. In a large frying pan, brown and crumble the sausage until no longer pink, about 5 minutes. In a medium-size mixing bowl, mix together the chopped mushroom stems, sausage, seasoned breadcrumbs, and parsley. In a small mixing bowl, blend cream cheese, Garlic Cream, Red Gold Hot, and Parmesan cheese. Add to the sausage mixture and combine. Generously stuff the mushroom caps. Drizzle the stuffing with olive oil. Bake for about 20 minutes, or until stuffing is lightly browned and cheese has melted.

Forgot to take the cream cheese out to soften? Just cut into small pieces and it will soften fast.

Serves 4

Preparation time 20 minutes

Cooking time 20 minutes

Ready in 40 minutes

A nice, crunchy bite of fresh veggies!

Veggie Cakes

ingredients

3 Tbs extra virgin olive oil

2 cups fresh corn kernels (or frozen kernels, thawed)

⅔ cup onions, chopped

½ cup red bell pepper, chopped

¼ cup green bell pepper, chopped

1 Tbs Univer Red Gold Hot

1 tsp Univer Gourmet Garlic Cream

1 tsp ground cumin

¼ cup low-sodium chicken broth

¾ cup flour

1 tsp baking powder

½ cup cornmeal

1 egg

½ cup milk

1 Tbs unsalted butter, melted

2 Tbs cilantro, finely chopped

Freshly ground black pepper, to taste

Vegetable oil, for sautéing

Preheat oven to 150° F. Heat olive oil in a large saucepan over medium-high heat. Add the corn, onions, and bell peppers. Add the Red Gold Hot and Garlic Cream; stir to combine. Sauté 4 to 5 minutes, until vegetables begin to soften. Add the cumin and broth, scraping up any browned bits. Cook until the liquid has evaporated. In a medium-size mixing bowl, sift together the flour, baking powder, and cornmeal. Add the egg, milk, and butter and mix until smooth. Add the corn mixture and cilantro to the flour mixture and season with pepper.

In a large frying pan over medium-high heat, heat oil to 375° F. Cooking in batches, spoon in large dollops of corn mixture and fry until golden brown all around. Do not crowd pan. Remove and drain on paper towels. Place in an ovenproof dish and keep cakes warm in oven until ready to serve.

Veggies cooked in water or broth will benefit from being put back in the warm pan to dry a bit before serving.

Serves 4

Preparation time 10 minutes

Cooking time 15 minutes

Ready in 25 minutes

Try these for a simple lunch sometime.

Summer Squash Boats

ingredients

4 large summer squash, cleaned and sliced in half, lengthways

4 oz cream cheese, softened

1 egg

1 Tbs Univer Gourmet Garlic Cream

1 Tbs Univer Goulash Cream Mild

½ cup seasoned breadcrumbs

½ cup crabmeat, real or imitation, chopped

1 cup shredded Italian cheese blend

Squash pulp, chopped (optional)

Olive oil, for drizzling

Using a small spoon, remove seeds from squash, leaving about ¼-inch of squash in the shell. (If the squash are large enough, chop any scooped out squash and reserve.) Set aside. In a mixing bowl, blend together cream cheese and egg until smooth. Add Garlic Cream and Goulash Cream Mild and stir to combine. Add breadcrumbs, crabmeat and cheese. Add reserved squash, if any. Mix until well blended. Spoon mixture into squash boats. Drizzle with olive oil and grill over indirect heat for 15 minutes or until heated through. Serve hot.

No crab? Use leftover shrimp or chicken.

Serves 6
Preparation time 10 minutes
Cooking time 30 minutes
Ready in 50 minutes

A great use for leftover spaghetti sauce with meatballs or sausage! Just chop the meat and return to the sauce.

Spaghetti Pie

ingredients

½ lb cooked spaghetti, drained

1 Tbs Univer Goulash Cream Mild

2 eggs

¾ cup grated Parmesan cheese, divided

1 cup ricotta cheese

1 tsp Univer Gourmet Garlic Cream

¼ cup fresh parsley, chopped

1 cup prepared spaghetti sauce

½ cup shredded mozzarella cheese

Preheat oven to 350° F. Lightly grease or spray a 10-inch pie pan. Toss hot spaghetti with Goulash Cream Mild in a large mixing bowl. Spread spaghetti into pie pan and form into a loose "crust."

In a small bowl, combine eggs, ½ cup Parmesan cheese, ricotta, Garlic Cream, and parsley. Spread ricotta mixture evenly over the crust but not quite to edge, and top with spaghetti sauce. Bake uncovered for 25 minutes. Top with mozzarella cheese and bake 5 minutes longer, or until cheese melts. Remove from oven and sprinkle with remaining ¼ cup of Parmesan cheese. Let set up for 10 minutes before cutting into wedges.

Use Garlic Cream in place of garlic cloves. Use it in dips, dressings, etc. One teaspoon equals about 2–3 cloves of chopped garlic.

"Univer has blended all the ingredients with the right proportions so everything comes out just right. The best thing is that it is so easy to use. I'm hooked for life!"
—Satisfied Paprika Fan

Creamy Orange Dressing with Horseradish, see page 226

Irén and the Tomato Sauce

In the 1930s and early 1940s, the only thing that a mother knew about rearing a baby or a small child is what she heard from her mother, or more importantly, the maternity nurse. Back in those days, most babies were born at home, at least in Hungary. Most mothers were told by grandma or the midwife, "Feed the kid spinach sauce as soon as you can. It will let them grow up good and strong—it's full of vitamins!" they would say.

Of course, you can't explain to a small child why he or she should eat that green stuff because they are not yet aware of the dietary science that a maternity nurse or grandma—someone who hardly finished elementary school—possesses. And of course, what does a young child do in defense of letting that awful looking and tasting green stuff into their mouth? They spit it out, not just simply rejecting it but spraying it out so everything in front of the mouth gets to be colored green including my mother. Oh boy, that was fun to do!

The proverbial saying of "He, who accepts nothing, has nothing to return" wasn't quite true in my case. I had all of it to return. The entire surroundings, including my unsuspecting mother, turned an amazing hue of green. And the little pot that had been placed in front of me that held the green stuff was soon turned over, too.

Of course, my poor mother soon discovered that if you force-feed a child with spinach sauce, that child rapidly displays a very loud voice of protest from the head at the top of the body, and quickly displays a hasty exit from the other end.

But I had to go through that battle of force-fed spinach sauce for all of my young childhood until my mother finally got tired of cleaning up half the kitchen and herself after these unwanted episodes. When that happened, I felt triumphant. Boy, that was a long battle that lasted for years. But I finally won!

I did not eat spinach in any form until my adult life, and even today, I can only eat it in a steamed form. To my surprise, it actually tastes good.

As a child in our household, we did not use a lot of sauces. We were happy with just having basic food. Sauces were a luxury. Tomato was the exception.

There are many sauces for a variety of dishes in the Hungarian culinary arts. The most common ones, especially in the summertime, included tomato or fruit. Included would be garlic tomato sauce, tomato sauce with olive, Mediterranean tomato sauce, sweet tomato sauce, spicy tomato sauce, tomato purée sauce, tomato sauce with cream, tomato sauce with onions—in the summer, if we had anything, it was tomatoes.

Summertime also had my grandmother and mother combining fruits from our trees and bushes: sauces were made with names like spicy apple sauce, lemon sauce with olive, plum sauce with red pepper, cherry sauce with orange peel, quince apple sauce,

gooseberry sauce, raspberry sauce, and many more. If it was edible and grew in our gardens, it found its way to our table.

In our household, the tomato reigned supreme and tomato sauce was king. It would enhance any meat or pasta dish. Every household with a backyard grew tomatoes for the family to be used in the kitchen. If one could grow enough during the summer and there was excess, than it was cooked and preserved for the winter. That process was always intriguing to me as a young boy. We picked the tomatoes as a family and if we didn't have enough, then Mother bought more from the farmers. She was a master at quickly assessing what we needed for the winter months, which was supported by the number of bottles that the family had to store it in … and then the creation of the bottled tomato sauce began.

I really enjoyed the process of converting the tomato into the liquid form. It all took place in the backyard. First, you had what seemed like a mountain of tomatoes—at least it was to my brother's and my eyes. Next, we washed them in cold water, peeled off the skin, cut each tomato in half and removed the seeds. A gadget that looked like a meat grinder crushed the halves into a large container that was sitting on a base made out of stone, with fire burning in the center under it. A little water was added and the ground-up tomato mixture was slow-cooked all day until it became liquid.

All the while, we had to constantly stir it. When it was close to being ready and the liquidity was right, my mother would appear from the house and start her part of the job. Lots of sugar was then dumped into the now liquid tomato mix, along with some salt—we then stirred it some more as it continued to cook. The bottles had all been cleaned, disinfected, and heated and were now all lined up. A funnel was used to put the hot tomato juice into the bottles and covered with cellophane tied to the neck of the bottles. The bottles were then placed in big boxes and covered so they stayed warm

and eventually cooled down. The next day, the bottles were transferred to the pantry for use during the coming winter. This was a process of capturing the summer's gift for the winter.

Mother created all kinds of different sauces and soups with the tomato juice. My favorite was stuffed peppers cooked in tomato sauce, as well as hot tomato sauce on top of mashed potatoes.

As young teenagers, my brother and I were always pulling pranks on our older sister. Irén was three years older than I was, and six years older than my brother Steve—with her "advanced age" she would act as though she was an adult and we were just children and not in her league. Her attitude became a major sibling rivalry—at times, it felt like we were declaring war on each other. Irén had a gift for music—when she was studying piano at the Academy of Musik, a high school that specialized in music, she began to perform in concerts. She really thought we were way out of her league. And of course, my mother was very proud of her and Irén used that distinction to the hilt. Every time she had to do a chore in the house, she would say she couldn't, because she had to practice piano for her next concert.

"Let the boys do it!" was the usual phrase that came out of her mouth. Mother always ruled against us, saying, "Irén is now a concert pianist and she needs to practice a lot." Steve and I weren't happy; we now had to do double duty, by doing her chores too. She began to get all kinds of privileges. Because now she was a Prima-Donna, and she had to protect her hands in order to play the piano well. And we were her slaves! What were two brothers who felt very put upon to do? Why, we retaliated by pulling all sorts of pranks on her to get even, especially when Mother was not around.

Then one day, the ultimate happened. She declared to the family that she had met a very nice boy who wanted to escort her home from school and carry her books. Oh boy, that really separated us from Miss Princess—especially me. It felt like an outsider was now invading our family. I liked girls, some in the neighborhood, but there was one in school that I really liked, but I wasn't about to carry her books—what would my friends say? They can do that very well themselves, thank you. A year later, my attitude changed about girls and their books, too.

One day our parents were not home and Irén told us she was getting ready to go for her piano lesson. Steve and I felt that something wasn't right and we didn't believe her. She had her best dress on, combed her hair for an hour, and we even saw her put on makeup and lipstick, something that was forbidden by Mother. And we both knew that something different was happening—we guessed that she was going on a date with the jerk that carried her books. As she was "preparing herself," she was giving us orders to do this and do that—things that were otherwise her chores in the house. Well, we wouldn't stand for that! We huddled together and devised a way to ruin her romantic episode.

Who did she think she was? We decided to really scare her for making us her slaves. She was in her bedroom and we were in the kitchen. I had an idea and set the scene. Getting a bottle of tomato juice from the pantry, I gave my brother a large kitchen knife telling him, "I'll lie down on the kitchen floor and you pour the tomato juice on my chest. Put some on the knife so it drips and then we'll both start screaming and yelling as if I was stabbed with the kitchen knife and the blood will look like it is flowing everywhere. I'll act as if I'm dying!"

Well, it was an Academy Award performance—Alfred Hitchcock could not have done it better. Miss Princess Irén ran out of the bedroom not knowing what she was going to see, what all the commotion was about. Needless to say, we achieved our goal. Her voice added to Steve's screaming and my moaning. Then she started crying and fainted right into a pool of tomato juice with her best dress on. What a scene. We showed her who was boss!

Ironically, about twelve years later, I was a participant as an actor in a similar scene, but this time in a television show called Alfred Hitchcock Presents, in Hollywood. The difference was that I got wacked on the head with a fire log and the blood was not tomato juice, it was chocolate syrup.

Although the tomato sauce was the main sauce in my home growing up in Hungary, I remember when my brother Steve and I brought my mother to visit us after we moved to the United States. She said that sauces are just used to cover up the taste of badly cooked foods or the taste of yesterday's leftovers. She claimed that they were some type of French concoction. "If you use a lot of paprika in whatever you are cooking, you shouldn't have to cover up the bad taste of your dish," she would say.

Now as an adult, I don't think she was entirely right in her opinion about sauces. However, she was a good cook with or without them. She thought that if you use enough paprika and garlic in your cooking, you'll have a dish fit for a king. That I can agree with!

Yield about 1½ cups
Preparation time 10 minutes
Ready in 10 minutes

Dried Tomato and Green Onion Butter

Serve over grilled vegetables and crusty bread.

ingredients

½ lb unsalted butter, softened

¼ cup sun-dried tomatoes, oil-packed, drained and finely chopped

3 Tbs green onions, minced

1 tsp Univer Gourmet Garlic Cream

1 tsp Univer Goulash Cream Mild

½ tsp coarsely ground black pepper

In a small mixing bowl, mix all ingredients together until well blended. Cover and refrigerate until needed.

butters

Yield about 1 cup
Preparation time 5 minutes
Ready in 5 minutes

Fresh Paprika Butter

Serve with vegetables, pasta, and meats.

ingredients

½ lb unsalted butter, softened

1 Tbs Univer Sweet Ann

Mix ingredients together; cover and refrigerate until needed.

Yield about 1 cup
Preparation time 5 minutes
Ready in 5 minutes

Garlic Butter

Excellent on steak and, of course, garlic bread! Serve with vegetables, pastas, and meats.

ingredients

½ lb unsalted butter, softened

2 Tbs Univer Gourmet Garlic Cream

Mix ingredients together; cover and refrigerate until needed.

Yield about 1¼ cups
Preparation time 10 minutes
Ready in 10 minutes

Garlic Butter with Parsley and Cilantro

Wonderful stirred into mashed potatoes.

ingredients

- ½ lb unsalted butter, softened
- 1 Tbs Univer Gourmet Garlic Cream
- 1 tsp Univer Goulash Cream Mild
- 2 Tbs parsley, finely chopped
- 1 Tbs cilantro, finely chopped
- ½ tsp freshly ground black pepper

In a small mixing bowl, mix all ingredients together until well blended. Cover and refrigerate until needed.

Yield about 1¼ cup
Preparation time 10 minutes
Ready in 10 minutes

Green Onion and Cilantro Butter

Great for grilled meats.

ingredients

- ½ lb unsalted butter, softened
- ½ tsp Univer Red Gold Hot
- 2 Tbs green onion, finely chopped
- 1 Tbs fresh cilantro, finely chopped
- 1 Tbs fresh parsley, finely chopped

In a small mixing bowl, mix all ingredients together until well blended. Cover and refrigerate until needed.

Gourmet Garlic Cream

Garlic is revered throughout the world for its flavor-enhancing qualities and is a staple in most kitchens. With Gourmet Garlic Cream, you can do away with messy cleaning and chopping. Just open the jar! Great garlic aroma, pure garlic flavor!

A few suggested uses:

- Add to soups, stews and gravies
- Mix into mashed potatoes for instant Garlic Potatoes
- Make garlic bread in a snap
- Add to sauces, dips and spreads
- Sauté onions and other vegetables
- Toss with hot cooked pasta before dressing with sauce
- Rub onto clean, dry potatoes before baking
- Brush onto pizza crusts before baking

Yield about 1 cup
Preparation time 5 minutes
Ready in 5 minutes

Horseradish Butter

Delicious on fresh corn and steaks. Serve with vegetables, pastas, potatoes, breads, and meats.

ingredients

½ lb unsalted butter, softened

2 Tbs Univer Horseradish with Vinegar

Mix ingredients together and cover and refrigerate until needed.

Yield about 1 cup
Preparation time 10 minutes
Ready in 10 minutes

Hot and Spicy Butter

Serve with vegetables, pastas, and meats.

ingredients

½ lb unsalted butter, softened

2 tsp Univer Strong Steven

1 tsp lime zest

1 tsp lime juice

In a small bowl, mix ingredients until well blended. Cover and refrigerate until needed.

butters

Yield about 1 cup
Preparation time 5 minutes
Ready in 5 minutes

Hungarian Butter

Serve with vegetables, pastas, potatoes, breads, and meats.

ingredients

½ lb unsalted butter, softened

2 Tbs Univer Goulash Cream Mild

Mix softened butter with Goulash Cream Mild. Cover and refrigerate until needed.

Yield about 1 cup
Preparation time 10 minutes
Ready in 10 minutes

Restaurant Butter

Serve with vegetables, pasta, and meats.

ingredients

½ lb unsalted butter, softened

1 Tbs Univer Goulash Cream Mild

½ tsp white pepper

1 Tbs fresh parsley, finely chopped

1 Tbs lemon juice

Mix softened butter with Goulash Cream Mild; add the pepper, parsley, and lemon juice and stir to blend. Cover and refrigerate until needed.

Yield about 1¼ cups
Preparation time 10 minutes
Ready in 10 minutes

Rosemary and Garlic Pepper Butter

Great on meat and seafood.

ingredients

½ lb unsalted butter, softened

1 Tbs Univer Gourmet Garlic Cream

2 Tbs fresh rosemary, finely chopped

2 Tbs freshly ground black pepper

½ tsp salt

Mix softened butter with Garlic Cream; add the rosemary, pepper and salt and stir to blend. Cover and refrigerate until needed.

butters

dressings

Yield about 1 cup
Preparation time 10 minutes
Ready in 10 minutes

Capers and Olive Dressing

Wonderful as a base for stuffed eggs.

ingredients

½ cup Univer Mayonnaise

½ cup plain yogurt

1 tsp Univer Gourmet Garlic Cream

1 Tbs capers, finely chopped

1 Tbs green olives, finely chopped

In a small bowl, mix together all ingredients; cover and refrigerate until needed.

Yield about 1½ cups
Preparation time 10 minutes
Ready in 10 minutes

Creamy Orange Dressing with Horseradish

A creamy dressing good for salads and as a seafood dip.

ingredients

½ cup plain yogurt

½ cup Univer Mayonnaise

¼ cup Univer Horseradish with Vinegar

2 tsp orange zest

2 Tbs orange juice

Salt and pepper to taste

In a small bowl, blend all ingredients together; cover and refrigerate until needed.

Yield about 1 cup
Preparation time 10 minutes
Ready in 10 minutes

Creamy Red Gold Dressing

Excellent for salads and as a sandwich spread.

ingredients

1 cup Univer Mayonnaise

1 Tbs Univer Red Gold Mild

1 tsp Univer Gourmet Garlic Cream

In a small bowl, blend ingredients together; cover and refrigerate until needed.

Yield about 1 cup
Preparation time 5 minutes
Ready in 5 minutes

Garlic Ranch Dressing

A great dip for Strong Steven Chicken Wings and as a dressing for salads.

1 cup ranch salad dressing
1 Tbs Univer Gourmet Garlic Cream

In a small mixing bowl, whisk together the ranch dressing and Garlic Cream. Cover and refrigerate until ready to serve.

Yield about 1½ cups
Preparation time 10 minutes
Ready in 10 minutes

Green Chile Dressing

Nice for salads and also as a dip for veggies and chips.

1 cup Univer Mayonnaise
1 Tbs lime juice
1 Tbs hot green chilies, finely chopped
1 tsp Univer Garlic Cream
1 Tbs cilantro, finely chopped
1 small green onion, thinly sliced

In a small mixing bowl, whisk the ingredients together. Cover and refrigerate until ready to serve.

dressings

Yield about 1 cup
Preparation time 10 minutes
Ready in 10 minutes

Jalapeño Mayonnaise

A wonderful topping for any Mexican dish!

ingredients

½ **cup** Univer Mayonnaise

½ **cup** sour cream

1 Tbs jalapeño pepper, finely chopped

1 tsp Univer Garlic Cream

1 tsp ground cumin seed

Blend together all ingredients. Cover and refrigerate until needed.

Yield about ½ cup
Preparation time 5 minutes
Ready in 5 minutes

Lime Mayonnaise

Excellent as a dipping sauce for shrimp.

ingredients

½ **cup** Univer Mayonnaise

1 Tbs lime juice

1 tsp Univer Goulash Cream Hot

Combine all ingredients; cover and refrigerate until needed.

dressings

Yield about 1¼ cups
Preparation time 10 minutes
Ready in 10 minutes

Mild Chile Mayonnaise

Yummy with chicken salad.

ingredients

½ cup Univer Mayonnaise
½ cup sour cream
¼ cup diced mild green chilies
½ tsp ground cumin seed
Salt and pepper to taste

Blend Mayonnaise with sour cream, green chilies, and cumin. Season to taste with salt and pepper. Cover and refrigerate until needed.

Yield 1 cup
Preparation time 10 minutes
Ready in 10 minutes

Mustard Dressing

Great as a starter for stuffed eggs.

ingredients

½ cup Univer Mayonnaise
2 Tbs Univer Mustard
1 Tbs green onions, finely chopped
2 Tbs parsley, finely chopped
Salt and pepper to taste

Blend all ingredients together. Cover and refrigerate until needed.

Yield about 1 cup
Preparation time 5 minutes
Ready in 5 minutes

Pesto Mayonnaise

Spread on warm bread on Italian Night!

ingredients

1 cup basil leaves, lightly packed
1 tsp Univer Gourmet Garlic Cream
2 Tbs grated Parmesan cheese
1 tsp Univer Goulash Cream Mild
¼ cup extra virgin olive oil
½ cup Univer Mayonnaise
Salt and pepper, to taste

In a food processor, process the basil, Garlic Cream, Parmesan cheese, Goulash Cream Mild, and olive oil until smooth. In a bowl, combine the basil mixture with the Mayonnaise; season with salt and pepper to taste. Cover and refrigerate until ready to serve.

dressings

Yield about 1½ cups
Preparation time 10 minutes
Ready in 10 minutes

Salsa Mayonnaise

Good with fresh green salads.

ingredients

1 cup Univer Mayonnaise

1 Tbs Univer Goulash Cream Mild

½ cup salsa, mild or medium, drained

1 Tbs cilantro, chopped

Freshly ground black pepper, to taste

In a small mixing bowl, combine Mayonnaise and Goulash Cream Mild. Stir in salsa and cilantro. Season with pepper. Cover and refrigerate until ready to serve.

Yield about ½ cup
Preparation time 5 minutes
Ready in 5 minutes

Spicy Red Mayonnaise

Great with crab cakes or grilled shrimp.

ingredients

½ cup Univer Mayonnaise

1½ Tbs salsa, medium heat

½ tsp Worcestershire sauce

In a small bowl, whisk together the ingredients. Cover and chill until ready to serve.

Yield about 1½ cup
Preparation time 10 minutes
Ready in 10 minutes

Sweet Ann Dressing

A creamy dressing suitable for any salad, including tuna and egg salad.

ingredients

½ cup Univer Mayonnaise

¼ cup Univer Sweet Ann

½ cup tomato, seeded and chopped

2 Tbs green onions, chopped

1 Tbs fresh parsley, chopped

Salt and pepper to taste

Mix all ingredients in a small bowl. Cover and refrigerate until needed.

Yield about ½ cups
Preparation time 10 minutes
Ready in 10 minutes

Artichoke Dipping Sauce

Not just for artichokes; try this as a dip for any vegetable.

½ cup Univer Mayonnaise

1 Tbs Univer Horseradish with Mayonnaise

1 tsp Univer Gourmet Garlic Cream

1 tsp Univer Mustard

1 tsp lemon juice

Dash Worcestershire sauce

Black pepper to taste

Whisk together all ingredients. Cover and refrigerate until ready to serve.

Yield about 1½ cup
Preparation time 5 minutes
Ready in 5 minutes

Bill's Zookie Sauce

Try this on Hungarian Meatballs (find recipe on page 47) or as a side for other meat dishes.

1 cup Univer Mayonnaise

¼ cup Univer Mustard

¼ cup grated Parmesan cheese

1 tsp Univer Gourmet Garlic Cream

Salt and pepper to taste

In a small mixing bowl, whisk together all ingredients. Cover and chill until needed.

Yield about 2 cups
Preparation time 10 minutes
Ready in 10 minutes

Creamy Horseradish Sauce for Meat

A simple dressing for meats, especially beef; also nice as a sandwich spread.

1 cup Univer Mayonnaise

½ cup Univer Horseradish with Vinegar

½ cup sour cream

1 Tbs Univer Mustard

½ tsp salt

¼ tsp white pepper

In a mixing bowl, whisk together Mayonnaise, Horseradish with Vinegar, and sour cream. Add Mustard, salt and pepper. Whisk to combine. Store covered in refrigerator.

Yield about 2 cups
Preparation time 10 minutes
Ready in 10 minutes

Creamy Seafood Sauce

Very tasty on seafood and baked potatoes, too.

ingredients

½ cup Univer Mayonnaise

½ cup sour cream

1 ripe avocado, peeled and mashed

2 tsp lemon juice

1 tsp Univer Red Gold Hot

1 tsp Univer Gourmet Garlic Cream

Salt and pepper to taste

Blend Mayonnaise and sour cream. Add in the avocado, mixing well. Add remaining ingredients and mix again. Cover and refrigerate until needed.

Yield about 1 cup
Preparation time 10 minutes
Ready in 10 minutes

Herb Vegetable Sauce

Nice over steamy cooked vegetables.

ingredients

½ cup Univer Mayonnaise

3 Tbs parsley, finely chopped

2 green onions, finely chopped

1 Tbs fresh tarragon, finely chopped

Salt and pepper to taste

Blend all ingredients together; cover and refrigerate until needed.

Yield about 1½ cups
Preparation time 10 minutes
Ready in 10 minutes

Horseradish Mustard Sauce

Nice as an all-purpose dip for vegetables and meats.

ingredients

1 cup Univer Mayonnaise

3 Tbs Univer Mustard

2 Tbs Univer Horseradish with Vinegar

1 tsp Worcestershire sauce

Salt and pepper to taste

In a small mixing bowl, whisk together all ingredients. Cover and refrigerate until needed.

sauces

Yield about ¾ cups
Preparation time 10 minutes
Ready in 10 minutes

Seafood Cocktail Sauce

Use as a dipping sauce for shrimp and scallops.

ingredients

½ cup ketchup

2 Tbs Univer Horseradish with Vinegar

1 tsp Univer Gourmet Garlic Cream

1 tsp onion powder

1 tsp Worcestershire sauce

1 Tbs parsley, finely chopped

Blend all ingredients together; cover and refrigerate until needed.

Yield about 1½ cups
Preparation time 10 minutes
Ready in 10 minutes

Tartar Sauce

The classic sauce for all seafood!

ingredients

½ cup Univer Mayonnaise

½ cup sour cream

¼ cup Univer Horseradish with Vinegar

¼ cup red onion, finely chopped

1½ Tbs dill pickle relish

3 tsp capers, finely chopped

Salt and pepper to taste

Blend all ingredients well. Cover and refrigerate until needed.

sauces

Yield about 2 cups
Preparation time 15 minutes
Ready in 2 hours, 15 minutes

Dried Cranberry and Jalapeño Relish

Great with chicken and pork.

ingredients

- 1 cup dried cranberries
- ½ cup orange juice
- ⅓ cup red onion, chopped
- ⅓ cup fresh cilantro, finely chopped
- ¼ cup freshly squeezed lime juice
- 1 Tbs Univer Sweet Ann
- 1 tsp Univer Gourmet Garlic Cream
- ½ tsp ground cumin seed
- 1 jalapeño pepper, seeded and finely chopped

In a mixing bowl, combine all ingredients. Cover and refrigerate at least 2 hours before serving.

Yield about 1 cup
Preparation time 10 minutes
Ready in 10 minutes

Garlic-Oregano Marinade for Chicken

Increase the amount of Strong Steven for a spicier marinade.

ingredients

- ½ cup extra virgin olive oil
- 2 Tbs vinegar
- 2 Tbs honey
- 1 Tbs fresh lemon juice
- 1 Tbs Univer Strong Steven
- 1 Tbs Univer Gourmet Garlic Cream
- ¼ cup fresh oregano, finely chopped
- ½ tsp black pepper

Whisk together all ingredients and pour over chicken; turn to coat. Cover and refrigerate until ready to cook, up to 4 hours; drain chicken and discard marinade. Prepare chicken as desired.

Yield about ¾ cup
Preparation time 10 minutes
Ready in 10 minutes

Sandwich Spread

A "secret sauce" kind of spread, or add some Univer Mustard and pickle relish to garnish your favorite hot dog!

ingredients

- ½ cup Univer Mayonnaise
- 2 Tbs Univer Horseradish with Vinegar
- 2 tsp ketchup
- 1 tsp Univer Gourmet Garlic Cream
- ½ tsp Univer Sweet Ann
- ½ tsp onion powder
- Pinch freshly ground black pepper

In a small mixing bowl, whisk together all ingredients, mixing until well blended. Cover and refrigerate until ready to serve.

and more

Univer Product Descriptions

Gift Boxes available

Four jar items of your choice plus seven tubes of your choice! Mix and match! (Univer products only–does not include Alamo Red products.) Please turn the page to make your selections. You may order up to four of any jar items, and up to seven of any tube items.

www.PaprikaRocks.com

www.PaprikaRocks.com

Imagine a sea of eye-popping red and the fragrance of rich loam. It's the vast, world-renowned Hungarian paprika fields ready for harvest.

Our paprika pastes and relishes capture the earthy essence of the fresh fruits, ripe and luscious from the vine. Never diminished to a chalky powder, our paprika is ripened on the plant, then harvested and crushed or made into a paste. It is available in mild and hot flavors.

There are two relishes, **Strong Steven** (hot) and **Sweet Ann** (mild). The pastes are **Red Gold,** mild or hot, and **Goulash Cream,** mild or hot. Red Gold and Goulash Cream are available in jars or tubes. Goulash Cream has just enough tomato and onion to create superb stews and soups, while Red Gold is pure paprika paste.

Now that you have these marvelous tools, use them to turn ordinary meals into gourmet meals. Add some to oil or butter when you are sautéing vegetables. Baste onto chicken for crisp and beautiful skin. Glaze a sizzling steak or chop while it rests. Mix into ground meats when making burgers or meatloaf. Stir into hot, fluffy rice. Add to dips and salad dressings.

The uses are nearly endless, and we have provided you with hundreds of recipes as a starting point; we encourage you to experiment, have fun, and create your own memorable dishes!

All products are gluten-free and have no trans fat

From Judi's Univer Store

All products are gluten-free and have no trans fat

Gourmet Garlic Cream

Garlic is revered throughout the world for its flavor-enhancing qualities and is a staple in most kitchens. With Gourmet Garlic Cream, you can do away with messy cleaning and chopping. Just open the jar! Great garlic aroma, pure garlic flavor! A few suggested uses:

- Add to soups, stews and gravies
- Mix into mashed potatoes for instant Garlic Potatoes
- Make garlic bread in a snap
- Add to sauces, dips and spreads
- Sauté onions and other vegetables
- Toss with hot cooked pasta before dressing with sauce
- Rub onto clean, dry potatoes before baking
- Brush onto pizza crusts before baking

Horseradish with Vinegar

Love the flavor of horseradish but not the 'sinusy' bite it usually has? This will become your favorite pony! Use it where you normally would, but try a little in coleslaw, potato salad, salad dressings, etc.

European Condiments

Univer Horseradish with Mayonnaise

If the love the boldness of horseradish, this will soon become your go-to choice. Toned down by the rich, creamy Mayonnaise, it's a unique blend to use on sandwiches, salad dressings, in sauces and more.

Tube packaging means less air can get in, almost eliminating that watery separation that happens with mayonnaise in jars. It means the last squeeze will be as good as the first. It also means environmentally-friendly aluminum packaging makes it easy to recycle. (5.64 oz.)

Mayonnaise

Rich, creamy mayo suitable for your adult palate (and kid-friendly, too). Tube packaging means less air can get in, almost eliminating that watery separation that happens with mayonnaise in jars. It means the last squeeze will be as tasty as the first. It also means environmentally-friendly aluminum packaging make it easy to recycle. (5.64 oz.)

Mustard

A sophisticated yellow mustard that will enhance any recipe or sandwich! Tube packaging means less air can get in, almost eliminating that watery separation that happens with mustard in jars. It means the last squeeze will be as good as the first. It also means environmentally-friendly aluminum packaging makes it easy to recycle. (5.64 oz.)

www.PaprikaRocks.com

Index

Meet the Paprika Rocks Team

Backing John Czingula is the amazing duo of Bill and Judi Monsour.

Bill Monsour is an expert in creation of a great meal. He loves good food, good times and good drink. As the past owner/operator of three gourmet restaurants in Vail and Denver, Colorado, he honed his love for entertaining for family and friends. His greatest fear is not having enough food on the table.

Taking his experience and understanding of what makes a great meal; he now heads up the Gourmet Specialty Foods division of Univer Foods USA and is its primary spokesperson. Because of John Czingula's extensive travels, Bill is the contact in the U.S. for *For the Love of Paprika* cookbook.

Judi Monsour first discovered the wonders of cooking when she was eight when she re-created her mother's meatloaf. By the time she was eleven, she was the cook for a family of seven and has never lost her delight in creating new recipes for friends and family alike.

Judi is the social voice of all things paprika. There isn't a thing that she doesn't know about the unique qualities of paprika and the amazing array in how to use it in a recipe. Creating Judi's Univer Store, she routinely posts new recipes, has an active blog, *Recipes from the Cutting Board,* and makes sure that all inquiries that come in online are immediately answered and orders for true Hungarian Paprika fulfilled. You can connect with her through *www.PaprikaRocks.com.*

John Czingula travelled extensively between Hungary and the U.S., and the one thing that his friends and business associates requested was that he return with a suitcase full of Hungarian Paprika. The suitcase soon turned into a few boxes, then a crate, followed by a pallet and then the light bulb went on. Being the entrepreneur that he is, Univer Foods USA was born. John owns the exclusive rights in the United States from the manufacturer located in the heart of Kecskemét, Hungary.